GEMIGNANI

GEMIGNANI

Life and Lessons from Broadway and Beyond

MARGARET HALL

Guilford, Connecticut

APPLAUSE
THEATRE & CINEMA BOOKS

An imprint of Globe Pequot, the trade division of
The Rowman & Littlefield Publishing Group, Inc.
4501 Forbes Blvd., Ste. 200
Lanham, MD 20706
www.rowman.com

Distributed by NATIONAL BOOK NETWORK

British Library Cataloguing in Publication Information available

Library of Congress Cataloging-in-Publication Data

Names: Hall, Margaret, 1997- author.
Title: Gemignani : life and lessons from Broadway and beyond / Margaret Hall.
Description: Lanham, MD : Applause Theatre & Cinema Books, 2022. | Includes index. | Summary: "GEMIGNANI tells the life story of Paul Gemignani, who is widely considered to be the most successful Broadway music director living today. A frequent collaborator with Stephen Sondheim, Kander and Ebb, Michael Bennett, and the Roundabout Theater Company, Mr. Gemignani is directly entwined with the history of American musical theater itself"—Provided by publisher.
Identifiers: LCCN 2021046403 (print) | LCCN 2021046404 (ebook) | ISBN 9781493061051 (cloth) | ISBN 9781493061068 (epub)
Subjects: LCSH: Gemignani, Paul. | Conductors (Music)—United States—Biography. | Musicals—Production and direction—United States.
Classification: LCC ML422.G433 H35 2022 (print) | LCC ML422.G433 (ebook) | DDC 784.2092 [B]—dc23
LC record available at https://lccn.loc.gov/2021046403
LC ebook record available at https://lccn.loc.gov/2021046404

♾™ The paper used in this publication meets the minimum requirements of American National Standard for Information Sciences—Permanence of Paper for Printed Library Materials, ANSI/NISO Z39.48-1992.

Dedicated to Jennifer Ashley Tepper
for paying it forward.
MH

Before you start looking for the juicy parts, I would like to pay tribute to a
few magnificent humans.

First, I would like to thank all the wonderfully talented and completely
undervalued members of every orchestra I have ever conducted for making
me look good in whatever performance we all were involved in, be it theatre,
concert, film, or recording studio.

I would like to dedicate this book to the teachers everywhere, especially the
ones who used their talents and energies to guide me toward my dreams,
sometimes before I even knew what those dreams were.

I dedicate this book further to Harold Prince and Stephen Sondheim for their
constant support and for giving me my career.

I also dedicate it to my son, Alexander, for being the best of the best of friends
and for making me proud every single day he's been on this earth. I continue
this dedication to my stepson, August, who has always held me accountable
and whose ambition and drive have always made me work harder to be a
better stepfather. Lastly to my beautiful wife, Derin Altay, for giving me the
support, love, and life I thought I'd never have.
PG

CONTENTS

I have worked with thousands of musicians over the nearly fifty years of my professional music career. Paul Gemignani is on the top of my very short, "You call me, I'm there" list.

While claiming to be a meritocracy, professional music is often driven by politics. Bucking those games, Paul chooses his musicians based on artistry. While others betray colleagues readily in quests for power or easy bucks, Paul stands up for musicians' rights. In an era of increasing mechanization, Paul fights hard and long, sometimes over years, to hire the musicians the works artistically need. Art and merit come first for him, always. He is a rare colleague who walks the walk of integrity, even when it means paying a personal price.

Paul is a rare conductor who can immediately hear the difference between an excellent player, an incompetent player, and a great player who had a bad moment. In a Broadway era largely defined by conductors who want players to sound like automatons ("like the recording") Paul is the anomaly who relishes the individual artistry of every musician, including substitutes. He hears the differences in each artist's voice, savors what they offer, and weaves new tapestries of sound using whoever is on hand, every performance.

He is the rare conductor who gives players what they need, when they need it. When things are going great, he gets out of everyone's way. But the moment there is the slightest unraveling, he immediately reins everyone in, bringing the company back, tight, en forme.

He is playful, creating living games with actors and musicians during every show, keeping everyone fully engaged; the most effective way to combat eight-shows-a-week-boredom. He does not just "do it the same every night." He knows art does not live in mindless, automatic repetition. Every performance with Paul breathes a new life, spinning new subtleties. Maybe tonight he will let a singer or musician float a bit longer on a particularly delicious note or push more forcefully through a moment of driving momentum. Infinitesimal changes that keep it all alive. There is no stagnation when Paul is at the helm.

But while savoring the details, Paul never sacrifices the whole to individual moments. Yes, he recognizes each artist's voice, relishes it, lets it be heard. But he never loses track of the fact that each phrase is building a Song, which builds a Scene, which builds an Act, which builds an entire Show. He conducts in multilayered phrases, always shaping layers on layers of larger and larger phrases that build the entire work. He does not just conduct a series of "numbers." Paul never loses sight of the story, and where we are within it.

Making music with Paul is a joy and highlight of my career. When he calls, I say "Yes," happily. Even if I am seriously ill. Even if other life demands make it very challenging or inconvenient. Because making music with Paul is always, and absolutely, worth it.

JENNIFER HOULT (HARP, ANVIL, KEYBOARD)

Introduction

What Is a Music Director?

In the musical theatre, there are few positions more elusive than that of the music director—a critical piece of the creative team, they oversee the music in musical to both carry out the composer's vision and collaborate with the performers onstage and in the pit to create a cohesive production. Many of the decisions regarding the score of a show are made by a music director, and they are often the member of the creative team who stays with the show furthest into its run, with composers, directors, and choreographers moving on to new projects after opening night. They regularly act as conductors for the shows on which they work, clocking in and out eight times a week alongside the performers, stagehands, and pit musicians, and they participate in the initial casting.

Their work, while incredibly important to the structure and success of a show, is regularly misunderstood by the industry at large. Considered by some to be the equivalent of a human metronome, their talent and insights can be overlooked by those who do not work with them directly. The Tony Award for Best Conductor and Musical Director was discontinued in 1964, and their efforts in the theatre have been left almost entirely unrecognized by the public ever since.

Paul Gemignani, whose life you are about to unpack, is widely considered to be the most successful music director living today. He is certainly the most awarded. With forty-two Broadway credits and sixteen films to his name, Gemignani has received a Primetime Emmy Award for Best Music Direction, a special Drama Desk Award for Outstanding Musical Direction, and a Lifetime Achievement Tony Award from the American Theatre Wing. He was awarded an Honorary Doctorate from the Manhattan School of Music in 2003 and inducted into the American Theatre Hall of Fame in 2011. And yet, even the most curious musical theatre aficionado is likely to know very little about the man who brought industry favorites such as *Sweeney Todd*, *Crazy for You*, *Sunday in the Park with George*, *Dreamgirls*, *On the Twentieth Century*, and *Into the Woods* to the stage.

He is something of a shadow, haunting the staves of sheet music strewn throughout rehearsal rooms, libraries, and concert halls across the world. Resistant to being photographed, he exits a room when a camera enters. To strangers, he is a burly bear of a man, imposing and impressive, with strong hands and ever-present tinted glasses. To those who know him, he is a gregarious and warm figure, with a glint in his eye as he slides a moment of wit in between the stories of a sage. He is deeply private, with a storyteller's heart.

When Paul began his career, he had no intention of working in the musical theatre. Becoming a music director was something that had never crossed his mind, until it was suddenly in front of him. Fifty years later, he stands as the looming figure at the podium, hands aloft and heart open. When he began his career, he had few examples to turn to; now, with this book in hand, we hope that his experiences will influence and inspire the next generation of music directors, many of whom do not know what lies ahead.

Paul, and people like him, are critical to the shows on which they work, and as you read this book, we hope that the curtain is pulled back from this most misunderstood of the creative collaborators.

CHAPTER ONE

Childhood

POST–GREAT DEPRESSION SAN FRANCISCO WAS A CITY OF DICHOTO-mies. In the 1930s, it was considered one of the rising cities in the United States, with the highest Eastern immigrant population per capita. By the beginning of the 1940s, it was nearly emptied by Executive Order 9066, which legalized the internment of Japanese residents in concentration camps following the events of Pearl Harbor. The dedication of the Golden Gate Bridge in May of 1937 was a moment of great architectural triumph, and the structure was considered to be a symbol of prosperity and status for Bay Area residents. Several short years later it was covered in military personnel and used as a last stop before military convoys were sent to Japan and the Pacific in World War II.

Immigrants across the city were cautious—the ground on which they stood could give way at any time, and as families were pulled from homes they had previously celebrated building, the instability of the country, and not the San Andreas Fault, proved the most dangerous.

It was to one of these families that Paul Gemignani was born on November 8, 1937, just outside of San Francisco. A second-generation Italian immigrant, he was the first son of Ezio Paul Gemignani and Margaret Helen Lewis, a couple as dissimilar as the city. Ezio was one of five children and had been raised fifty miles north of San Francisco in Valona, an Italian enclave in the town of Crockett. His father, Cesare Gemignani, had immigrated to America at the turn of the century, fleeing the poverty that had surrounded him and his wife, Orsalina. A chef, Cesare had received word in New York that one of the first mainland cane sugar processing plants was to be built in Crockett, and the family swiftly transplanted to the West Coast, intent on creating a boarding-house for businessmen and workers who would come to visit the plant.

It was there that Cesare built what was to be the family's first American legacy—the Gemignani House became one of the most profitable places to stay in Valona, and it was run primarily by the family itself, with Orsalina working as the bartender and money handler while Cesare prepared the food. Cesare and the children maintained the house itself, and a handyman was brought in only for work too dangerous for untrained hands. Ever aware of the poverty they had left behind in Italy, Cesare was careful with money and did not hire work out if he had any chance of completing it himself. At age fifty-eight, Cesare was beating rugs on the roof of the house when a gust of wind came, and he was blown from the roof, dying on impact.

This first tragedy, the death of the patriarch, greatly affected the Gemignani family. Orsalina sold the boardinghouse, unable to live in the home that had quite literally killed her husband, and moved into the house immediately behind it. A dark and somewhat dingy place, she lived in this house with her sons and the family friend who had acted as the handyman for the now defunct hotel and restaurant. Her eldest son, Alfonso, lived with her for extended periods, and the family centered around tragedy for a time. The youngest brother, Dino, died at eighteen months old, and Ezio's twin sister, Cesira, died at age fourteen during a routine tonsillectomy, when she bled to death on the operating table.

Ezio, now the youngest surviving child of the Gemignani family, had two paths before him: Remain with his brothers, Alfonso and Mondo, so as to care for Orsalina and support the family, or grasp at his father's sense of possibility and strike out on his own. He was a bright boy, with a strong work ethic, and he made the decision to press on in search of his own life, free of the family's precarious position. Ezio became the first member of the family to graduate college, attending San Francisco Catholic University and the University of California, Berkeley, where he majored in English and Education and became a schoolteacher.

Paul's mother, Margaret, could not have had a more different background. Raised in Rodeo, a small town north of San Francisco that had been devastated by the 1906 earthquake, she carried herself with a sense of decorum that suited the upper classes of the Bay Area. A claimant of Irish and Welsh ancestry, she prided herself on being a member of the right kind of family. This intense desire to fit in, and to be seen as a member of the right group, was to be expected for a woman of Margaret's age and background. As families were being torn apart by divisions of identity and class, the strict adherence to one's social position was one of the few areas of control in which a woman could wield power. Margaret's job within this society was to marry well, in order to safely entrench herself in the community she had been born. An Italian immigrant from a lower-middle-class family who held a respectable, if not high-earning, job teaching children, Ezio was not the kind of man Margaret would have been expected to have married. A businessman perhaps, or a lawyer, someone with higher social standing than a small-town teacher would have been the match made for her at birth. But against all expectation and prejudice, she chose Ezio.

Margaret was a bright woman—a trained pianist, she had attended the San Francisco Conservatory of Music before marriage put a stop to any artistic ambitions. She had settled, somewhat fitfully, into the role of homemaker, and as the teacher's wife, when young Paul arrived. Ezio was the sole teacher in a one-room schoolhouse forty miles outside of Crockett, and the living was tight. Tensions were high as the violence ramped up in Europe a few short months after Paul's birth; Ezio knew that he would be one of the last to be drafted, thanks to bad knees, but that didn't stop the family from worrying as Italy entered the conflict. Paul's sister, Marie, was born, and they relied on Margaret's family in Rodeo to make ends meet.

In Rodeo Ezio found a job teaching at an elementary school, and it was at that school that Paul was formally enrolled as a student. A fiercely curious child, he immediately received blowback from his kindergarten teachers for his refusal to blindly follow rules. Once they had been explained to him, he had no problem obeying, but blind faith had never been one of his virtues. Toward the end of kindergarten, a particularly distressing incident occurred in which a teacher roughly bound six-year-old Paul to his school chair with rope, leaving him tied down until his father found him, horrified. By the end of the year, plans were put in place for Paul to continue his studies at the Catholic school in Albany. A private institution, Ezio wouldn't be there to protect Paul as he had been able to when he was teaching down the hall, but he and Margaret hoped that the structure of a private education would be good for Paul.

Unfortunately, a strong sense of logic and justification did not easily mesh with a religious education. From a very young age, Paul had personally rejected a religious framework to his life—petitions and prayers had never seemed as logical as solving the problem himself. He had never lashed out over this belief—in fact, he had spent hours of his life sitting and watching Orsalina repeat the rosary twice a day as a personal ritual. He had no problem with others finding solace within the church, but he was endlessly frustrated by the nuns who refused to grant him the same freedom to find solace elsewhere. He spent almost every afternoon at the front of his classroom, writing out contrite phrases on the blackboard for hours at a time. Physical discipline was common, both in and out of school, as Margaret took to placing welts on any open skin the nuns had missed. After a year of constant verbal and physical attacks, Paul was expelled from the Catholic school and the family relocated to the Alameda Projects.

As the family moved for the fifth time in seven years, Paul began to nurture his independent streak, preferring to remain alone in his room than out with the new neighborhood children with whom he never had enough time to forge real friendships. Music quickly became his refuge—Margaret was constantly playing hymns throughout the day, and the family owned a player piano that young Paul would bang away at, fascinated by the mechanics. Every Sunday they would visit his maternal grandparents, and Paul would make a beeline for his grandfather's garage, where the old Victrola player and boxes of '78's were kept. He would play the records over and over, with songs such as "Animal Fair" serving as a popular music contrast to the classical music his mother filled the house with. When visiting Orsalina and his father's family, he would see Alfonso. Al was the oldest of the Gemignani boys, and the opposite of Ezio in ambition. More laissez-faire in his attitudes, he lived in the flat above Orsalina for most of his life and was married to a local band singer named Doris. He worked in the sugar mill and played in a dance band at night, living the life of a wayward musician happily even as Ezio fought to provide a more "respectable" lifestyle for his family.

The Alameda Projects were not the kind of place Ezio had wanted to raise his children, and as Paul and Marie grew, he found an unorthodox solution—a yacht club, aimed at the families to which Margaret aspired, had an opening for a club captain. Ezio seized the opportunity in addition to the three other jobs he was already working. To be club captain meant that Ezio and the family would live in the club itself—they lived in an apartment attached to the cantina. Ezio oversaw the upkeep and maintenance of the club, and during the summer months the family would run the cantina, with Paul and Marie acting as lifeguards for the affluent members of the club. It was a child's paradise. They would ride their bicycles freely through the club after hours, and Paul had a small sailboat that he would take out on the water whenever he wasn't on duty, sailing the coast alone as Marie socialized on shore. This freedom was the closest Paul and Marie came to the upbringing Margaret had anticipated for her children, and the family was happy for a time, as Ezio labored to keep their new lifestyle together.

During this time at the Yacht Club, Paul began to get serious about music. In sixth grade, under the guiding hand of Howard Hanson, the music teacher at the Haight School, Paul began his musical education. Howard first started Paul on a particularly creaky violin, and then a cello, encouraging the cacophony as the students found their way to musicality. Hanson was the rare teacher who was more interested in the process than the final result—he sought to train musicians, rather than players of music. He searched for hidden talent in every corner of his life and celebrated his students when they found it themselves. The support and care Howard offered were the push that Paul needed to jump headfirst into his love of music—first with the cello, and soon to the orchestra itself. Paul lived for the early morning rehearsals and soaked the music up like a sponge, even as his family cautioned him against a career in music.

While his mother was trained, she had never intended to work professionally as a classical pianist—it was merely a passion with which to occupy herself before marriage to a man who would provide for her and the family they would form. Margret's talents were useful insofar as getting her a job as the organist and choir director for the St. Patrick Catholic Church of Rodeo, a position that solidified the family's social standing. Ezio worked hard to create stability for the family during the immense upheaval of the 1940s, and that his son would continue to live a stable life was the expected reward. That Paul might become a music teacher was as far as was accepted—education was a solid career, and one that Paul's parents could picture. As they warily observed their son's burgeoning enthusiasm, they begrudgingly sated his curiosity, bringing home vinyl records and taking him into the city to see performances when finances allowed.

One of these records was the original cast recording of *South Pacific*, starring Mary Martin. The grand sweep of the score was palpable even through the family's tinny turntable, and the orchestral elements jumped out at Paul as theatre music was presented to him for the first time. The music of Richard Rodgers was as artistically complex as much of the classical music they played in his classes, but unlike Brahms or Beethoven, Rodgers was alive and actively working. Paul wore out the recording learning every exciting nuance. He never tired of the grandeur and held *South Pacific* as close to his heart as any childhood story. The family's period at the Yacht Club came to an end, and they moved to Oakland as Paul made the decision to venture further into popular music, against his mother's orders.

Now in high school, a teacher named Jewel Lord took the foundation given to Paul by Howard Hanson and expanded it monumentally. Paul went to him, no longer happy with the cello, and asked to join the school's band, which would require him to play a non-stringed instrument. Jewel, shrewdly recognizing that Paul's interest in the band was related to his having several friends in the marching line, offered him a deal. Jewel would teach him another instrument on the side, provided he remained in the orchestra, and he would be able to be a part of both groups the following semester, playing both instruments. Paul took the deal, and a mentorship of immense influence began. They started with the French horn, which Paul rejected almost as thoroughly as he had the piano, and the trumpet soon followed into the rejection pile. The trombone lasted somewhat longer, in an effort to learn embouchure and take advantage of the bass clef knowledge Paul already had from playing the cello. Finally, at the San Francisco Symphony with his mother, Paul saw the timpani player. The sheer power it gave the music affected Paul deeply, and the very next day he went to Jewel and told him he would be a percussionist. Jewel, trusting Paul to be serious about the decision, moved him immediately and gave him a percussion lesson to start him on his way.

From that point on, Paul was in love with rhythm. Jewel continued to give him private lessons, encouraging his ambitions and helping him explore the world of music that Paul had fallen for. Unlike his strictly regulated home life, Paul found a sense of relaxation and belonging in music, and he was intent on remaining there. Soon, his work in class wasn't enough; Paul needed his own instrument to practice on at home.

He worked for a year, mowing lawns and picking up early morning paper routes to save enough to rent a drum set for the summer. Once it arrived, Paul spent every free moment in his room, practicing along to such favorite artists as Spike Jones and the City Slickers, Harry James, Tommy Dorsey, and anything else he could snag from his parents' record collection. These included recordings of Danny Kaye, from which he could learn the rhythm of comedy and following a performer. At the end of the summer, the drum set had to be returned, but Paul was determined to get it back, and for good. While still working with Jewel and devoting much of the school year to the orchestra and the band, he worked odd jobs and gave the entirety of his earnings to his father, intent on buying the drum set outright from the rental company.

Paul's father had always conditioned his son to hard work and to support himself—if Paul wanted something, it was up to him to earn the money to get it. Ezio's salary was just enough to keep the family stable, and there was no excess for unnecessary things like drum sets. The money Paul gave his father was the bottom of the barrel amount that a full set could fetch, even used. Somehow, Ezio brought it home to Paul; the question of whether this was due to a generous manager of the rental company or Ezio scraping together enough money to make the deal is lost to history. Ezio wanted the best for Paul, and in spite of his own reticence, he was willing to support Paul in this all-encompassing passion—just so long as Paul found stability in a steady job. Alfonso had struck a balance between millwork and nighttime gigs as a musician—while it was not the kind of life Ezio had pictured for his son, it was at least a dynamic he could comprehend.

Paul soon formed a dance band with some friends from the jazz band at high school. They would rehearse in the front room, under Margaret's critical eye, before going into downtown Oakland every Friday and Saturday night to play at the USO club, a job they held from their junior year in high school to their sophomore year in college. A five-piece band, they mostly played Glenn Miller and other Top 40 Big Band hits to dance floors packed with servicemen and their girlfriends. In the summertime, they would up the ante, playing college dances for local fraternities in addition to the USO work. These bandmates were some of Paul's closest friends, and they would remain together until college when their lives began to separate from Paul's ambitions.

Jewel saw the initiative Paul was taking in addition to his passion and began putting him up in front of the band and orchestra classes, having him conduct pieces as Jewel would look on. It was the first time Paul had stepped up to the podium, and under Jewel's careful guidance, he found his footing as a conductor. Paul became the drum major of the marching band and conducted the entrance march at his high school graduation, cementing the idea of becoming a professional conductor, rather than the small-town music teacher as his parents expected.

Paul was not the only one of his peers who was rattling against the constraints of the world he was stepping into. The Korean War had come and gone during his high school years, and attitudes toward what became known as American Exceptionalism were changing. And Paul, a healthy eighteen-year-old man, was graduating directly into one of the greatest nonviolent draft pulls in US history.

Chapter Two

College Years

WHILE THE KOREAN WAR HAD COME TO A CEASE-FIRE IN THE SUMMER of 1953, the military presence of the United States in Southeast Asia had not faded. Instead, South Korea became a key location for the US military, in part because of its proximity to Soviet strongholds. The American public were both cognizant of this military benefit and of how unprepared the country had been going into the conflict. Previously, the United States had remained diplomatically neutral in foreign conflicts outside of the World Wars; Korea was one of the first combat scenarios in which the United States intervened in the "name of democracy," a battle cry that would become increasingly loud over the following decades as the Cold War heated up.

Paul wanted to stay uninvolved. He had no interest in the military, and with the Korean War effectively in a standoff, he wanted to try his chances at avoiding the draft. Instead, he wanted to go to college and start his professional career in music. To Ezio, this was too great a chance to take.

In the forty-six years Ezio had lived in the United States, he had lived through two World Wars and the involvement of the United States in the Mexican Revolution, the Russian Civil War, the Philippine-American War, and the Korean War. The country seemed eager for a fight, with less than a decade between large-scale wars. That the draft would come calling for Paul felt less like a risk and more like a certainty—Ezio himself had only narrowly avoided World War II due to a knee problem, and Paul was a healthy young man, ripe for being pulled into a future conflict. Ezio was of the mind that it was better for Paul to enlist and serve his time willingly, rather than be drafted and sent out during a more dangerous period.

Paul did not have his father's concerns. Yes, he was healthy, but so were hundreds of thousands of other young men across the country, many of whom had aspired to a life of military service, unlike himself. Paul was not, and is not, a violent man, and there was little allure to the life of base camps and military strategy. In fact, Paul considered himself to be a borderline pacifist, and the idea of shooting at nameless faces was repugnant to him. The Navy held some interest, if only for the seafaring life and the peace being on the water brings, but that his passion for boating would be twisted into warfare was far from ideal. Ezio was firm in his wish for Paul to enlist now that his precollegiate schooling was complete, and the pair went back and forth, fighting in a way rare for either man, before a compromise was finally reached.

Paul would join the Army as a member of a newly instituted program—in exchange for six months of voluntary active service, enlisted men would serve twelve years in the reserves, rather than the traditional two years of active service with eight years in the reserves. Gritting his teeth, Paul went to training and served his active time, a chasm opening between him and his parents.

As a child, Paul had always been independent. Ezio's philosophy was more to lead by example than lead by hand, and Margaret's influence had been one of a strict Mother Superior. Paul's free spirit and his mother's strong will clashed, in contrast to Marie, who had always remained closer to home in ambition. Paul had his sights set higher. While his parents had wished for him to follow his father into education, Paul knew that teaching was not for him—while he adored his music teachers, the monotony of doing the same job for fifty years did not align with his soul. The life that he had tasted with his dance band was far more appealing—with an ever-changing setlist and rotation of audience members with which to engage, the unpredictability gave Paul the sense of security his father had found in stability. Music itself was Paul's home base, not Oakland, and he knew that in order to make the life for himself that he was picturing, he had to find his way out of California.

Once he returned from active duty, Paul enrolled in San Francisco State University (SFSU)—while other, better-known colleges had been tempting (in particular Stanford), SFSU's connections with the San Francisco Symphony Orchestra won Paul's affection. By remaining somewhat close to home, Paul was able to maintain his weekly gig with the dance band at various venues, and he began establishing himself in the San Francisco jazz scene. Paul was not sure exactly what avenue he would be following, but he knew it would be in music, and by situating himself at the intersection of these three influences, he figured he would find his target with time.

At SFSU, the majority of the teachers were the first chair musicians of the San Francisco Symphony Orchestra, and their influence was strongly felt in the structure of the curriculum. There was next to no downtime throughout the entire year, whether school was in session or not. SFSU prepared its students for the most hectic periods of a professional musician's life, with each year's curriculum containing two orchestra concerts, two band concerts, a book musical, a book opera, and a student-written revue, all of which were mandatory, in addition to touring throughout California during term breaks with the Concert Wind Ensemble. Rather than returning home during breaks, the students were expected to instead take the time off to focus on their life as professional musicians on tour, putting into practice all that they had learned during the rigors of their training. Somehow, within this period of immense learning, Paul was able to maintain his weekly schedule with the dance band for two years, until his work in downtown San Francisco picked up to such a pace that he had to choose the professional work over the gig circuit with his friends.

This attitude of hard work, instilled by Jewel Lord, quickly brought Paul to the attention of the staff at SFSU, in particular Dr. Edwin Kruth and Roland Kohloff. Dr. Kruth was the director of the bands, and he picked up where Jewel Lord had left off—the band program was audition only, and quite competitive, but Paul was selected for the percussion section in his first semester. Dr. Kruth was no-nonsense and demanded 100 percent from his students at all times, treating them the same as he would professional musicians who had been working under him for years.

The expression of music and commitment to the craft were paramount in Dr. Kruth's eyes, and Paul quickly rose in his esteem.

Roland Kohloff, Paul's percussion teacher, was an incredible musician and an even more devoted teacher. His passion and dedication for sharing his all-encompassing love of music was infectious, and in Paul he found a kindred spirit. Kohloff knew that Paul had the potential to reach great heights as a musician, and he worked hard to help Paul reach his full potential as an artist. He expanded what being a working artist could be for Paul and, in conjunction with the heavy course load, opened up a world of opportunities before him.

As this artistic osmosis was happening on campus, Paul was continuing to report to his reserve meetings, and to summer boot camps in which his skills as a soldier were maintained for four weeks, while playing with and conducting the post's Army band. The distance between Paul and his family remained somewhat stable, and he settled into his half-student, half-professional lifestyle, when a representative of the USO came to see one of SFSU's student-written revues, titled "Campus Capers." Why a representative was in the audience is unknown, but the talent of the students made quite the impression, as the representative went to the college and requested six students to form a revue to take out on a USO tour of East Asia. Paul was one of the students selected, and among his peers, including one of his high school buddies from the old dance band, a revue was cobbled together from fresh writing and prewritten material they hoped would land with the servicemen. They went on a summer tour, visiting Hawaii, Taiwan, various military bases in Korea, Okinawa, and finally Tokyo, where they had a weeklong sit-down in a Naval Officers Club.

The tour proved mostly uneventful. However, while stationed in Okinawa, a typhoon ripped through the day before they were to depart for Tokyo. The band was given the day off, and Paul went out to swim in the Pacific Ocean outside his barracks room, unaware that the strength of the typhoon had blown away the protection of the cloud layer, making the sunlight much more intense. Paul's pale skin was practically fried, leaving him with scars across his shoulders that did not fade for decades.

Upon returning from tour, Paul went to his reserve meeting as normal and was pulled aside by his sergeant. Unbeknownst to Paul, a USO tour was considered additional active duty; his four months overseas nullified his status as a reserve member, and he was honorably discharged. Paul walked out of his final meeting in uniform and never put it on again.

With his military career gracefully cut short, Paul turned his attention fully to his professional career. He took conducting lessons from Earl Bernard Murray, who was the trumpeter in the San Francisco Symphony, the music director for the San Francisco Ballet, the conductor for the San Francisco State orchestra, and the conductor for the San Francisco Opera. These lessons helped Paul refine his approach to being at the podium for more classically structured music, even as his jazz career began to take off. Along North Beach, a neighborhood in northeast San Francisco, Paul found work at such clubs as the Hungry Eye and The Purple Onion. In particular, The Purple Onion became a home base, and Paul worked there for three years as a member of a trio, backing up various vocalists. Kohloff was thrilled and supported Paul's professional activities, helping him to balance them against his education. This day life of classical and concert music and nightlife of jazz brushed against the world of theatre when his mother insisted Paul accompany her to the national tour of *Gypsy* at the Curran Theatre, starring Ethel Merman.

Margaret had told Paul that Ethel was the best musical theatre performer that had ever lived, and Paul went in curious, only knowing the theatre from the cast recording of *South Pacific* that had so greatly impressed him years earlier. While the idea of working in opera and operetta had occurred to Paul, primarily in the works of Gilbert and Sullivan, or traditional opera, the musical theatre had never held much interest for him outside of an appreciation for the scope of the *South Pacific* score. His interest was piqued by his mother's investment, as she had always leaned more toward classical music, but Paul was less than impressed. Ms. Merman, theatrical legend she was, had never been at her happiest while touring. Her performance as Rose had become one of legend, in part because of her insistence on never missing performances. *Gypsy* had run 702 performances on Broadway, of which Ethel had missed none. Immediately after embarking on the national tour, she had seriously injured her back at the top of the San Francisco run, as her exhaustion caught up with her. She walked through the performance, hitting her marks with little enthusiasm, but bellowing out the score in a fashion only she could ever achieve.

While Ethel's performance did not captivate Paul in the way his mother had hoped, the music intrigued him. After the show, Paul went to the orchestra pit to express his admiration and met Milton Rosenstock. A member of the Broadway cavalcade, Milton had music-directed ten shows on Broadway, including the original production of *Gypsy*, before bringing it out on the road. A sweet man, Milton was happy to talk to Paul, taking note of the burly man and his diminutive mother as pleasantries were exchanged. When they would meet again, much later in Paul's life, Milton would remember every detail of the encounter, down to the way they had been dressed—he put value on every interaction he had, and his ironclad memory endeared him to everyone who worked with him. It was the first time Paul had met a theatrical music director and the first time Paul had seen a professional musical production, but their influence did not affect Paul at first.

He was far too focused on his career as a jazz musician and on the residency he had built at The Purple Onion.

Chapter Three

Rhythm Section

The Purple Onion was a cozy underground jazz club, owned and operated by Keith Rockwell, in the North Beach area of San Francisco. With its intimate, eighty-person setting, the club had been a popular hangout for local musicians and comedians during the Beat era of the 1950s, with artists as diverse as Maya Angelou, Bob Newhart, and Woody Allen getting their starts during the early days of the club. The Smothers Brothers, a popular folk music duo, had recorded their first album, entitled *The Smothers Brothers at The Purple Onion*, live at the club, and that had cemented the public perception of the club as one of the best local cellar clubs in the city.

In 1960, Rockwell's sister and brother-in-law, Ginnie and Bud Steinhoff, took over the management of the club and closed it for a time to renovate and regroup. The Beat Movement had come and gone, and they were aiming the club toward local musicians rather than poets when Paul stepped into the picture.

A recent graduate of SFSU, Paul had gotten together with Gus Gusterson and Tommy Beason, forming a jazz trio with the hope of becoming the house band for a club. They would cut tapes on an old recording machine in Tommy's garage, and Paul would send them out to clubs, acting as the trio's de facto manager as they searched for work. One of these tapes made it into the hands of Bud, and the boys were brought in to audition in the middle of renovations. After a bit of cajoling, Bud agreed to bring them on as a house band, but he could afford only two of them under contract—Tommy would be brought in on a case-by-case basis when a performer specifically requested a bass player, and Paul and Gus would be there six nights a week as the drummer and pianist.

It was Paul's first long-term professional job as a musician, and he never held a civilian job again.

Upon reopening, the club was busy, with Paul and Gus playing from 7:30 to 1:30 every night, every day but Sunday. Every week netted about $300, and Paul managed to live on that sum, but Gus taught at a college down the peninsula, and Tommy worked at a barbershop during the day. Before the club would open for the night, Paul would reach out to record companies and send out the audition tapes they had previously cut, hoping to elevate the trio beyond being a house band, but to becoming recording artists themselves. Paul knew they were good, and he believed that if they caught the eye of a record executive from RCA or Warner Bros., they had a chance of being invited down to Los Angeles to cut a proper demo and possibly get a recording contract of their own. They wouldn't be the first band The Purple Onion had launched, and Paul had ambitions that went much further than maintaining a steady house gig for the rest of his life.

Unfortunately, Gus and Tommy did not feel the same way. They had begun to put down roots in San Francisco, and the idea of leaving their day jobs to go to Los Angeles for a week on a chance was unfathomable for them. Paul understood but was disappointed at the realization that the people he had surrounded himself with saw the world differently than he did. He had again found his way into a group that was content to remain in place, the very thing he had pushed away from in Oakland.

Wonderful musicians would come in and out of the club, including Toni Lee Scott, a chanteuse who had been a close friend of cultural icon James Dean before his untimely death. She had made quite the name for herself, appearing on *The Tonight Show with Johnny Carson* and *The Mike Douglas Show* both as a vocalist and as a guest in her own right, and she was a popular act in California when she came to the relaunched Purple Onion. With the full trio backing her, she played a number of gigs and came to like the boys, in particular Paul. She was older than the boys, but she fit in well with their rough-and-tumble lifestyle, and Gus and Paul would take care of her as the pressure of life on the road, and a life of loss would get to her. Scott had lost her leg in a motorcycle accident at age nineteen and hid her prosthetic from audiences in a myriad of gowns, as well as hiding her grief behind an impressive repertoire of blue jokes.

When Toni was asked to take on a three-week residency in Minneapolis, she approached the trio to ask them to accompany her for the duration. Gus and Tommy declined, choosing to remain with their day jobs, but Paul eagerly agreed, effectively dissolving the trio. Unlike Gus and Tommy's day jobs, taking three weeks off from The Purple Onion would not necessarily cost Paul his job, and he went to talk to Bud about taking a month off with Toni before returning. Paul had made himself essential to the club, acting both as the head of the trio as well as the lighting designer and announcer from a microphone and a dimmer switch set up next to his drum set. Replacing him wouldn't be easy, even in the short term, but Bud walked Paul through everything he and Ginnie had been thinking regarding the future of the club—bringing it back to its spoken-word roots by opening up for comedians and comedy acts. They would open up the music to more than jazz performers and lounge singers, including a residency by The Irish Rovers, a band out of Toronto that had begun to popularize Irish music in North America.

Paul knew that this new direction did not particularly interest him, and he made a snap decision—he wouldn't be taking a leave of absence but was instead handing in his resignation. He had the gig lined up with Toni and trusted he would figure out his way forward from there, as he had before with the dissolution of his high school dance band. Bud, understanding Paul's greater ambitions, gave him his blessing and a promise that if Paul got back from Minneapolis and needed a job, one would be waiting for him. Paul never had to take him up on the offer.

Paul had already begun to taste the world of music outside of club and session work, and traveling with Toni was the excuse he needed to take that next step. He had become a common figure at clubs across San Francisco, in particular an after-hours club under The Fillmore. There was no set performer list, and Paul would find out on the street who was in town and going to play the day of the performance. The club was tiny and mostly filled with musicians themselves, rather than the traditional audiences of a jazz club. Performers would rotate who was onstage, and anyone had the ability to hop up and start playing before the end of the night. It was a surreal thing, a community-wide jam session, and it took a long time of going to the club before Paul built up the courage to play. Everyone in the room was incredibly good and at the top of their game in a way that creates a family atmosphere through the love of music alone. Career musicians such as Cannonball and Nat Addlery, Anita O'Day, and Miles Davis would filter in on occasion, but they were treated the same as any other member of the family, even as *Milestones* and *Kind of Blue* became seminal jazz hits across the globe.

Few of the musicians Paul played with at the underground club stayed around for very long, and Paul did not intend to either. Toni's hired bass player and Paul loaded up all of the instruments in a rented station wagon and drove straight to Minneapolis a week and a half before the start of the residency, when Toni would fly in. They would play nightly, but during the day Paul was left to his own devices, the farthest east he had been in his life. Paul had only ever left California with the USO, and the freedom of exploration given to him in Minneapolis was a new experience for him. There was no Margaret looking over his shoulder, no sergeant with orders and expectations. So long as Paul showed up every night, Toni and the boys gave him his space to be truly independent and untethered for the first time in his life. Paul had an old friend, Richard Ramos, who was working at the Guthrie theatre, and Paul took one of his days to go and see him in Shakespeare's *Titus Andronicus*, alongside a young Len Cariou.

Paul had met Richard working at San Francisco Actor's Workshop shortly after college. Founded in 1952 by two professors from San Francisco State College, Herbert Blau and Jules Irving, the San Francisco Actor's Workshop rapidly became the city's major theatre, putting on a wide variety of shows. Paul had taken a handful of elective courses in college, including an acting class with Irving, and he had approached Blau and Irving, asking to assist with the music responsibilities for the plays the company produced. He had been hired, and his duties had ranged from raising and replacing the needle on records for key moments, to playing percussion on the back bumper of a Chevrolet during a particularly esoteric production of a restoration comedy with a fresh score by

Morton Subotnick. Paul befriended the majority of the company, in particular Richard, Robert Symonds, Priscilla Pointer, and Edward Winter, who had since moved to New York to pursue a career on Broadway.

As the three weeks with Toni began to wind down, she approached Paul with another offer—she was going on a tour across the country and wanted Paul to accompany her. Again trusting his gut, Paul declined. He had seen the state of disrepair the Minneapolis club was in and knew that the other clubs were likely in a similar state, as jazz was lessening in popularity compared to the bustling folk and rock movements. He stayed in Minneapolis as Toni moved on, and he never saw her again.

Paul stayed with Richard and his wife for a few days as he decided what he was going to do. A storm whipped through Minnesota, the largest Paul had ever seen, which strengthened his resolve. In an effort to put off returning to San Francisco, he made the decision to visit Edward Winter in New York, taking a bus to Chicago and a train across the Midwest to complete his journey across the country. He didn't know what he was going to do once he got there, other than meet up with Ed for a drink, but he knew it would buy him time to figure out his next move, and allow him to see more of the world than he had ever seen before. He was thirty-one years old, and was in full control as he ventured out into the unknown.

Paul packed his drum set into a storage trunk, all of his clothes in a single suitcase, and set out for New York, intent to see Ed in his new show—a story set in a Weimar Republic–era cabaret club aptly titled *Cabaret*.

Chapter Four

Next Stop, New York

The New York City that Paul was traveling to was a city in flux. Economic and social decay was beginning to rise to the surface as the postwar building boom swiftly slowed and Robert Moses' infrastructure plans were brought to a close. The New York Mets were newly formed in 1962 and had found a home at Shea Stadium in Queens, which was experiencing an influx of Manhattanites moving out of the heart of the city. The Immigration Act of 1965, which abolished Nation of Origin quotas, had opened the door to increased immigration from East Asia, leading to many new businesses opening throughout the city as previous stalwarts went under. Industries that had previously been the backbone of the city's economy, such as textile manufacturing, were shut down and moved elsewhere, leaving blue-collar neighborhoods in a state of near-immediate deterioration. Decaying facilities and infrastructure led to widespread blackouts, as well as a spike in the downtown guerila art scene. Strip clubs and other adult-oriented businesses had begun to filter into Times Square, and a moral panic had set in, causing a population shift to the suburbs.

New York was a national center of protest movements against the Vietnam War and in support of the emerging feminist and LGBT movements. Hundreds of thousands of Black and Puerto Rican people moved into the city, breathing fresh life into communities as they were revitalized in the face of withering postwar prosperity. Labor unions, in particular the transit workers, teachers, and sanitation workers, went on strike, and tensions were high across the city as it was reshaped before its occupants' eyes. There were few places on the planet more rife with change than New York City in the late 1960s.

Like the city, Paul was entering into a future that was uncertain. Having called Ed Winter to tell of his arrival, he had the afternoon to walk across the city before going to the theatre. August in the city was, as always, hot, and the sanitation strikes had hardly helped the sensory ambiance. Paul left his drum set in a storage locker in Grand Central Station, dropped his single suitcase off at a Howard Johnsons on 8th Avenue and made his way to pick up his ticket at the Imperial Theatre.

The Imperial, situated on one of the most congested theatre streets in Midtown Manhattan, was the second home of *Cabaret*. The show had been evicted from the Broadhurst to make room for *More Stately Mansions*, starring Ingrid Bergman, but had proved popular enough to necessitate a transfer rather than a closing. A ticket waited for Paul at the box office, at the behest of Ed, and with it, Paul's first true experience with Broadway.

Paul's earlier experience at *Gypsy* in San Francisco paled in comparison to *Cabaret* at the Imperial. While many of the structural elements within the Imperial were actually the same from *Gypsy*'s 1960 run in the theatre, the dramatic elements were worlds away. Whereas *Gypsy* had been a traditional book musical in sonic style and construction, *Cabaret* broke new ground, blending the avant-garde theatre that director Hal Prince had experienced in postwar Germany with the sinister and satirical lens of the John Kander and Fred Ebb collaboration. The creative team had barely scratched forty years of age, and with only one previous collaboration between them (1965's *Flora the Red Menace*, which had introduced Liza Minnelli to professional stardom), they had struck gold, winning Best Musical, Best Original Score, Best Direction, Best Choreography, Best Scenic Design, Best Costume Design, and a host of acting awards, including the Tony Award for Best Featured Actor for the then-fresh-faced Joel Grey (who had beat out Paul's pal Ed Winter for the honor).

Of course, none of this was weighing on Paul as he watched the story of Sally Bowles and the Kit Kat Klub unfold before him. What made an indelible mark was the score itself. The biting nature of the lyrics, bald-faced in their poetry, captured the imagination, as did the deceptively complex nature of the characters' musical styles, and the ways they came together only to be torn apart, both harmonically and textually. It was a glorious show, and Paul was taken in.

After the performance, Paul went around to the stage door of the Imperial to wait for Ed, as he processed what he had just seen. Unlike today, a theatrical stage door was a semiprivate place, without fans congregating for a glimpse of their favorite performers. Paul and Ed were able to have their friendly reunion behind the theatre, in the light of the stage door, when Music Director Harold Hastings exited for the evening. Ed introduced the pair; it proved to be an introduction that changed Paul's life forever.

Harold Hastings was a soft-tempered man who had music-directed fifteen Broadway musicals prior to *Cabaret*. Having met Hal Prince behind the scenes at the short-lived musical revue *Tickets, Please!* Hastings had quickly become Prince's go-to man at the podium, with ten of Hastings' credits being under Prince's employ. Known throughout the community for his kind heart and flexibility, Harold was the type of man to put the art before his ego, and he was eager to reach out and help, extending his assistance to anyone who might need it. When he met Paul, the typical pleasantries were exchanged, but both men quickly found footing with each other, in particular after Paul expressed his admiration of the score. The pair swiftly progressed from small talk, and Harold asked Paul about his previous experiences and how he planned to get back to San Francisco.

Paul had been trained to always carry a résumé with him in his back pocket by his professors at SFSU. On the train ride into the city, he had penciled in the tour with Toni, updating the résumé on the off chance he would need an up-to-date copy before returning to California, and his typewriter. His preparation proved priceless. He handed the résumé off, explaining that he had no set plans to return to San Francisco just yet. Harold was impressed with Paul's playing experience and told him to come by the theatre the next afternoon so they could talk privately. Paul agreed, and Harold left Paul and Ed to enjoy their night, Paul's résumé in hand.

The next day, Harold had an offer for Paul. The first national tour of *Cabaret* was going out in December, and they needed a drummer. He knew Paul was a conductor at heart and not a career percussionist, so he cut him a deal. He would be the drummer for the tour and would have the additional credit of assistant conductor. While the additional position had no pay bump, and Paul would not conduct a performance unless the tour conductor dropped dead, it was a significant concession to give an as yet untested musician within the world of theatrical music. Paul agreed, so long as he could find some sort of employment in the four-month interim. Harold arranged with the accordion player from the Broadway company for Paul to join Harry Simeone, the writer of "The Little Drummer Boy," on tour for ten weeks prior to the beginning of the *Cabaret* tour, and the deal was done.

Paul had come to New York on a whim and had snagged a job as drummer and assistant conductor on the first national tour of the reigning best musical on Broadway in less than forty-eight hours.

The Simeone tour served as a stepping-stone for Paul, both logistically and artistically, as he moved from playing jazz clubs to playing more theatrical music. The structure of the production itself was not dissimilar from the musician and performer setups Paul had grown accustomed to in dance and USO bands, only the music was much more set in stone, with less room to improvise around the repetitive nature of consistent schedules. They played one-night-only shows, hopping from city to city throughout the eastern seaboard. Paul had never seen any of the East Coast before coming to New York, and less than three months later, he had seen the overwhelming majority, going as far south as Florida. The tour itself was unremarkable, but it was Paul's first real touring experience, outside of the Minnesota residency and touring with his college peers. When he arrived back in New York, two weeks before *Cabaret* was set to begin rehearsals in Connecticut, he had just enough time to horse around and learn the city as he prepared for untested musical waters.

Paul's drums were taken to New Haven in the company truck, and Paul drove himself in a rented car the day before rehearsals were to begin. The musicians were to get a standard eight-hour rehearsal to work through the score on the first day, the second would serve as a dress rehearsal with the cast, and then the tour would be off and rolling. Paul made it to New Haven around eight that night and found a bar where he could sit, eat a quick dinner, and watch TV as he drank a few beers in celebration. A few beers turned into a handful, and he made it back to the hotel next to the theatre late that night.

All musicians were to report at 10:00 a.m. for rehearsal. Paul awoke five minutes before ten, hungover. He was able to pull himself into a functional state in about fifteen minutes and made it to rehearsal a quarter past late. Unfortunately, unlike a brass player, Paul could not just whip out his instrument and begin. Instead, in front of the entire company, including a disapproving Harold, Paul had to assemble his drum set. He got through it with minor visual embarrassment, but the experience rattled him. He made it through the rehearsal, picking up the show and executing the complex rhythm sequences swiftly, and he assured Harold that the incident would never happen again. Thankfully (and in gratitude to a good alarm clock) this proved true.

The *Cabaret* tour was a fantastic experience for Paul. The company bonded, as many shows do, into a tight community, and it was Paul's first taste of the nebulous Theatre Family. They traveled through the United States, and up into Canada for a stop in Toronto, expanding Paul's knowledge of the continent further. Paul saw more of the world on tour than he had in the thirty-one years leading up to it. But even as so many things were different from what Paul had known, much was the same.

In Cincinnati, there was a small jazz club down the alley from the theatre where *Cabaret* was playing. *Cabaret* was in town for two weeks, and for much of the run, Paul would break down and transport his drum set after the show into the club in order to jam with the local musicians and other members of the *Cabaret* orchestra. He would leave his drum set in the club around 2:00 a.m. and collect it the next afternoon to disassemble and return to the theatre, as if nothing had ever happened. What had been Paul's life, playing in jazz clubs, had become something more like a moonlight passion—something that he did to scratch his own back artistically before returning to the theatre, where his greater needs were beginning to be met.

On the San Francisco stop, Paul received a call from Harold Hastings. Kander and Ebb had a new show, called *Zorba*, and he needed Paul back in New York to play drums in the pit. Paul was reticent—he was back home, and by returning to New York, he would be creating a life on the East Coast, away from the foundation he had built in California. He wanted to conduct, and to return to play in the pit was not a move that made sense to him. They reached a compromise. Harold would give Paul the road company of *Zorba* to conduct, in exchange for Paul coming to play *Zorba* in New York. Paul had proved himself to be an immense talent, and Harold was adamant that Paul take this second job. Trusting him, Paul got on a plane and went back to New York.

Paul's Broadway debut as a musician was a pleasant one—the pit of *Zorba* was a happy place to be, if less flashy than *Cabaret*. Based on the 1964 film *Zorba the Greek*, *Zorba* followed the friendship between Zorba and the American Nikos, who had inherited an abandoned mine in Crete. Along the way, both friends fall in love, and the show takes a turn befitting a traditional Greek tragedy when Zorba kills himself after finding Nikos sleeping with the woman he loves. The show was steeped in Hal Prince's research and Kander and Ebb's particular panache, and, just like *Cabaret*, it captured the energy of a European country that exemplified "the old world" that the 1960s had begun to leave behind. *Zorba* opened in 1968, in the same season as *Hair*, *1776*, and *Promises, Promises*, and lost all but one Tony Award that season, blown into the shadows by the perfect storm that was their competition.

Zorba's score was an interesting one, and Paul had plenty to do, with multiple different percussion setups surrounding him. Three musicians played onstage at various times in the show, playing traditional Greek music sequences, and they would exit and enter the pit via a door to Paul's left, as would the goats that were used for certain pastoral sequences.

Yes, goats. Well-behaved (and fairly well trained), they were tied to a metal grate in the pit when not onstage, content to rest and watch when not in use. One night, in the middle of an extended book scene, Paul felt a tap on his shoulder. When he looked behind, he saw that the tap had come from a hoof. One of the goats had cheerfully chewed its way through the rope that tied him to the grate, and he had come to inspect Paul before making his way up the stairs to explore. Much to the suppressed laughter of those that surrounded him, Paul grabbed the goat and petted it for a while, keeping it quiet and entertained until the time came for Paul to have to play again. The rope that the goat had been tied to, although chewed through, was fairly long, and shortly before the next musical number, Paul was able to get up and refasten the goat under the snickers of his fellow musicians, including Harold Hastings at the podium. Thankfully, the goat made no bleats or cries, and the show continued on as if nothing had happened, and a note was made to tie the goats up with metal dog leads instead of chewable rope.

When *Zorba* closed a mere nine months after opening, much of the original company stayed on to do the tour. For many of the Greek musicians and actors in New York, *Zorba* was a rarity—a show that directly dealt with their heritage and let them perform a piece of their own artistic culture. The principal players stayed in New York, and so Chita Rivera, John Raitt, and Barbara Baxley were brought in to head the tour. *Zorba* had the same tour route as *Cabaret*, only with the city order jumbled around. It was the perfect show for Paul to begin his journey as a musical theatre conductor. Coming directly out of the pit in New York, he quickly assimilated into the touring routine and was able to guide the company through, forging his first real friendships in the theatre with the tour's stars. They had a month-long residency in Detroit, and the three Greek musicians found a small club where they could sit in and play, much as Paul had during *Cabaret* in Cincinnati. Paul, Chita, and John would go to the club after the show to support them and to have dinner. The three of them grew close on tour, becoming a family both inside and outside of the show, and the nights spent huddled together in that small Detroit club became the bedrock of long-lasting friendships. Paul's friendship with John Raitt lasted until Raitt's death in 2005, and his friendship with Chita continues to this day.

Nine months into the tour, *Zorba* had reached San Francisco. At the Curran Theatre, one of the most important theatres on the West Coast, *Zorba* was set to run for forty-six performances, the longest stop of the tour. Paul took Chita out to see the city, and they went to Fisherman's Wharf, a sort of boardwalk with amusements, tourist traps, and great local food. While walking, they stumbled upon a man dressed as the

Universal Monster iteration of Frankenstein among the other street performers in front of Madame Tussauds. Locked still, almost as if he were a statue waiting to be reanimated, he was an impressive sight. Wearing high platform shoes to make his height imposing, he wore a suit near exact to the one from the film and a wonderfully constructed rubber mask that made him look exactly like Boris Karloff. At the sight of him, frozen against the sky, Chita had one of her clever ideas.

Chita's daughter, Lisa Mordente, who was playing Tasso on the tour, was turning eleven. Her first birthday out on the road, the company had been searching for a way to make it special, and Chita decided that she and Paul had found it. They hired the man to come to the theatre and sing "Happy Birthday" to Lisa with the company that night: a real-life movie monster, straight off the screen. Paul and Chita returned to the Curran, getting everything ready for the celebration, but when the street performer made his grand entrance, things did not go as planned.

Lisa, unprepared for the sight of a monster appearing from the shadows, bolted for the basement, panicking. But even more surprising was Chita, who, caught off guard by the man's appearance out of the light of day, ran in fear alongside her daughter. Lisa locked herself in a basement bathroom, terrified, as the company tried to make sense of the sudden hysterics. After what felt like an hour, the pair were talked out of the bathroom and the birthday celebration was completed, the poor street performer now the accidental subject of a preteen girl's nightmares. Chita's reaction to her own planned surprise has, fifty years later, still not been fully explained.

CHAPTER FIVE

Picking Up the Baton

WITH LESS THAN A MONTH LEFT IN THE *ZORBA* TOUR, PAUL RECEIVED another call from Harold Hastings. Harold had a new show in New York that he said would allow Paul to meet everyone he would ever need in his career. The catch? Stepping down as music director and conductor for the *Zorba* tour to once again play drums in the pit.

For Paul, it was out of the question. To leave the podium was to leave everything he had fought for, and a new show in New York wasn't worth it—*Zorba* was playing well in San Francisco, and to go back to New York for anything less than a lateral career move didn't make sense. *Zorba* had been the last show he was willing to be a pit musician on, something he had made clear to Harold when he had received the call to do *Zorba* in the first place. Hastings cajoled him, listing off the names of the creative team—"Michael Bennett, Stephen Sondheim, Hal Prince!" Paul was hardly impressed. He was already working for Hal Prince and had now done two shows with him. Bennett and Sondheim weren't recognizable names to Paul, and regardless of what Harold said, Paul refused to play in the pit for *Follies*. The two men butted heads, with Harold fighting to pull Paul back to New York, until finally telling Paul that if he did not come back, he would fire him from the road show of *Zorba*. Paul hung up.

Naturally rattled, Paul called friends to explain what had happened, as he questioned if Harold would actually carry out the threat. But instead of support, he was met with incredulity on the other line. "You mean he handed you the opportunity to work with Michael Bennett on the new Stephen Sondheim and Hal Prince musical, and you *refused?*"

It was a golden opportunity, an absolute gift that Harold was offering Paul, and as each friend lectured him, Paul slowly realized his mistake. He had a healthy respect for Hal Prince, and he knew Ed Winter had left *Cabaret* to work with Bennett on *Promises, Promises* while Paul had been playing drums on the tour of *Cabaret*. And Stephen Sondheim, his friends forcefully explained, was someone who Paul should know.

Swallowing his pride, and sleeping on it for a night, Paul called Harold the next morning. He would come back to New York at the end of *Zorba*'s run in San Francisco, leaving the tour early, and accept the demotion from music director to pit percussionist. Harold, happy that Paul had seen sense, told him that he was doing the right thing, and the pair never spoke of the fight again.

Follies was Sondheim's love letter to the Ziegfeld era and the grandeur that had been lost to the decay of time. At the time, it was the second-most expensive musical that had ever been produced, only narrowly edged out by the Katharine Hepburn–led *Coco*. Paul had, by the skin of his teeth, slipped into a piece of theatre history *about* theatre history. As the rehearsal drummer, Paul was in the room as the show was built, collaborating with choreographer Michael Bennett to create the rhythmic underscoring to the "Loveland" dance sequences. After eight hours of rehearsal, Paul would load his drum set into his VW Bug, and he would drive the dance team to Feller Studios, in which Boris Aronson's set was being built. Alongside Michael, his assistants Bob Avian and Graciela Daniele, actor Gene Nelson, and the rehearsal pianist John Berkman, they would work through Gene's extended tap sequences for hours, perfecting every step to make sure Gene was as comfortable as possible on the raked set. When everyone was thoroughly exhausted, they would pile back into their respective cars, Gene, John, and Bob in one, and Graciela and Michael in Paul's cramped coupe. Graciela laid claim to the passenger seat, leaving Michael to wrap around the snare drum and partially disassembled cymbals in the backseat, his hair wild and limbs contorted in the pattern of a cubist painting to avoid kicking a hole through the drumhead during their animated discussions. This diligent routine was repeated for three weeks, and Michael never opted to take the other car's open seat, much to everyone's amusement.

When *Follies* held its out-of-town tryout in Boston, Paul and Michael continued with their late-night rehearsals, going up to the roof to try to create a brand-new opening number after performances. Slowly, the cast got in on the action, changing out of costume and into rehearsal clothes to devote even more time and energy to a show that everyone was invested in making work. Michael loved his dancers, his dancers loved him, and the can-do attitude of the show was infectious. These late-night sessions built a sense of camaraderie that has remained for much of the cast to this day, and Paul and Michael struck up a devoted friendship that lasted until Bennett's death in 1987.

Within the show, there is a sequence in the middle of the song "Who's That Woman." Commonly referred to as "Mirror Mirror," the leading women are pulled back into their memories of their young lives performing in the Follies, and they perform a tap number mirrored by the reflection of their younger selves. It was complex choreography, and the performers had to be exact in their execution to present a unified tap sound. Dorothy Collins and Alexis Smith, the actresses playing Phyllis and Sally, were not world-class dancers, and neither were many of the young women in the ensemble. They had been cast for their vocal and acting talents, and while some were good tappers, if even one of them fell out of sync it would ruin the sound. Normally, when a tap number is happening onstage, a microphone will be put either in the stage or attached to the tap shoe of a performer, to ensure that the sound of the tap rhythms is presented loudly to the audience through the sound system. To present a more cohesive sound, and to avoid any audible slipups in the choreography, Michael had a small dance floor installed in the pit, next to Paul's drum setup. The dance captains, who were not being utilized onstage, would come down and tap the number directly into microphones, giving a crisp and controlled sound for the sound engineers.

This trick worked flawlessly, giving audiences the appearance that the aging stars were truly returning to their young and hopeful selves, both in memory of the routine and in technical execution of the tap steps. But a problem came that winter, when the flu swept through the cast. Performers were calling out left and right, and it wasn't unusual for five people to be out per performance. One day, during the "Mirror Mirror" sequence, the tap section sounded different—there was a sharpness to the rhythm that Paul had not heard before. He turned and was greeted by the sight of Michael Bennett and one of his assistants personally tapping out the number. Both of the normal dancers had called out at the last minute, and they had stepped in, performing for an audience that was none the wiser to Michael's presence, months into the run. Surprised, Paul greeted Michael, and the two held a hushed conversation, without Michael missing a single beat of the complex choreography.

Follies swept the Drama Desk Awards and was nominated for eleven Tony Awards, winning seven, including Best Choreography for Michael Bennett's work. They lost Best Musical to *Two Gentlemen of Verona*, a Shakespearean rock musical adaptation by Galt MacDermot, the composer of *Hair*. It is, to date, one of the most contested wins in Tony Awards history, and you would be hard-pressed to find a room of theatre fans today who universally agree with the outcome.

Shortly after the Tony Awards, Hastings left *Follies* to work on a new show, *The Selling of the President*. His assistant conductor was promoted to conductor of *Follies*, and bombed. Hard. He conducted the orchestra as if they were chained to a metronome, rather than a living part of the show. His style of conducting was very difficult to follow, and his tempos made the show drag on, frustrating the cast and the pit musicians to no end. Everyone loved Harold, and word quickly got back to him that his replacement was not up to snuff.

Harold freed up some time from his new show to check up on *Follies*, and it did not take long for him to see the problem. What was meant to be a driven score was being conducted with no passion. Hastings found Paul in the musicians' locker room before the matinee the next day and told him that he would be conducting the next matinee, much to Paul's shock.

Paul had not been in the line of presumed ascension to the podium, but after two days of intense preparation, he got up in front of the colleagues he had been playing with for five months and conducted the show well. Not perfectly, but well. Harold congratulated him and left, leaving Paul confused, until a week later, when he got the call that the assistant conductor had been removed, and that Paul was to take over as conductor until Harold Hasting returned from opening the new show. *The Selling of the President* opened and closed in ten days, and Hal Prince decided that he had other work for Hastings, which left Paul to conduct for the rest of the run of *Follies*. Paul was now a conductor of a major Broadway musical, and he had been there from the start to see how Hastings had pulled the show together as music director.

Paul then took the show out on the road. The tour of *Follies* was extremely tight financially—they had lost a significant amount of money on Broadway, and no new investors had sprung up to finance the tour. The original Broadway set was reworked to travel, and they were sent to California with hopes that fans of classic Hollywood would gravitate toward the larger-than-life story. *Follies* was to be the inaugural production in a new Shubert Theatre in Los Angeles—at 2,100 seats, the theatre was to be massive, and much of the space was built around the requirements to stage *Follies*. Shortly before the show left New York, the Shubert Organization requested specifications from Paul for exactly how he wanted the pit to be when they arrived—he provided the measurements from the pit at the Winter Garden Theatre, which had been approximately eight feet deep from the top of the orchestra rail. This gave clearance for any musicians to stand in the pit if need be without their heads being visible, and it gave him room to conduct from atop the podium without blocking an audience member's view.

Unfortunately, when Paul arrived in Los Angeles the day before the first dress rehearsal, he found that there had been a miscommunication, and the contractors had dug a ten-foot-deep pit from the floor of the audience—approximately a fifteen-foot drop from the stage, painted pitch-black. This could absolutely not do—Paul had to be able to see his performers to conduct, and even if he stood on his tiptoes in the chasm, he wouldn't have been able to see anything but the sides of the hole. After receiving a firm promise that they would build a wooden platform to raise the pit to the proper level, Paul asked to go down into the pit to inspect the other elements. There was one more problem.

They had neglected to leave space for doors when pouring the concrete for the pit, and it was quite literally a massive hole you either fell into or climbed out of, with no proper entrance and exit.

His hands tied, Paul rehearsed the touring company (which included his old friend Ed Winter as Benjamin Stone) as best he could the next day through the cacophony of carpet being stapled to the floor and dynamite blasts in the oversized pit to create entrance and exit doors. A $5,000 wooden platform was built to raise the pit six feet, and the musicians were left to wander a maze up and down staircases to eventually enter the pit. Finally, the show opened to decent crowds, and the company settled into a six-month sit-down engagement.

In an atypical act of parental pride, Ezio and Margaret decided to come to Los Angeles from San Francisco to see the show. They had never seen Paul conduct and were finally ready to engage with what he had been doing on the East Coast, even if they didn't understand what it was that he actually did. When he went to pick up a pair of tickets for them, the box office informed him they were sold out. Surprised, he took it in stride and phoned home for a different date, but when the original date came, he glanced over his shoulder and saw hundreds of empty seats. The same thing happened, date after date—somehow they were sold out, while playing to increasingly anemic audiences.

The Shubert Organization had told their box office workers to instruct anyone who attempted to purchase a ticket to *Follies* that the show was sold out, regardless of the actual sales. They had decided that they wanted *Follies* out of the theatre in order to make room for a more popular tenant, and by decreasing the grosses they could activate the stop clause that would allow them to evict *Follies* before the end of the six months. By the time Paul figured out what was happening, it was too late, and the tour of *Follies* was forced to close two-and-a-half months into the run.

What was supposed to be a career boon had turned into a fizzle, and when Paul returned to New York, there was no work for him. He had conducted on Broadway, which was no small feat, but it meant that no one was looking to hire him to play percussion in the pit. He had gotten what he wanted—to be known as the person at the podium, but with only the *Zorba* tour and *Follies* under his belt, no one was willing to take the chance on hiring him from the outset. Hastings had already started work on *A Little Night Music* and had hired a new assistant conductor and pit drummer, having expected Paul to be out on the road with *Follies* for at least a year.

Paul was unemployed, and he had very little saved up—tours of musicals didn't pay musicians very well, and the *Follies* tour had been so short that the salary didn't stretch very far. By now Paul was attached to New York, and he refused to admit defeat by moving home and leaving Broadway behind. He found an ad looking for school bus drivers and was preparing to take the test to be certified when Kurt Peterson, one of the young actors from *Follies*, gave him a call. Some people had come together to do a concert for Stephen Sondheim, and they wanted Paul to music-direct. Paul said yes and prepared to work on a small benefit for the York Theatre, with just a piano, a bass, and drums (which Paul would play himself, to increase his salary slightly). Rehearsing in apartments around the city, the show sparkled, and as word got out, more people asked to join. What started as a little revue blossomed into a huge production, with more and more numbers and more and more stars attaching themselves. It quickly outgrew the York benefit and moved to the Shubert Theatre, where *Sondheim: A Musical Tribute* played as a sold-out one-night event. Using the sets of the currently playing *A Little Night Music*, the night was positively star studded, with representation from every avenue of Sondheim's career up to that point, from Larry Kert (the original Tony in *West Side Story*) to Glynis Johns (who was bringing the house down every night with "Send in the Clowns" at *A Little Night Music*). And in front of them all, Paul was at the podium. Paul not only conducted the variance of scores with skill, but as music director, his name was directly attached to the creation of this "little concert that could," responsible for the structure and flow of the evening's music. The show was recorded live by RCA Records and sold very well, with the distinctive Scrabble Tile cover instantly memorable. However, the majority of the press coverage omitted Paul's involvement altogether.

This was not due to any kind of intentional plot against Paul—quite the opposite. It was the norm for a music director to remain unacknowledged—you almost never saw a music director's name listed outside a theatre alongside the rest of the creative team, and music directors were primarily treated like human metronomes, separate from the cast and creative team as more utilitarian than artistic. The work of a music director is difficult for an audience to see, but it is critical to an audience member's experience, and this tight line of near-invisible power has kept music directors near-invisible as well.

During the concert, Paul was not invisible to other music directors in the crowd. No longer the upstart with a handful of touring credits to his name, he had proved himself a highly capable conductor to everyone who had watched him, including Elliot Lawrence. Lawrence, who had served as music director for the original productions of *Bye Bye Birdie*, *How to Succeed in Business Without Really Trying*, *The Apple Tree*, and *1776*, had just opened what was to be his final show on Broadway—*Sugar*, an adaptation of the film *Some Like It Hot*. Lawrence called Paul to give an incredibly kind review of the concert and Paul's hard work.

About a month after the concert, when Paul had taken and passed the school bus driving test, Lawrence called again. He needed a replacement conductor at *Sugar*, and Paul immediately agreed, leaving his bus-driving career behind permanently.

CHAPTER SIX

Does That Mean I'm the Music Director?

PAUL WAS IN THE BACK OF THE MAJESTIC THEATRE ON MAY 30, 1973, familiarizing himself with *Sugar* and preparing to take over from Lawrence the next day, when an usher came to him at intermission. There was a call for him on the box office telephone. Paul went, confused as to who would be contacting him there, and took the call from Howard Haines, the general manager of Hal Prince's office. He declined to give Paul details, but asked him to come to Hal's office after the matinee. Paul agreed and was greeted by a stone-faced Howard when he arrived. The pair quickly went to Haines's office, where Howard shared a critical announcement.

Harold Hastings was dead at age fifty-six of a heart attack. He had died with little warning, at home with his wife and two daughters. Paul's mentor, who had boosted him up the ladder so many times, was gone, and the void left was near impossible for the Prince office to fill. His assistant of twenty-five years was not going to fill the position, and they needed Paul to take over—he had proved himself on *Follies*, and again at the concert, that he was incredibly adept at conducting Sondheim's work, and that they could trust him to do what needed to be done. As one of Hastings' protégés, it honored his memory, and his relentless faith in Paul, to hand Paul the baton.

Paul called Elliot Lawrence, explained the situation, and Lawrence released him from *Sugar* immediately, in an act of kind understanding that went on to define their working relationship for the rest of their careers. The next day, when Paul had been scheduled to take over *Sugar*, he began to learn *A Little Night Music*, and within five days he was conducting.

Hours before Paul's first performance conducting, Stephen Sondheim invited him out for a drink—Downey's Irish Pub was conveniently located near to the Shubert Theatre stage door, and it was known for hosting theatre types before and after curtains. Nervous, Paul tried to maintain his concentration on the show as the pair shared a few dark jokes to pass the time. Paul and Stephen had always been friendly since *Follies*, but the dynamic was not lost on Paul that Sondheim was the boss. The Prince office might sign off on his paychecks, and bring him on board, but as conductor, it was Sondheim's music that was being entrusted to him. The job before him was to take over the helm from Hastings, to present what Stephen had written, and here he was, an hour before curtain, nursing a drink alongside his nerves.

As the time came to return to the theatre, Paul asked Stephen for any advice he might have, expecting a note on the score or on the show itself—some kind of key that as composer, Sondheim would be able to impart. Instead, Stephen took a moment, inclined his head, and told him quite plainly to "just do what you do." It was simple enough advice, and hardly what Paul was looking for as he prepared to take this step into the unknown, but the trust of the remark was inadvertently an omen of their working relationship from that day forward.

The pit musicians had a pinch of trouble adjusting to the sudden shift—Harold was beloved, and his sudden death coupled with Paul's sudden takeover had everyone on edge. But Paul stuck it out, slowly winning over the company with his collaborative approach to creating a stronger whole. Paul would check in with everyone following a show, visiting dressing rooms to personally deliver notes and to hear any concerns anyone might have had from onstage.

Hermione Gingold, the eccentric English actress who originated the role of Madame Armfeldt, had a dressing room on the ground floor, next to the stage manager's desk. At the end of his daily rounds, Paul would come to Hermione, who had a habit of stretching his last name into an entire musical phrase of a greeting. One night, after being urged to enter, Paul was greeted by the septuagenarian in nothing but her stockings.

Shocked, Paul whipped around as she cackled, alerting leading-lady Glynis Johns and the rest of the company as to what had happened. Soon, Paul was being greeted by the same breathy *Gemignani* from other members of the company (although thankfully, they remained clothed). The joke stuck, and to the majority of people Paul has worked with over the years, he is known by his last name.

A portion of Paul's energy during the show was always focused on the needs of Hermione and Glynis. As the leading ladies of the company, they required a particularly deft hand. Both had remarkable sweet tooths, and they equally adored the boccone dolce (an Italian meringue, chocolate, and strawberry dessert) served at Sardi's across the street from the theatre. One day, Glynis sent word to Paul during intermission, asking him to go across the street and fetch her one, since she couldn't leave the theatre in costume. He obliged, and when Hermione heard of the incident, she was incensed. From that point on, Paul had to carve time into his intermission schedule to pick up the dessert for *both* women when the craving would arise.

Paul was just beginning to settle in with *A Little Night Music* for the long haul when he received a call from Hal Prince. He needed Paul to take over a production of *Candide*, again on short notice. John Mauceri, a former student of Leonard Bernstein's, had been assigned to the project but had had to exit, leaving Hal with no one at the podium. Paul took over, marking his second emergency replacement in a Prince show, with his former conductor from the tour of *Cabaret*, Joseph Lewis, acting as his assistant conductor.

The cast, made up of almost entirely new talent straight from classical-training programs, took to Paul immediately. Paul's classical training at SFSU made him adept at communicating with the cast, while his more open approach from his jazz training made him a favorite of the musicians. He began casually dating a member of the company, and the show moved forward steadily under his baton.

Leonard Bernstein, the composer of *Candide*, took a firm liking to Paul. Giving him the tongue-in-cheek nickname "Gem of the Sea," he came to a dress rehearsal of the production once Paul had taken over. He was one of the few people to ever shake Paul's steady stability at the podium. Bernstein had been one of Paul's conducting idols—growing up, Paul had eagerly watched broadcasts of Bernstein conducting, and when he had decided to be a conductor, it was Bernstein he had planned to emulate. To do the show in front of him was nerve-racking, and it was the closest Paul ever came to bowing under the sudden pressure that had been placed on his back following Harold Hastings' death. Paul got through it, and the two men had a frank and friendly conversation, with Paul doing his best to appear comfortable as he struggled to suppress his awe.

The two men had a similar philosophy musically, over which they connected—rather than approaching music in a tyrannical manner, they preferred to collaborate, leaving room for interpretation and nuance. Bernstein, a composer revered for his skill, was not married to one interpretation—in fact, it was quite the opposite. He loved the sound Paul had gotten out of the pit for the revised orchestrations of *Candide*, and how that sound delivered in a much brighter, natural way to the audience.

The key of that delivery was Paul's trust in his musicians. Paul's philosophy was and is simple—if a person is in the room, you need to treat them as if they deserve to be in the room. A person's individual attitudes and approaches are a part of them—to become so good a player as to be working professionally requires a long period of study and practice, and every musician has a different way of approaching their craft. By showing that he trusted them, Paul had built an attitude of collaboration and trust, and the camaraderie in the pit felt more like a team than a competition. They were all working together to make the strongest product, and what resulted was a cohesive sound.

While working on *Candide*, *A Little Night Music* announced a closing date, in part due to a musicians' strike. Paul put Joe Lewis on as conductor at *Candide* and conducted the final performance of *A Little Night Music*, wrapping up that company and preparing it to go out on the road as he helped to guide *Candide* to its end. In the midst of balancing the two productions, Hal called upon Paul one more time. The New Phoenix Repertory Company was in its second season, and as one of the artistic directors, Hal had three plays to direct for the 1973/1974 season. The company was fledgling at best, and Hal needed Paul to handle the music on a shoestring budget.

The three plays—*Holiday*, *The Visit*, and *Love for Love*, posed new challenges. *Holiday* and *Love for Love* were not unlike Paul's previous work in San Francisco, with the incidental music provided by records he would adjust the needle on throughout the show. But unlike San Francisco, it was Paul who was selecting the records. Hal gave him free rein to find recordings accurate to the period, and Paul would present the options to him for approval. This curation process gave Paul an opportunity to call upon the immense musical knowledge he had absorbed as a teen and a creative freedom he had not previously enjoyed as a conductor—as a replacement music director, it was his job to keep the ship stable and watertight, not build it from scratch.

The Visit gave Paul the chance to build from scratch. There were two live musicians, and Paul was tasked with composing the pieces they were to play through the three acts. Paul had previously composed some in college, including a handful of the classes' revues, but he had never considered it as a viable career path. Working on *The Visit* confirmed that judgment. He was able to produce a score that fulfilled Hal's needs, but the amount of painstaking effort did not give him an equal sense of achievement. Paul was, and is, an interpretive artist.

There is a tremendous amount of pressure put on artistic people to be creative—to generate new ideas, new thoughts, and new approaches. The problem with that rhetoric is that it often drowns out the contributions of interpretive artists. A composer, who is by nature a creative, can sit with a piece for months, constructing something that presents perfectly on paper, but it is up to interpretive artists such as performers and musicians to elevate the piece to a consumable reality. Paul's gift as an interpretive artist was to breathe life into a score with his passion and never-ending investigation; working on *The Visit* underlined to him that he belonged with the baton rather than the pencil.

Paul worked on the three plays with Hal as he wrapped up *Candide*, proving himself adept under pressure and capable of handling an immense number of projects. Now, why Hal brought Paul on for all of these projects is debatable. Hal himself was known for always staying busy, to the point that he started on new shows before the dust had even settled on a previous project's opening night. However, even with Hal's tendency to swift work, it is hard not to see this period as a test for Paul. He was replacing the late Harold Hastings, Hal's musical right hand, and Hal wasn't going to trust Paul to fill his shoes permanently without a few trials. Of course, Paul was not aware of any of this at the time—he took the offers at face value and assumed Hal simply needed his help, knowing that Paul would respond to last-minute calls. This ready-for-anything attitude proved handy, and it served as the foundation for the busiest fifteen years of Paul's life.

This period jump-started when out of the blue Paul received a phone call from Stephen Sondheim.

Sondheim was working on a new show, about the Westernization of Japan over a hundred-year span. A blend of classical Asian theatre and quasi-Japanese music styles, it was a challenge quite different from the score of *A Little Night Music*, which was steeped in European polyphonic composition traditions and three-quarter time. Shortly after that, Paul also received a call from Hal Prince to set up a meeting. By the third call from Howard Haines, confusion had set in. Howard ironed out details with Paul about the project and the meeting between the men, but when the time came to make it official, Paul did not know exactly what it was he was agreeing to.

He liked working with Hal and Stephen and was happy to hear that they had a new show in the pipeline, but this time it seemed that Paul was being included on the project from the outset. Not as an emergency fill in, but as a collaborator. Unsure of what this meant, Paul stopped Howard to clarify.

"Does that mean I'm *the* music director? Because this is the sixth show in a row for the office now."

Howard paused, and with a slight smile of exasperation in his voice, replied, "Yes, Paul. You're the music director."

Chapter Seven

Pacific Overtures

He is always my first choice—he is almost everyone's first choice.
—Stephen Sondheim (Composer, Lyricist)

Pacific Overtures was an immense challenge for Paul's first show as full-time music director. While he had been in the room for the rehearsal process with *Follies* and was used to the workload of conducting after *A Little Night Music*, a music director's responsibilities go above and beyond those visible aspects. The music department, headed by the music director and the orchestrator, have a mountain of responsibilities to bring a new musical to life, and *Pacific Overtures* was a particularly treacherous climb. Jonathan Tunick, Sondheim's long-term orchestrator, was tasked with arranging the score for performers and musicians alike, including a traditional Japanese shamisen. Paul was tasked with filling the requirements of Jonathan's orchestrations, both in the pit and onstage, as well as serving as the musical representative in the audition room for every actor Hal considered.

Casting is much more complex than handing the job to the best auditionee. It requires a careful balancing of the scales between artistic and functional requirements, with the balance constantly changing as different members of the creative team pull in different directions. *Pacific Overtures* had a very specific set of needs from the outset—they were committed to having an entirely East Asian cast, consisting primarily of men with experience in traditional Japanese Kabuki theatre, who had to sing in traditionally Western and Eastern musical styles, in addition to being strong actors who could keep up with the complexity of the historical story line.

Of those four requirements, the most difficult proved to be musical styles, which was Paul's purview. There is a specific difficulty to the task—while most musicians are skilled at shifting between methodology, traditional Japanese music is an entirely different language to the Western music canon on which most Americans are raised. Eastern music is based on a pentatonic scale, consisting of five notes, and has little interest in the Western fascination with harmony, instead putting value in line and rhythm orientation and counterpoint. Western music is based on a heptatonic scale (seven notes to an octave) and is driven by melody and harmony, with rhythm often serving as an undercurrent rather than the driving force.

These structural differences mean that, for the majority of performers, it is difficult to switch between the two. A person primarily trained in traditional Japanese music may be incredibly talented at navigating complex rhythms and tracks but be at a loss during moments of eight-part harmony. Likewise, someone trained in the Western tradition may approach the complex choral sections with ease but quickly lose their place during songs that rely on a deep understanding of contrapuntal rhythms.

While talent can play a part in this disconnect, it goes much deeper. The music a person is raised listening to gets into their bones. It becomes the foundation for how they engage with music—a sort of artistic first language. While a person may learn different styles of music throughout their lifetime, the music of their childhood is often the one they return to again and again as a source of comfort and a source of stability. Paul needed to find performers who were at home with the traditional Eastern music motifs that grounded the show, but who could disappear thoroughly into the Western sequences. And as if these were not strict-enough requirements, they had to be strong vocalists.

They saw thousands of performers, many of whom checked three of the four boxes—concessions were made from different members of the creative team to bring on fantastic singers with unpolished acting talent and brilliant actors with less than stellar vocals. As music director it was Paul's job to take the actors and turn them into singers, and his skill at shaping a song around the skills of a vocalist has become one of his professional calling cards.

There was one performer, brought in from a regional production of Rodgers and Hammerstein's *Flower Drum Song*, who checked all four boxes. Alvin Ing, a tenor born and raised in Honolulu, Hawaii, had played the role of Wang Ta in countless tours and regional productions of *Flower Drum Song*, and he had become synonymous with the show, performing in more licensed productions than any other performer. He was brought in to audition for *Pacific Overtures* and found his second long-term theatrical home. His high tenor perfectly suited him to several of the feminine roles within the show, and the strength of his voice was arresting as he employed a strong understanding of the rhythms and harmonies presented to him as the Shogun's Mother, the Observer, and the American Admiral. Alvin was hired, became the primary tenor of the original production, and went on to perform in every official tour and Broadway revival of the piece, with the role of Shogun's Mother forever tied to his voice.

The cornerstone of the show's storytelling was Makoto Iwamatsu, commonly known as Mako. Born and raised in Kobe, Japan, he had split his adolescence between his grandmother's care in Japan and his parents' in the United States before becoming a naturalized US citizen in 1956. He had quickly become a rising film star, nominated for the Academy Award for Best Supporting Actor in 1966 for his work in the film *The Sand Pebbles*. He had formed the East West Players, a Los Angeles theatre company dedicated to Asian American actors, and was deeply invested in the exploration of art between the Eastern and Western traditions. He had been brought on before auditions had even begun, and he was to be the leader of the company as the Reciter, Shogun, and Emperor.

A cast was slowly unearthed from every corner of the globe, with the majority making their Broadway debut. *Pacific Overtures* was the first Broadway musical with an entirely Asian cast, with one glaring error— James Dybas, a Caucasian man, lied to the team about his ancestry, falsely claiming Filipino heritage. As performers were selected and signed, Paul was deeply involved in research. He had seen traditional Japanese theatre while on tour with the USO, in particular an all-female production of a traditional French play where the lead woman's hyper-specific movement had blown him away. Her precision became the basis for his approach to the show, both in teaching and conducting it. The sharpness of each moment in contrast to the elegance of each sequence became a defining characteristic of the piece, and Paul had to pick up the Eastern musical tradition as quickly as possible. He hired two classically trained Japanese musicians, Fusako Yoshida and Genji Ito, who served as the bedrock of the show's Eastern musical sequences. Genji spoke English and would translate between Paul and Fusako (known as Sako) when elaborate hand signals would not suffice in sharing information.

They had assembled a cast, they had assembled an orchestra, and they had assembled a creative team. With those hurdles cleared, *Pacific Overtures* moved into rehearsals in preparation for an out-of-town tryout in Boston. Paul knew he was in for a huge challenge. He had to teach an incredibly complex show to performers of various skill levels, and he had only just begun to grasp the complexities of the show himself. Thankfully, Sondheim and Prince believed in a free music department—rather than dictating to Paul and Jonathan what they wanted, they were trusted to figure out the necessities on their own, fostering a truly collaborative experience between the four men.

The score initially delivered by Stephen was almost exactly the same score they presented in Boston. Moments were expanded, and lyrics were tweaked, but the core of the show was there on arrival. The stability was a blessing as Paul worked to teach the show, as the complexities were challenging enough without the addition of constant changes and cuts. Two numbers were particularly challenging—"Four Black Dragons" and "Please Hello."

"Four Black Dragons" is the third number of the show and is primarily underscored by an insistent drumbeat, propelling the number forward. If any one performer missed a count, the entire number was lost. So much of the piece relied on a deep understanding of the rhythms of the song, and it was almost impossible to get back on track if someone dropped a line or jumped a beat ahead. In "Please Hello," the problem was almost exactly opposite. The number is a pastiche of various Western music styles as traders come in contact with Japan, and the music sharply switches between parodies of an American Sousa march, a British patter song, a clog-dancing Dutchman, a gloomy Russian, and a bright Frenchman. The sheer number of musical threads at play were at risk of unraveling, and the company rehearsed the number regularly to get the styles into the bones of the performers.

Paul worked with Sako and Genji to create the music that would be played onstage during the more traditional Kabuki sequences. Sako was a brilliant musician, and her compositions would be presented to Sondheim, who would approve them before they were finalized. Traditional Japanese music is written in a style similar to the notation used in Gregorian chants, and Paul was tasked with taking Sako's work and translating it to Western notation in order to place it in the official copies of the score.

When the show opened in Boston, the company's primary focus was clarity. They knew the show was out of the ordinary, and that the overwhelming majority of their audiences would be ignorant of the styles being utilized to tell history that most Americans were unaware of. To refine the piece to make it as clear as possible to an observer was the aim, and by the end of their run in Boston, they had found something close to crystal transparency. The show covered more than a hundred years, steeped in cultural traditions and patterns, and they had created a piece that both taught and expanded the interests of its audience.

Much of this clarity was achieved through simplification. Boris Aronson, one of the most talented set designers in the history of the American musical theatre, had created a beautiful set for the Boston run, including a realistic teahouse, da Vinci–inspired contraptions people could walk into and operate, functional wagons and rickshaws, a giant ship, and a hanamichi that extended over the pit and through the center of the audience, transforming the stage into a traditional Kabuki setup. It was visually stunning but made it harder to follow the story, so Hal made the decision to cut all but the ship, the hanamichi, and the set dressing for "Four Black Dragons." Paul found out about this particular change when he came to the theatre one day, arriving before the rest of the company. There was a parking lot next to the theatre, and it was filled with the set piled up against itself. Paul assumed that they were painting the stage floor until Hal pulled him aside to tell him that they were starting over. This was not an inexpensive decision, but one that proved worthwhile. Boris changed his design concept midstream, and the theatre was draped in a parachute material that hung from the ceiling, making it easier for an audience to know where to focus (different settings were delineated by different props, such as tables). Still, what was left of the set was complex, and it held a number of secrets that a viewer could discover through repeat study.

Boris approached Paul during a rehearsal and pointed out the large boat that had become the centerpiece of the design. Boris asked Paul what he had noticed about the waves painted on the boat and pressed Paul to look beyond their beauty. After weeks of study and mounting confusion, Paul finally saw it. Hidden between figures of dragons formed by the waves were small sketches of Shunga, erotic scenes from the era of Edo Japan that echoed the song "Welcome to Kanagawa" toward the end of Act 1. They were so artfully rendered as to blend in with the rest of the design that it is believed that only those Boris pointed toward the feature noticed it, outside of the performers onstage who could see it up close.

These figures were hardly the only secret hidden onstage. *Pacific Overtures* was told almost entirely through male actors, playing both the masculine and feminine roles as is traditional in Kabuki. In the final song, "Next," a cast of female actors join as the swift period of expansion and modernization is dramatized. The women seem to appear from the ether, a new ingredient added at the finish. In fact, they had been onstage almost as long as their male counterparts. Swathed in black cloth and positioned with their faces hidden from view, they had filled crowd scenes and moved set pieces, acting as the silent heartbeat behind the rhythm of the show's visuals. Only Freda Foh Shen had been visible, momentarily, as the Shogun's Wife during "Chrysanthemum Tea." Through their disguised effort, the show continued to glide smoothly, with their work hidden from the audience to preserve the illusion.

The company was under an immense amount of pressure to make sure the show worked. Everyone, from the youngest ensemble member to Hal Prince, as director and producer, had a responsibility. Rather than letting the stress keep them apart, the company held tightly together, working toward their common goal—to bring *Pacific Overtures* to life, and by extension, bring the history itself to light. Friendships abounded through the company, including a bond between Paul and Mako. Paul acted as the sort of creative manager of the company—while Hal and Steve were always the bosses, Paul would take their requests and present them to the company, working with them day in and day out to maintain the musicality of the show. Similarly, Mako was the leader of the cast both in role and in respect. Mako led by example, and the cast was eager to follow.

Mako was the pinnacle of discipline. Every performance, he would arrive early, shave his head to ensure clean physical presentation, and be onstage, ready to begin before the doors had even been opened to the public. Traditionally in a musical, the half-hour mark is when everyone begins to settle in and prepare as the audience filters into their seats. For Mako, the half-hour mark was the moment he had to be ready. There was no messing around backstage, no late check-ins and hasty preparations. He would come out to the stage, seat himself in his opening position as the Reciter, and meditate for the entire half hour, listening to the sounds of the theatre surrounding him. The rest of the company followed suit, preparing early and leaving the half-hour time frame for reflection and focus—even the stagehands would whisper into their mics, the hallowed energy of the space permeating everyone around it. The stage would be ready at half hour, with everyone in place, waiting with bated breath for the curtain to rise and for the show to begin. This routine of reverence eight times a week, performed before every performance, fostered a sense of purpose in the company that is incredibly hard to achieve without a leader as esteemed as Mako.

This isn't to say Mako was all business all the time. He was a kind man, and quite funny, telling jokes with Paul in his dressing room before the half-hour call. He was simply aware, as was the rest of the company, of the gravity of the story they were presenting. Paul understood this weight and worked with Mako, both as music director and friend, to create an environment in which Mako could best do his job. Mako almost never left the stage, phasing from role to role, and he spoke the first and last phrases of the piece. It was his lines that underwent the most tweaking in Boston, in particular his first sequence in the opening number, "The Advantages of Floating in the Middle of the Sea." He presented a spoken monologue to underscoring before transitioning into a rhythmic song, full of tongue-twisting pitfalls for a native Japanese speaker. In particular, his third line, "the realities remain remote" proved troublesome. Steve had gone to Paul when he had first written the lyric change, concerned that it could sound like a joke in bad taste if not delivered properly. Paul was tasked with helping Mako navigate the phrase, and the change was given to him shortly before a performance (although Paul had the presence of mind to tell Mako to put down the straight razor before hearing the news). Mako stumbled over it at first, practicing it in his dressing room with difficulty, but swiftly rose to the task, and after a few weeks of focus he had it down cold, successfully delivering a sequence of words that became one of the more iconic phrases of the entire piece.

As the Reciter, Mako served as the narrator of more than a hundred years of Japanese history, and the weight of that responsibility was not lost on him. This company, composed of Asian performers, telling a distinctly Asian story, was far from the Broadway norm, and they knew that it was going to take every ounce of their focus and dedication to do the story justice in a way that would open the minds of its audiences. By the end of their out-of-town run, they knew that they had produced a gem of a show. Concise, clear, and respectful, it was as digestible as possible. Unfortunately, audiences did not necessarily feel the same. *Pacific Overtures* is a deeply poetic show, and much of the audience went into the experience expecting to be confused. Boston was a hard sell, with the majority of the audience there not interested in complex stories of Japanese history told honestly. New York was only slightly better, and the novelty of the piece brought enough people in to see the show to keep it open for six months. They were nominated for ten Tony Awards, winning two, including Boris Aronson for his magnificent set.

The unfortunately stunted Broadway run was far from the end of *Pacific Overtures.* A video recording of the original Broadway cast was made and broadcast on Japanese television, and it was so successful that subsequent recordings of Sondheim's work were made for VHS release for the next decade. The production transferred to California and positively glowed. People traveled across the Pacific to see the show live, and the company was greeted with the respect and admiration they had deserved from the very beginning. Hundreds of young Asian and Asian American artists saw themselves presented on the musical theatre stage, and it has become one of the most influential musicals in history for the East Asian community. It has been revived once on Broadway, with Alvin Ing reprising his role as Shogun's Mother, and Paul again picking up the baton as music director. In 2017, it was successfully staged Off Broadway, with George Takei taking Mako's place. Stephen Sondheim has gone on record that "Someone in a Tree" is his favorite song he has ever written, and pieces of the show have deeply influenced the way non-Western music has been incorporated into the musical theatre tradition ever since.

Paul had successfully rehearsed, opened, closed, and toured his first musical from start to finish. Paul's drum set was in storage, collecting dust as Paul stepped steadily into a different kind of light. When Genji, the young drummer of *Pacific Overtures*, expressed interest in American jazz music, Paul gave him the set, passing on the luck that it had brought him. Paul had loved his time in jazz, and he loved playing percussion, but the time had come to pass the mallet on to the next generation. With *Pacific Overtures* under his belt, Paul no longer had to question if this was where he belonged. He had unquestionably risen to the challenge and found the right home for his lifestyle of constant change. He married his girlfriend of two years, and put down roots in New York. He had found stability in chaos, the very thing that he had searched for since playing USO gigs in Oakland, and he was ready to commit to the commotion of the theatre, leaving his life as a jazz drummer behind for good.

Chapter Eight

A Little Night Music (Film)

Paul has such a great love of music. He knows how to help make it come alive through you. Paul creates life.
—Bernadette Peters (Actor, Singer)

Shortly after *Pacific Overtures* closed on Broadway, work on the film adaptation of *A Little Night Music* began. Hal Prince was directing, and he had brought his music department with him from the Broadway production, as well as a good chunk of the cast—Len Cariou, Hermione Gingold, and Laurence Guittard reprised their roles from the original production, and Elizabeth Taylor, Diana Rigg, and Lesley-Anne Down were brought on to add film star gravitas to the project. The film was plagued with problems from the start, and as Paul's first experience on a film set, it set the tone for how difficult it can be to capture the energy of a musical onscreen.

Much of the film's success hinged on Elizabeth Taylor, both for her immense star power and the immense pressure that came with the role of Desiree. The breakout song of the show, "Send in the Clowns," fell on her shoulders, and as a non-singer, that was quite a nerve-racking position to be placed in. Paul worked with her in earnest, helping her find a sense of calm and confidence from the ground up. They would sit together in the Viennese recording booth, recording every line over and over until it finally came out the way Elizabeth needed it to sound. Her trust in Paul to be honest with her soon blossomed into a friendship, and during a night off from production, she invited Paul to a concert with her. Sammy Davis Jr. was playing, and Paul agreed, escorting Elizabeth alongside a handful of others.

It was one of the best live concerts Paul had ever seen. Sammy had seemingly endless reservoirs of energy and did not leave the stage for two hours, tap dancing and singing to the rafters, with the pedal to the floor for the entire night. After the concert they returned to Elizabeth's seven-room suite in the Hotel Imperial, where a large silver tub of Beluga caviar was waiting, a gift from the Shah of Iran. The group worked through the sea of caviar, and countless bottles of wine, enjoying each other's company until the early hours of morning, when Paul finally made the decision to return home.

As he waited for the elevator, good humored from the night, he ran into Sammy himself. Paul expressed his intense enjoyment of the show, and Sammy offered to have his driver take Paul home. Sammy and Paul discussed music and life for the length of the drive, and Paul was safely returned home from the whirlwind of upper-echelon Hollywood celebrity with the genuine kindness of Sammy and the luxuriant company of Elizabeth echoing in his mind forever.

Working on *A Little Night Music* was not all caviar and limousines, however. The Viennese producers caused significant roadblocks in production and micromanaged Paul and Jonathan in a way Hal and Steve never had. The two men, now well-worn colleagues, had a particular way of working together, and they had to invent ways around the interference to produce as high a quality product as they could. A new scene was written for the film where Desiree is the guest celebrity in a provincial town, and a small-town band playing a military march in the background was required. Jonathan composed the march, and Paul was tasked with conducting the band made up of an actual Austrian Army band that had been hired by a producer. Unfortunately, as can happen when musicians are hired by people outside the music department, the Army band was not good enough to be good, but not bad enough to be funny—the two options of playing the sequence. Jonathan had an idea and quickly passed it to Paul, knowing that improving the quality of the musicians would take much more time and effort than lowering their quality into the "so bad it's good" range. They told the musicians to transpose Jonathan's composition up a half tone on sight, and enough mistakes were produced that a charming chaos was created, sending Paul into hysterics and giving the team the truly questionable background music they needed to make the scene funny.

On nights after shooting, many of the original company members would go to Café Central in the first district of Vienna. A favorite of Hal's, it served fantastic pastry and German food, and the team would filter in as they finished their work for the day. Paul and Jonathan were often some of the last people at work, tweaking moments ever so slightly. One of these nights, Hal called them at midnight and told them to come down to the cafe. They arrived to an already jovial group, several glasses in, and Paul took a seat next to a happy Hermione, who handed Paul her champagne glass, insisting he start the night.

Unfortunately, with her eyesight somewhat fuzzy from age, she had not noticed the bits of food from her dinner that floated in the glass. Paul declined as the rest of the table watched, holding back snickers, as Hermione insisted. After a brief back-and-forth, and an indulgent shake of his head, Paul took the glass and downed it, much to Hermione's delight and the table's laughter.

In the midst of playful antics in Vienna, Paul was flying back to Los Angeles to oversee *Pacific Overtures* and ensure all was well with the company as the show opened to rapturous crowds. His schedule was changing constantly, as was the filming schedule, and a cameo that had been planned for him within the film had to be shifted. During the opening overture, he was supposed to be seen dressed up as Johannes Brahms, but *Pacific Overtures* urgently needed him back in the States, and so Jonathan filled in as Richard Strauss.

Although the movie was being filmed in Vienna, the decision was made to use the London Symphony Orchestra (LSO), and Paul spent much of his time in the recording studio next to Wembley Stadium, where they had to pause recording whenever the crowds would cheer. The Viennese producers wanted the original tapes used in the mixing of the LSO with the performers' voices, but Paul and Jonathan had the presence of mind to make a copy to hand off, just in case they needed to return to the unaltered version, without having to fly back to London to rerecord. This move, while potentially risky, paid off. While putting everything together, a government worker in the Viennese recording studio accidentally pressed mute and wiped the tape, destroying an entire sequence of the orchestral accompaniment. Paul admitted to the copy, and it saved the production schedule, much to the chagrin of those who had demanded there be no copies made for safety.

This experience, punctuated by moments of fun and laughter, unfortunately resulted in a film that is middling at best. It was Hal's final time directing a feature film, and Elizabeth was lambasted by critics for her fluctuating weight and inconsistent focus. Diana was somewhat more praised, but the film itself could not be saved critically. Adapting a musical for the screen is an intensely difficult task, and a person has to think differently between the two mediums, leaving a gulf of disconnect between the company members who had come from the Broadway production and the film stars who had been brought on to "legitimize" the project. What resulted was a labor of love, with an emphasis on the labor.

Still, it wasn't all for naught. Jonathan won an Academy Award for his work, the first of the awards that would lead to his EGOT (Emmy, Grammy, Oscar, and Tony awards), and Paul had learned how to work with traditional movie stars, a skill that would prove invaluable on future projects.

CHAPTER NINE

Side by Side by Sondheim

Paul has the sharpest ear in the business. He is highly intelligent and is not a cheap laugh. You have to impress him, and he does not suffer fools; his exacting tastes mean that when he says it's good you know it's really good. You can trust him.
—CHRISTINE BARANSKI (ACTOR, SINGER, COMEDIAN)

As PAUL AND THE REST OF THE PRINCE OFFICE WERE BUSY IN VIENNA filming *A Little Night Music*, a revue of Sondheim's career entitled *Side by Side by Sondheim* had opened in London. It was essentially an updated version of *Sondheim: A Musical Tribute*, only with a core cast of four performing all of the songs, rather than a star-studded night of single performances. Put together by Ned Sherrin and David Kernan, selections from eleven Sondheim projects were presented with the backing of two pianos, in an intimate examination of his career that was always climbing to new heights.

This was an exciting development. As adored as Sondheim was (and is) in artistic circles, he had suffered for many years under the popular (and incorrect) assumption regarding the "hummable" nature of a show tune. London didn't have the same holdups as New York, and *Side by Side* was a love letter to the poetry and storytelling he committed to music. Initially produced by Cameron Mackintosh, Hal Prince picked up the US rights before editing had even commenced on *A Little Night Music*.

Within a few months, Hal had successfully lobbied the American Actors Equity Association to allow the original London cast to come with the show to New York, and Paul was assigned to supervise the show and the handling of the music. With no orchestra, his day-to-day workload was significantly different than on any other project—instead, his skills at interpersonal management of a company came to the forefront. Millicent Martin, Julia McKenzie, David Kernan, and Ned Sherrin comprised the entire company, and with the show already on its feet and functional in London, Paul's primary job was to simply keep the house of cards from collapsing. Two new pianists were brought on to play the show, Daniel Troob and Albin Konopka, and Danny rearranged all of the piano charts to expand the size and scope of the sound produced by the two instruments. Those piano charts were the only significant change from the London production—songs, narration, and organization remained the same, with a few small tweaks and additions to tailor the show to American tastes.

It ended up being one of the most straightforward jobs Paul ever worked. The quartet knew what they were doing and knew how to approach their work—in particular, Millicent and Julia were on their A game, bringing their decades of stage experience to the piece in a way that lent a gravitas to the narratives they had interwoven. When they first opened, Paul attended every performance, nestled in the audience as he kept track of the show and its development. After a month of little to no change, Paul called a company meeting. It made no sense for him to continue coming every day, when coming twice a week would make it easier for him to notice changes, rather than his experiencing the same drift as the rest of them.

For the rest of the run, he would pop by, unannounced, entering with the throng and hiding in the balcony to check on the show. No one was ever aware of when he was in the room, and he was able to see the shape the show was in when no one felt like they were being graded. This technique of secret observation became Paul's modus operandi for checking in on touring companies for the rest of his career, and it was not uncommon to find him in the rafters of a theatre, a benevolent phantom.

Side by Side by Sondheim has the distinction of being one of the only shows in history to have every actor nominated for a Tony Award—both David and Ned were nominated for Best Featured Actor in a Musical, and Julia and Millicent for Best Featured Actress in a Musical. Of the five nominations, no wins were taken home, but the revue was successful enough with crowds to transfer from the Music Box Theatre to the now-demolished Morosco Theatre, and to experience two rounds of full cast replacements, including stints by Larry Kert and Hermione Gingold.

Paul's biweekly vigils meshed nicely with the addition of Hal's next project, *On the Twentieth Century*, which Paul would rehearse and open before *Side by Side* closed. Outside of *Zorba*, it was to be Paul's first journey outside of the world of Stephen Sondheim as music director and a feet-first dive into the world of the bold and brassy musical comedy.

CHAPTER TEN

On the Twentieth Century

Paul is one of the most prolific and important musical theatre conductors of the modern era. There are a lot of incredible music directors who have done a ton of wonderful work, but Paul is our history.
—JANE BROCKMAN (ACTOR, SINGER)

BASED IN PART ON THE 1934 PRE-CODE FILM *TWENTIETH CENTURY, ON the Twentieth Century* was a screwball comedy with shades of operetta that openly embraced and poked fun at the farcical backstage stories of the early Hollywood studio system. Written by duo Betty Comden and Adolph Green, it was a true-blue comedy, and a departure from much of the theatre Hal, and by extension Paul, had been making. It was theatre designed for entertainment and escapism, rather than historical or psychological exploration, and its sunny disposition was a tonic.

Comden and Green were theatrical stalwarts by the late 1970s, with *On the Town, Singin' in the Rain*, and *Bells Are Ringing* having been adapted into immensely successful MGM films. *On the Twentieth Century* was to be their triumphant return after eight years away from the New York theatre scene, and it was exactly the type of show the community was craving from them. Much of the character of Oscar Jaffe, the bankrupt theatrical producer, was based on David Belasco, one of the infamous eccentrics of early Broadway, and the book of the show was razor-sharp comedy, filled with references and jokes for almost every pop culture category.

Cy Coleman was brought on as composer, with four Tony nominations and multiple pop hits under his belt, including the seminal hit "Witchcraft." Cy had initially turned down the show, keeping clear of the musical theatre since the death of his writing partner Dorothy Fields in 1974, but he was won over when he recognized the comic opera potential of the melodramatic 1920s pastiche.

Once the trio of Comden, Green, and Coleman was assembled, Hal Prince came on board as director, bringing Paul with him to music-direct. Working with Cy stretched a very different muscle for Paul than working with Steve—whereas Sondheim was, and is, deeply entrenched in the connection between lyric and melody, Cy was firmly focused on his work musically, trusting Betty and Adolph to handle the text. While Paul had found his footing on *Pacific Overtures*, *On The Twentieth Century* promised to keep him on his toes.

Cy had perfect pitch, and it showed in how he composed. He was able to write music in a manner akin to stream of consciousness, naturally flowing between keys without a second thought. As it wasn't something he had ever needed to see written out, he almost never wrote in these changes for the benefit of whoever might be reading the music. When asked what key a song was in, it wasn't uncommon for him to shrug and say A♭ (his key of choice)—of course, just because he started there didn't mean he stayed in it for very long. This made his score hellish work to compile for an orchestrator, in this case Hershy Kay, who had orchestrated the production of *Candide* Paul had been swept into four years earlier.

Because of his perfect pitch, Cy was very particular about ensuring his music came out exactly the way he heard it in his head. Adjusting the key of songs and shifting pitches to accommodate a performer was something that he did not take lightly, and Paul had to be absolutely sure of a change before suggesting it.

Thankfully, few changes were necessary with the casting of John Cullum as Oscar Jaffee and Madeline Kahn as Lily Garland. Immensely talented, both had classically trained voices and could sing nearly anything put in front of them. Cullum, fresh off his first Tony for *Shenandoah*, was poised to be the next Richard Burton, with a rich baritone that could transform into a number of character inflections with ease. Madeline Kahn had a gloriously warm soprano, having trained with Beverley Peck Johnson and performed in several Broadway shows before exploding as the star of three successive Mel Brooks comedies—*Blazing Saddles*, *Young Frankenstein*, and *High Anxiety*. Now beloved by America for her on-screen comedic talents, she was returning to the staged musical comedy, with much fanfare.

Soon a cast formed around the two stars, including Imogene Coca, who was nationally adored for her involvement in *Your Show of Shows*. Kevin Kline was brought on to play Bruce Granit, Lily Garland's boy-toy lover, and the company was filled with some of the best classical singers and comedians in the city. Four dancers—Keith Davis, Quitman Fudd III, Ray Stephens, and Joseph Wise—were brought on to play The Porters, the tap dancing, harmony-singing heartbeat of the show. Theirs were perhaps the most perilous roles in the show. All four had to remain perfectly aware of one another, synced in extremely stylized dance, as they maintained tight vocal harmonies that relied on absolute precision.

That is not to say the show was easy for anyone else. It was a beast of a show, with a high-octane requirement of its entire company. From the moment the show left the station, everyone had to keep the energy bouncing, or risk the show skidding off track. Thankfully, with Cy's dynamic score and Comden and Green's sparkling punchlines, the company quickly found the required rhythm. The greatest risk of derailment came in the show's repeatability. Cy's score was a complicated one, clearly written on a piano by someone who experienced music as though he himself was the instrument. Placing this vocally was a challenge, to say the least. While a piano is strung with steel, human vocal cords are much more fragile, and the cast risked damaging themselves during the out-of-the-gate eight-part harmonies that trended toward the stratosphere. It was Paul's job to assign performers the correct vocal track to keep them healthy, and *On the Twentieth Century* was an incredibly difficult show on which to ensure everyone's good health.

Had the cast been performing the show once or twice, as if making a studio album or a film, it would have been less of an issue. But a Broadway musical is a marathon, not a sprint, and the constant wear and tear of performing the score eight times a week was very risky. Paul had to institute a rolling cycle of "silent singers," chorus members who would mouth their way through certain songs to preserve their voices, while keeping the stage looking as full and bustling as a Twentieth Century Limited train. Thankfully the cycle did not prove aggressively necessary, but whenever a flu would come through the company, spots on the approved list would become hot commodities.

Betty and Adolph's contributions were thankfully less taxing on the health of the performers, though the demands of the lyrics and book were no less grueling artistically. Betty was intensely focused, and Adolph a true song-and-dance man, resulting in a text that could be endlessly mined for comedic beats. Like Cy, they knew exactly how something should be delivered and could see the performances in their heads. During the out-of-town tryout in Boston, a new number for Lily was added to the second act, called "Babette." With Madeline and the rest of the creative team, they tucked into a room downstairs in the theatre. Betty and Adolph took on the roles of Lily and Oscar, throwing themselves into the material. Whenever they performed their own material, it expanded to practically burst the space they occupied, over the top in the most delicious way possible. Betty and Adolph made you love them, and made you love their work even more—to capture their energy was Madeline's job, and thankfully she was one of the only actresses in the industry who was truly up to the job.

Madeline was, in a word, a genius. With a natural talent for timing, she could work her way through a comedic scene with such gusto that she practically glowed. Where other performers might anxiously jump from punch line to punch line, she relished in the silence between gags, pulling laughter out of thin air with something as small as a flick of the eyes. She could sing anything put in front of her, with a voice that was seemingly limitless, extending effortlessly into the stratosphere of clarion soprano. To see Madeline perform was to adore her, and to work with her was to love her. If any actress was to have the self-important airs of excellence, it was Madeline, but ever rebuking expectation, she was unassuming offstage, quiet and soft spoken. She lived with her mother and kept mostly to herself, leaving the larger-than-life antics on the stage or screen, depending on the job.

In contrast, Imogene was exactly who you would expect her to be offstage. Quick-witted and quirky, she had a wild sense of humor, even as the oldest member of the company. As the suspiciously religious Leticia Primrose, she would regularly stop the show with her lament against modern impropriety, "Repent," as the seventy-year-old rubber-faced her way through the entire show.

With this company of powerhouses assembled and rehearsed, the show prepared for a bang-up opening in Boston at the Colonial Theatre at the start of 1978. Housed in the Plaza Hotel, the cast could watch the comings and goings of cars and pedestrians on one of the main streets of Boston through floor-to-ceiling windows installed in the lobby. The morning of the show's first preview, the company descended to the lobby to find a thick slurry of snow pressed against the glass, stacked several feet high. The blizzard of '78 had descended on the city without warning, and much of the city was rendered untravelable, with the company walking together as a unit down the center of the street where the snow was best packed.

When Hal went out to welcome the audience to the first preview, which had been sold out in anticipation, he was greeted by a small smattering of rosy faces loosely dispersed through the massive theatre. Travel had been made next to impossible by the storm, and no one had been able to make it into the city but these few city dwellers who had braved the trek. To Hal's credit, rather than canceling the performance outright, he carried on as if nothing was odd, encouraging the audience to come down front, and presenting the show in full.

It was quite possibly the best audience *On the Twentieth Century* ever had. So raucous was the energy of the happy few that it reflected deeply on the company, who performed with full luster directly to them. By the next day the city had begun to excavate itself, and roads were reopened, but that first audience experienced the show in an intimate way never experienced by audiences in fuller theatres.

That was not the only thing they experienced differently than any other audience that followed. Robin Wagner, set designer extraordinaire, had designed a show curtain that looked like the train itself, complete with smokestack and wheels. When the driving rhythm of a train began to filter into the overture, picking up speed, the wheels of the curtain would spin, copying the rhythm as steam would come out of the smokestack, whistle blowing as Imogene waved out of the train engineer's window. A strident roar of applause would then echo through the theatre as the train drove away, revealing the company onboard the train for the rest of the evening.

Unfortunately, this marvelous effect called for more energy than the small generator backstage could provide, and the motors were burnt out after its first public presentation. More substantial motors could not fit on the set, and the curtain effect was cut, with the small crowd of the first preview serving as the only witnesses to the full creative vision.

On the Twentieth Century opened in New York to mixed reviews but an eager audience. However, tensions began to rise backstage as the company settled into the routine of an open-ended run. Madeline, ever the comedienne, would slide into moments of improv with John, creating new bits in character before the two would return to script. These moments were absolutely hysterical, and the freshness of the surprise kept the rest of the cast on their toes, although it put the more pattern-preferring members on edge. Paul found these moments endlessly entertaining, a master class in someone who had come as close to perfecting the comedic artform as anyone, but his opinion was unfortunately not shared by Hal.

Hal had a very specific vision for the show, and Madeline's bottomless bag of tricks was not a part of that vision. He had created and frozen a show at opening, and the constant tweaking on Madeline and John's part undermined what he had created. He approached her several times, reminding her to stick to script, but Madeline simply couldn't help herself, expanding and exploring moments as they came, pulling laughs from the audience with each invented sequence. After a particularly caustic conversation, it became clear that she and Hal were never going to agree on her purpose in the show, and nine weeks after opening, Madeline left, feeding a story about vocal damage to the *Times* as a way of explaining the sudden departure.

This greatly upset Paul. In his view, Madeline *was* Lily Garland, and to censure her for fully engaging with all of the variations she contained left a bitter taste in his mouth. Madeline was a star, and she knew it. She had her own concept of the show, and of her performance, and the constant attempts to contain her into what was expected was simply too much for her to bear. Although John had been involved in the improv as an equal partner, he was given more leeway, and Hal's issue with the episodes was leveled directly at her. Madeline, the ultimate professional, left before things could get ugly or uncomfortable for anyone else in the company.

Her understudy, Judy Kaye, was elevated to the role, launching her career. She would go on to become one of Hal's preferred sopranos, and she later originated the role of Carlotta in *The Phantom of the Opera*, cementing her as one of the most recognizable sopranos in musical theatre history. The sudden casting of Judy proved to be a brilliant marketing move, and she was promoted similarly to how fresh studio finds had been presented to the public during the height of the classic Hollywood studio era.

Hundreds of acquaintances came to see the show throughout its run, either to say hello to a cast member or to wave at Paul deep in the pit. One day, after a standard evening performance, an older man came shuffling down to the pit rail, balancing on his cane to shake Paul's hand. His dark and expressive eyes glimmered as Paul greeted him.

"Marvelous performance. You are a marvelous conductor, I admire you greatly."

Paul thanked him as the man nodded to the rest of the orchestra before turning to make the long ascent back up the aisle, shuffling against the support of his cane. Paul sat down, trying to place where he may have met the man before, when the oldest member of the string section caught his attention, eyes wide.

"You do realize that was Richard Rodgers."

The vague familiarity crashed over Paul like a ton of bricks. *The eyes!* A stroke and an extended bout of jaw cancer had muddled his visage, but the mischievous eyes had been the very same eyes Paul had stared at on the back of the *South Pacific* LP as a child. By the time he could whip around to catch another glimpse, Richard Rodgers was gone. He died the next year.

Approximately a year into the run, Imogene had to leave the production for a week to film a television pilot. The Prince office decided to bring in a star for the short stint to boost box office, before Betty Comden phoned the office and said that she wanted to do it. Hal, always eager for a cost-effective publicity stunt, loved the idea, and Betty stepped into the role, exploding out with her usual energy in an aggressively bombastic performance that mined every moment she had written, much to the appreciation of the audience.

The show ran comfortably for a respectable thirteen months and won five Tony Awards, including Cy's first win for Best Original Score. Madeline was nominated for Best Actress, but much of the voting committee did not see her performance before her departure, leaving her to be passed over for Liza Minnelli in *The Act*. Madeline did not return to Broadway for another decade, and she never did another full musical in New York before her untimely death in 1999 of ovarian cancer.

CHAPTER ELEVEN

Sweeney Todd—The
Demon Barber of Fleet Street

Paul is the Jolly Green Giant. He is an incredible musician, with a great sense of fun, and a great sense of the dramatic. The first time he saw the score for "Epiphany," during a break on a rehearsal day, he came into the rehearsal room and came over to me and said "You are not going to believe what I've just seen. You are going to shit yourself." It was absolutely brilliant.
—Len Cariou (Actor, Singer, Director)

In the midst of opening *On the Twentieth Century* and closing *Side by Side by Sondheim*, Paul received a call from Sondheim. The new show he had been working on was ready, and they made a date to meet at Steve's town house in New York to hear the score. Excited, the week-long wait felt endless, and when Paul was presented with the score, in a state of near completion, his high expectations were superseded. It was an overwhelming thing to be introduced to. Based on a Victorian pulp horror novel and Christopher Bond's 1973 melodrama, it was to be a sharp departure from anything else Broadway had ever seen. A story of violent retribution with extended periods of blank verse, *Sweeney Todd* married the nihilistic aesthetic of Jacobean tragedy with the unhinged justice of *The Count of Monte Cristo*. Borderline operatic; it had the scope of a great film score, with an almost unexplainable sweep to its grandeur;

69

and clocking in at nearly two hours of music, the score was certainly grand. Played on piano, with Sondheim singing all the parts, the show shined. Complex, convoluted, and at times caustic, *Sweeney* demanded a focus and an investment from its listener that was slowly becoming the calling card of a Sondheim score. In particular, the Act 1 closer, "A Little Priest," required a rapt audience to catch the more than sixty laugh lines delivered in a little more than seven minutes.

A score as brilliant as *Sweeney* required an extremely capable cast—while middling shows with great performances often survive to be considered successes, it is incredibly rare for a fantastic show to overcome a poor performance. *Sweeney* required brilliant actors of its principal players, as well as classically trained vocalists in its chorus, and the show proved to be one of the most difficult Paul ever had to cast. Angela Lansbury and Len Cariou were quickly brought on board to play the murderous Mrs. Lovett and Sweeney Todd, and they were soon followed by Victor Garber as Anthony Hope and Sarah Rice as Johanna, but the chorus and supporting male principals proved elusive.

To get the operatic sound out of a musical theatre chorus that *Sweeney* required was the chief struggle. Opera singers with the vocal technique were not trained to act as the pseudo-Greek chorus needed to, and by the late 1970s, the majority of actors had stopped training in classical voice. Alongside casting director Joanna Merlin, Paul had to find the best trained voices in the city, who had acting chops to match. In particular, the search for two Basso Profundo proved difficult, as the score insisted on a richness of sound that was uncommon, even among more traditional scores.

The search for principals was more straightforward—keys for individual songs were adjustable, and much of the leading characters was defined by their text rather than their vocal lines, with the stratospheric harmonies written into the chorus parts. This was not the case for the secondary antagonists, the Beadle and Pirelli. Pirelli, a high tenor, was adjustable as a final resort, but the Beadle required a performer of incredible technique, with vocal lines ranging across octaves that, if altered, would change the scope of the songs themselves. With time, Joaquin Romaguera and Jack Eric Williams were found to embody Pirelli and the

Beadle respectively, and the show began rehearsals in a theatre adjacent to the ANTA (American National Theatre and Academy).

It was a difficult show to get on its feet—so complex is the story, in conjunction with the score, that even the seasoned professionals among the cast struggled. Regardless of the difficulty, everyone was firmly on board with the project. In particular, Angela Lansbury, as leading lady of the company, set the tone for gratitude in hard work. Having worked with Sondheim previously on *Anyone Can Whistle*, *Sweeney* was to be Lansbury's unveiling as a brilliant vaudevillian, in contrast to the chanteuse-like roles she had been inhabiting since the success of *Mame*. The music hall comedy of the piece, which seemed so British to early audiences, was a performance touchstone for Lansbury, and an archetype that she was eager to occupy. This can-do energy affected the entirety of the cast, and they jumped in headfirst, ready to climb the mountain together.

Len Cariou was the only performer Paul properly knew going into the process, having worked together on *A Little Night Music*. Angela had featured on the *Sondheim: A Musical Tribute* concert that had launched Paul, but their interactions had been extremely limited. It did not take long for Paul to become beloved by the company. While clear with notes, he was never cruel, and he gave performers time to figure out their path, rather than insisting on an aggressive approach.

As a music director, one of the most defining aspects of your career is how you treat your performers. As the member of the creative team tasked with being true to and protecting the composer's vision, the music director's choices have far reaching implications on the piece as a whole. Once a show is up and running, however, it is impossible to entirely prevent drift. Performers and musicians are not robots, and with each performance, things are likely to change ever so slightly. With time, these changes can pile up, and what started as a clearly delineated arrangement can alter. While a conductor, who is often the music director, is at every performance, supposedly leading the pit and the performers in tandem, they have no actual control to force their conducting to be both understood and completed. They are perched at a podium, gesturing with a stick that makes no sound, and it is up to the musicians and the performers to follow. Should they not trust their conductor, it is well within their abilities to ignore them altogether (although such a choice rarely makes for a good show).

This trust starts at the very first day of rehearsal and is shaped by the rehearsal process itself. When Paul, or any other music director, sits down with the chorus and begins assignments, it is up to them to judge what is and isn't going to happen. And it is their judgment that can create either confident or diffident performers. Paul is blunt, but rarely harsh with his performers, and his honesty is almost always met with appreciation. Many performers struggle with self-confidence, and to know that Paul was not only in their corner, but would actively tell them if something wasn't working, was the safety net they needed to try things outside of their comfort zone. He took the time and care to ensure that performers sounded their best, regardless of their vocal training up to that point, and would work with non-singers so that, by the end of the process, they felt like singers. His support and confidence in their abilities allowed them to let go of the cycle of judgment and self-doubt many performers harbor, and they loved him for it.

Paul attracted a similar loyalty from his musicians—rather than conducting notes on a page, Paul conducts themes, and his work has an uplifted forward motion to it that keeps a listener on the edge of their seat, rather than relaxed back and passive. Energy coming from the pit in turn gives performers a deck of security on which to stand, making it possible for them to live in the moment and try things, because of their confidence that if something happens, the musicians will be listening, and Paul will be watching them intently to follow their lead, rather than forcing them to stick to their initial interpretation.

This is possible due to Paul's habit of memorizing the scores of the shows he conducts. Having his eyes on his performers, rather than down on his score, is critical, and this eyes-on approach makes it possible for him to be with his actors in every moment and able to turn the pit on a dime should something happen onstage that requires an adjustment to the score. A music director, in Paul's view, is there to support and uplift everyone around them. Music directors aren't there to tell someone they are not good enough, or that they messed something up. They are there to help performers and musicians alike get into the headspace they need to do their best, and to get them out of any problems that might arise from this. A music director is the undercover guardian of a production, with their eyes and ears open to keep anyone else from falling into any traps or pits of confusion and disconnect. This is not an easy method for a music director to adopt. It requires a silencing of the ego and a love for the process that demands investment. It is far simpler to lay out the pieces of the show and expect that they will look the exact same once you turn your back. To live and breathe with a show, keeping it buoyant with life is a difficult task, and it is Paul's hard work in this arena that made him such a natural fit for the complexity of Sondheim's work. No show, from a one-person show to a three-hour epic should be dragged down by an uninvolved music director.

And *Sweeney* was surely an epic. The show moved into the Uris (now known as the Gershwin) on 51st Street, which is the largest theatre on Broadway, seating 1,933 audience members. The Uris is also one of the more recent Broadway theatres, and it was borderline new at the opening of *Sweeney Todd*, having been built on the site of the former Capitol Theatre in 1972. With a sixty-five-foot proscenium arch and an eighty-foot-wide stage, its playing space is massive, and many shows struggled to fill its expanse, as well as reach the back rows of the stadium-style seating.

Such a large theatre required a masterful orchestration to fill the space without overpowering the delicate moments of the score. Jonathan Tunick, in a feat almost unimaginable, took the score and orchestrated it perfectly in twenty-four days. That speed is unheard of, and when the orchestra met to play through the orchestrations for the first time, not a single note was incorrect. What Tunick had created in those twenty-four days is the licensed orchestration today. The size of the space also meant that the scope of the sound being produced could be increased. Paul went to Sondheim and expressed disappointment that the gong heard to open the show couldn't be a factory whistle, as it would have been in reality. Stephen gave him permission to change it, and the prop master, George Green, found a real Victorian-era factory whistle to attach to the set. So earsplittingly loud was the whistle that when first played, the sound caused ears to ring, and the whistle had to be moved to the far back of the set to keep from hurting everybody in the theatre.

Normally the stage manager would trigger the whistle offstage, reading the score to play the cue exactly, but Paul insisted on being the one to trigger it, as locking the cue for the whistle would prevent Len from having any freedom of time with the murders throughout the show, as the whistle sounded at each death. They ran a hose from the whistle, through the top of the lighting grid, down through and across the floor, and down into the pit, to where a button was installed at Paul's feet. When the time came for the whistle, he would step on the button, sending the signal to the whistle to ring out through the theatre at the exact right moment to startle the audience. The shriek of the factory whistle went on to become one of the most iconic aspects of the *Sweeney Todd* score, but it was never officially notated into the show's original licensable orchestrations, as Tunick's were not altered after that first rehearsal.

Eugene Lee's set certainly took advantage of the space as well. A massive re-creation of Industrial-age London, the sharp ironwork angles that made up the two-tiered set ascended into the rafters, in which a metal bridge weighing two tons waited for release on thick motorcycle chains. Soot-stained and rough, there was nothing about the visual of the set that projected comfort. While functionally sparse, the placement of pieces gave the illusion of overcrowding, and when the entire company took the stage, it felt as though they were going to burst out into the audience itself. The metal roof of an actual factory in Vermont was brought in and installed as the overhang of the set, which jutted over the heads of the performers, the pit, and the audience for four rows of seating. The installation of this roof proved particularly difficult, as the weight of the metal could not be supported without the front end dipping down into the audience, nearly touching the seats themselves. An engineer was brought in, and massive four-inch holes were drilled through the walls of the theatre and into the office building next door to secure the roof to the other building's foundation with rods, earthquake shields, and washers and nuts the size of a fist. It was an incredibly dangerous set, both in look and function, and an immense amount of effort was put into ensuring the performers' safety. Still, one of the first previews of *Sweeney Todd* nearly ended in an unscripted decapitation.

Toward the end of the show, Sweeney and Mrs. Lovett venture out into the London fog to search for Tobias. With only Len and Angela onstage, creeping with lanterns through the stage fog, a soft clicking sound could be heard. In character, Len was able to look up and see that the chains holding the two-ton bridge had come loose, and that the bridge was swiftly descending directly on top of where the two of them were supposed to play the scene. Len was the only person aware of this, due to the fog and dim lighting, Paul was unable to see what was happening in the above stage space, and Angela had not noticed the sound. Acting swiftly, Len grabbed Angela and pulled her to the front of the stage, much to her and the rest of the company's confusion, as the bridge came undone behind them. So great was the crash that it cracked the show deck itself, and if Len had not acted, it is likely that they both would have been seriously injured. It took eight stagehands to lift the bridge enough to move it to the very back of the stage. The company finished the show for the aghast audience, and a fleet of workers were brought in to both repair the set and increase security measures before the next performance. Following this dramatic incident, there were no other safety issues.

As is his custom, Paul had memorized the score by the first preview, and he was conducting without it on the music stand in front of him. At this point, the technology used to create video monitors was low quality at best, and so Paul lined his music stand with white butcher paper, so that what little light was in the pit would reflect up on him to illuminate his hands enough that they showed up on the camera. The visibility of his hands on camera was key, as the stage manager had to have a clear visual from the monitor to sync the lighting and sound cues to the cues Paul gave in the music. In the middle of Act 1, at the front of the stage, Sweeney slits the throat of Pirelli, and the fake blood sprayed far enough so as to stain the white butcher's paper with blood splatters. Paul left it like that for the rest of the show's run, and audience members who peered into the pit during intermission were often heard exclaiming with surprised disgust when they saw it, much to the delight of Paul and the musicians. It was these small moments of levity that defined the backstage and behind-the-scenes environment of the company of *Sweeney*—so heavy was the show, that the lighthearted antics were rampant.

A few weeks into the run of the show, something started going awry at the end of "The Worst Pies in London." In the transition into "Poor Thing," small projectiles were hitting Paul, enough that he could tell they were there but soft enough not to cause actual damage. Befuddled, he would look around the podium to try to find what it was but was unable to decipher what was somehow coming loose. What made it even more confusing was the lack of regularity to the hits. What started as a one-off incident started happening once every two weeks, then twice a week, until eventually he was hit ten performances in a row. At his wit's end, Paul scoured around his podium after performances, and one day he found a tiny dough ball.

During "Worst Pies," Angela had to keep bustling and busy, and she had begun making the tiny projectiles as something to do while delivering the number. When the lights would black out, she would search for Paul's dimly illuminated hands and take aim at where she imagined his head would be. With time, her target accuracy had increased, leading to more consistent hits. Paul brought the remnants to her dressing room after a performance, placing the dough on her vanity table—after about thirty seconds of playing the innocent child, she let out a laugh of pure childish glee, and Angela moved on to a new activity to keep busy during the number.

At the opening-night party, Bloody Marys were served, and the show was deemed a critical darling, receiving praise-laden reviews. Richard Eder, then-critic at the *New York Times*, wrote, "There is more artistic energy, creative personality and plain excitement in '*Sweeney Todd*,' which opened last night at the enormous Uris Theater and made it seem like a cottage, than in a dozen average musicals." Five months later, glasses were again raised, this time in celebration of the birth of Paul's first child, a son, Alexander Cesare Gemignani. Overjoyed, Paul quickly fit into the role of doting father, magnanimous as he balanced the responsibilities of the show and a newborn.

That holiday season, Angela threw a big Christmas party for the company onstage at the Uris, and Alexander was brought along, a cherubic six-month-old. He was introduced to the company and doted on, as most theatrical children are, when Paul carried him over to Angela.

Angela had two children of her own, Anthony and Deirdre, and offered to hold Alexander for Paul so that he could refresh his drink. By the time Paul returned, Angela had disappeared into the party, and he did not see them again until three hours later, when he tracked down Angela, still holding a happy Alexander, and requested the return of his son. It was a family atmosphere at *Sweeney*, and they teased and cared for each other just as family members do, with a camaraderie formed through their devotion to the show.

Unfortunately, the public was not nearly as devoted to *Sweeney Todd*. Walkouts were rampant, with the gruesome subject matter and dense material putting off more casual theatregoers and tourists. They responded to the show on a visceral level and, instead of examining their reaction, left the show in droves. Paul would come out for the conductor's bow after intermission, and the audience would have shrunk significantly from his view at the top of the show. Eventually people stopped coming altogether, regardless of the strong critical support, and the size of the theatre only highlighted the shrinking audience.

A few months into the run of *Sweeney*, Paul began auditioning people for *Evita* during the day, as Hal was always eager to move on to the next project shortly after opening night. Once that process was through, Hal asked Paul to go to Los Angeles to open *Evita*'s out-of-town tryout, which Paul questioned. He loved *Sweeney*, and to abandon Len and Angela just as they were settling into the run felt like a betrayal of what they had built from the ground up. Hal acquiesced, Paul stayed with *Sweeney Todd* for the rest of its Broadway run, and he was put in charge of setting up the touring company for the musical. Paul helped rehearse and prepare the company and then handed the conducting and maintenance duties over to Jim Coleman.

Coleman had previously worked with Paul on a production of *A Little Night Music* starring Hermione Gingold and Jean Simmons, and he had seemed the natural fit to take over conducting *Sweeney* when he came backstage following a performance. Angela, however, was less than convinced. She had committed to staying with the production on the road and was nervous to do the show without Paul, and without the musicians she had grown to know over the yearlong run. It was arranged for Jim to conduct an "audition" of sorts, from the opening number through "Wait," to allow Angela to experience his style before giving her approval.

Auditioning via hopping onto the podium is a stressful situation for a conductor in any show. But in *Sweeney*, the problem is tenfold. So complex is the score that it can deceive a conductor if it is simply read through the sheet music. "Ladies in their Sensitivities," the Beadle's Act 1 ballad, accompanied only by celeste and harp, required complete connection between performer and musician to sync, and the final scenes were perilous, requiring a conductor to take a section written in six, subdivide it into nine, and then sync them to the vocal lines, written in a completely different time signature. To conduct *Sweeney Todd* properly is to know the score inside out, and Coleman haunted the pit for some time, observing Paul and the musicians as if to learn through osmosis. Finally, the day came that Jim felt comfortable enough to conduct his chunk at the next matinee. Paul and Jim walked to the train together after that night's performance, as had become their custom, and Jim asked questions of Paul as they came to him—mostly innocuous, Jim felt rather prepared when Paul turned to him, a slight twinkle in his eye.

"Well, you know you're the whistle then?"

The whistle? What whistle? Jim had been given a copy of the score, including Jonathan Tunick's full orchestrations, and had been memorizing them as best he could in preparation. Nowhere in the score was a whistle notated. The factory whistle had never once been mentioned to Jim as his responsibility, and he had assumed the stage manager controlled the cue. Had Paul not mentioned it, he never would have known to press the button on the podium at the very top of his audition, or for any of the murders that followed. Panicked, Jim went home and circled the "gong" cues in red ink, knowing that missing such a crucial element of the show's sound scape would dissolve his chances of Angela trusting him. Coleman conducted his chunk of the matinee and managed to make every whistle cue, having arrived early to locate where the button was that he had not noticed in all the weeks of observation. Angela was sufficiently pleased, Jim got the job as conductor for the *Sweeney* tour, and he also conducted the Broadway company for a week, giving him his Broadway debut.

On March 22, 1980, Sondheim turned fifty. In celebration, Judy Prince rented out the Belasco Theatre, formerly owned by eccentric impresario David Belasco, in order to throw a raucous get-together. As the plans for the party began to shape up, Jonathan Tunick and Paul decided to weave a joke into the night, with Judy Prince's approval. Steve had always admired Latin music, in particular the bossa nova, which had influenced much of his early work (including the pastiche song "The Boy from . . . ," which parodied "The Girl from Ipanema"). Paul and Jonathan volunteered to be the house band for the evening, playing only Latin rhythm covers of Steve's work. Pianist Tom Fay and bassist John Beal were roped into the deal, and the four men tucked into a corner, Paul at the drums and Jonathan on the saxophone, as they worked their way through almost every song Steve had written up to that point in his life, all while wearing Desi Arnaz–style ruffled performance shirts that had been obtained by the *Sweeney Todd* costume department. By the end of the night, Sondheim was finally able to worm his way through the throng of partygoers to find the four men, laughing.

Through his own raucous laughter, Steve joined the men upon the stage. "You know you have real friends when they will make fools out of themselves for you."

While in Los Angeles, the touring company (which was the majority of the closing Broadway cast, alongside Angela as Mrs. Lovett and George Hearn as Sweeney Todd) was filmed and released to the public, marking the third major production of Sondheim's work that was given a filmed release (following the *A Little Night Music* film adaptation and *Pacific Overtures* broadcast). Paul was scheduled to conduct the company for the recording, as he had for *A Little Night Music* and *Pacific Overtures*, but scheduling changes due to *Merrily We Roll Along* prevented Paul or Stephen from being present for filming, leaving Jim to captain the ship. This film was the first of its kind to be televised publicly through the Entertainment Channel, and it was followed by a successful VHS release. Much of *Sweeney Todd*'s devoted fan base can be traced back to this VHS—fans across the country were able to get their hands on a tangible version of the show that had lasted a little more than a year on Broadway, and they were able to pick it apart, rewinding and replaying moments until they had it committed to memory. *Sweeney* has proved to be one of the most accessible productions from Sondheim's repertoire, through this VHS, its RCA Cast Album release, and the 2007 film that spread the story of *Sweeney Todd* across the world.

CHAPTER TWELVE

Evita

*Paul is a man of the theatre. He cares and understands what perform-
ers go through. It is a rare quality for a music director to consider the
performer the way he does. Paul is the standard-bearer.*
        —PATTI LUPONE (ACTOR, SINGER)

BASED ON THE LIFE AND TIMES OF EVA DUARTE, INFAMOUS WIFE OF
Argentine dictator Juan Peron, *Evita* had been a hit in London before
transitioning to Los Angeles, with a new cast taking the helm. Patti
LuPone, who was primarily known as a founding member of The Acting
Company, became the American Eva while the original London com-
pany remained in England, and a cast was swiftly compiled, including
Mandy Patinkin as Che and Bob Gunton as Peron, along with Mark Hsu
Sayers from *Pacific Overtures* as Magaldi.

A part of Paul's deal with Hal to stay on *Sweeney Todd* was to help
cast the Los Angeles transfer and provide him a conductor to work the
show while Paul stayed in New York. In time, Rene Wiegert was selected,
and Paul functionally handed the show to him, naming him official music
director as Paul took the role of music contractor. Paul set up the show
and worked with the house contractor, Irving Berger, who hired the
orchestra that the three men agreed upon, but otherwise he gave Rene
free rein. He sent the company, under Rene's watchful eye, to California,
and focused on *Sweeney*, and the rumblings of Sondheim's follow-up
show.

Working double duty on *Sweeney Todd* and *Evita* was a difficult thing. As Paul would audition performers for *Evita* during the day and conduct *Sweeney* at night, there was very little time in between to rush back to New Jersey to see young Alexander. Once the Los Angeles production was up and running, he had a slight reprieve, until *Evita* came into New York and proved a smashing success.

Producers normally have three courses of action in terms of handling a hit musical. They can keep the Broadway production exclusive, resisting tours and external companies to continue to drive business to New York; they can send out touring companies once the initial buzz around the show dies down; or they can hit the ground running, launching as many companies as possible before the general public loses interest. Hal Prince made the decision to use option three on *Evita*.

The show came to New York with much fanfare, and engagements in California were maintained as a new company was assembled for a Chicago sit-down. A year into *Evita*'s blockbuster run, Rene needed to leave for a rest before beginning work on *Cats*, having become a favorite of Andrew Lloyd Webber. As a result, Hal enlisted Paul to come back on board. Paul handled New York, and all touring and sit-down companies. He became the main touch point for many of the casts, as Hal hopped between companies and numerous other projects, and camaraderie quickly developed regardless of his absence during the development process.

Patti LuPone had an immensely difficult time during *Evita*. As Eva, she had the weight of the entire show on her back, and the score had been written with a concept album in mind, making it intensely taxing on the voice. Alternate Eva's had been instituted, but six shows a week was still an immense ask of Patti's full belt. There are not many people who can sing like Patti can, and with good reason. No woman is born with a belt voice. In reality, a woman has a chest voice and a head voice, and belting is a technique that can be implemented once learned. Not all women are meant to have belt voices. Patti had a great teacher and her voice was in good shape, but even with all the training and preventative measures, she still, like anyone who ever sang Eva, had to be very careful to limit the use of her instrument. It is very easy to ruin the voice for a very long time if you do not heed the pitfalls of overusing or misusing your voice. Eva put a lot of pressure on all the ladies who played her, but as the American introduction, Patti had made her performance so iconic that she had to maintain the athleticism of her initial choices. Now, long into her interpretation, Paul came in and made different requests of her than Rene, who she had come to trust.

Paul and Patti have immensely similar temperaments. Both being raised staunchly Italian, they had no problem expressing their frustration at the lack of communication. In particular, shortly after Paul had taken over, they reached an impasse. Much of the music in the show is triggered by voice cues, and Paul had to time the pit exactly to the actors, breathing as a single organism. At one of these critical cues, Patti consistently turned upstage, making it impossible for Paul to see her mouth and judge the entrance. He asked her to turn out just enough for him to see the corner of her mouth, to which she agreed, and promptly forgot about it by the next performance. He reminded her, and when she forgot a second time to angle out, he was frustrated. Paul does not often have to give notes twice, and a third time was unheard of. He stormed out of the pit during intermission, heading straight to her dressing room. Both overwhelmed and overworked, they reached a sort of "Italian standoff," staring at each other with fury in silence until Paul threw up his hands, spat out a "fine," and stormed out of the room, slamming the door.

There was an immediate crash, echoing through the halls of the Broadway Theatre. Patti had had a mirror attached to her door for final checks, and the slamming of the door had cracked it as a literal breaking of the tension. Paul stood, frozen as the sharp sound rattled, before hearing a full chest laugh echo in its place. He turned, opened the door, and the pair embraced, repairing any harm done and setting the basis for a working relationship that has lasted fifty years.

Paul and Patti have always made a point of listening to each other— unfortunately, that was a courtesy not extended to Patti by every member of the *Evita* production team. Broadway theatres in the 1970s were rarely air-conditioned backstage, and a large number of the costumes within *Evita* were made of wool, making the show incredibly uncomfortable to perform during the hot summer months. Ensemble members narrowly avoided fainting in the wings as they attempted to catch a breeze between numbers, and for several weeks Patti fought with management to have fans installed in the wings to get some kind of air circulation. Finally, after a particularly stifling "Rainbow High," Patti stormed off for her next entrance with a bellowed *"WHERE ARE THE FUCKING FANS?"*

So loud was her plea that Paul was able to hear her from the podium. The next day, Patti entered the theatre to find stagehands hanging fans in the wings that Paul had demanded they purchase immediately following the show. From that moment forward, he became the unofficial key point of contact for the company, someone who was willing to listen to any concerns that had been previously ignored.

Of course, Patti couldn't stay with the show forever. At the end of her yearlong contract, she made the decision to leave, extending four months to give the creative team time to replace her at the start of 1981. Thankfully, with so many alternate productions of *Evita* running, it was fairly simple to pluck the matinee Eva from Los Angeles, Derin Altay, to take over.

Derin had had quite the journey with Eva up to this point. At the age of twenty-five, she was a fresh face on the Chicago theatre scene, playing Laurey in a production of *Oklahoma!* when she was first called in to audition for *Evita*, as Peron's Mistress. She was stunningly pretty—short, with richly dark hair, she reminded Paul of a young Barbara Stanwyck the moment she entered the audition. She practically glowed, entrancing Paul and Joanna Merlin. They called her back, and John David Wilder, one of the assistant stage managers who was helping to run the auditions, escorted her out. John David gave her "Another Suitcase in Another Hall" to learn, but Derin stopped him at the door.

"Have all the Eva's been cast?"

"Can you belt an F?"

"Yes."

Derin had no idea if she could belt an F—she had never even tried! But she knew in her gut that she was more of an Eva than a Mistress. Sure she could play the tragic ingenue, but she had a fire to her that she refused to hide behind the waifish and wilting women she was usually called in for. John David turned her right around, walked her back to the audition panel, and talked to Paul.

Deciding to give her a chance, Paul ran her through "Can't Help Lovin Dat Man" from *Show Boat*, raising the key as they went until she was belting the final stanza, easily gliding through a high F. Her adrenaline had taken over, and she soared, shocking the panel who had just heard her effortlessly work through a more classical soprano sound. Paul practically threw the music for "Rainbow High" at her and told her to come back the next day.

Paul and Joanna called Derin back multiple times, testing all of Eva's material on her before finally calling Hal Prince and Ruth Mitchell. They flew Derin to New York and presented her to the panel among a number of other options, assured that Hal would pick her out immediately. Hal was blown away, and Derin was immediately plugged into the rotating cast of Eva's, first as the Matinee Eva in Los Angeles. Once she was off to the races, Paul didn't see her again until her return to New York.

Though she was far away physically, she was never very far mentally. Her presence had performed a sort of alchemy on Paul. While he had never been one to believe in fate or predestined paths (his refusal to adhere to a prescribed plan had gotten him kicked out of Catholic school, after all), he could not shake the instinct that something momentous had happened the moment Derin had walked into the audition room. Married as he was, he had difficulty denying the immediate emotional reaction he had had to her presence, both in the audition room and working with her on the show before sending her off. In her prescence, he was sustained. Paul had never trusted emotion, especially when it came to romance—his track record with women was less than ideal, and he had been taught from an early age that the purpose of a relationship was not an intense emotion such as love, but to raise a family. He and his wife had done this—married, and had a son, carrying on the Gemignani name for another generation. But still, Derin flitted on the edges of his consciousness, even as he shut it away.

When Derin came to New York to replace Patti, the spark was slowly fanned. Paul would go from dressing room to dressing room before every show, checking in with everyone, and as the star, Derin was naturally the last in the lineup. Note sessions steadily extended in length, punctuated with moments of flirting and coy glances, both avoiding the first move.

Derin knew it was a dead end. Paul was married, and she knew better than to mess with a married man, especially when he was also her coworker. Still, he began to filter into her dreams, and the intensity of their working relationship slowly transformed into a different kind of passion. Finally, after months of dancing around each other, Paul let go, tossing out a half-rendered piece of beatnik slang from his teenage days that was akin to asking her to bed. She was shocked, laughing as he picked at the door frame behind him, but it worked.

It didn't take long for the pair to become absorbed with each other. While Paul would go home at night to his family, their time at the theatre together was sacred, even as Derin lost sleep alone in her apartment. He would spend as much time as was publicly appropriate in her dressing room, the pair's humor meshing well as they enjoyed the honeymoon phase. Soon they started flirting in front of the cast, with Paul jokingly trying to look under her skirt in the opening number of the show where she walked across the front of the stage, camouflaged as a mourner.

Derin had an immensely difficult job, filling the shoes of Patti LuPone in a role that was enough to make any actress blanche. She was young, making her Broadway debut, and living in New York for the first time, but seeing Paul every day kept her grounded and focused. His humor kept her from being tossed to the winds, and they stayed on course, making the hard work enjoyable for each other.

Their hidden affinity would unfortunately not last long. Derin was moved across the country to the California production, and Paul couldn't fight to keep her in New York without revealing the coupling to the rest of the creative team.

Paul was trying immensely hard to navigate the situation—his love for Derin battled against his responsibilities to his family, and he stood frozen between the two, going through the motions at home until Hal would send him to San Francisco to check on the show, when he could be reunited with Derin for a few short days. He never talked of leaving his wife for Derin, and Derin never asked it of him. He was a father, and

Derin knew that that would trump any emotion he personally felt. Paul would do whatever it took to ensure a happy and healthy life for Alexander, and his own happiness was only a footnote to that devotion.

Paul would occasionally make phone calls, reaching out to Derin for a few minutes under the guise of work questions, but as Derin was moved from company to company, their fragile relationship was ripped apart. They would find small moments, but they became few and far between until she was moved to the international tour of *Evita* and sent to Europe.

As Paul was wrestling with his turmoil at being apart from her, Derin struggled under the weight of the knowledge that there was nothing she could really do to stop the severing. She started loosely dating a member of the *Evita* company, and when he proposed to her, she called Paul to tell him.

She was bereft, needing some sign from Paul that all of the pain they were putting themselves through was worth it. She wept on the phone, telling Paul that she thought she cared for the other man enough to try to build a life with him, all the time expecting Paul to finally wake up and tell her not to do it. Instead, he remained silent, shattered as he accepted that he couldn't give Derin what she deserved, and that he couldn't leave Alexander to do something about it. He wished her luck, accepted his own despair, and hung up, leaving Derin alone with nothing but the sound of the dial tone, dreaming of a time line where he would have fought for her.

Paul threw himself into work, running from the emotional anguish by working himself to the point of exhaustion. They would not speak to each other again for more than a decade.

Chapter Thirteen

Merrily We Roll Along

Paul's heart and emotional life is so open and pure and joyous. He downplays everything about himself. He thinks of himself as good, but not special, when he should. He values the lives he is intertwined with so much. Sure, he has a great love affair with the bigger stars he works with, but Paul remembers every chorus kid, everybody who didn't get another gig after the one they did with him. He has great affection for the people he has worked with. You may not always know that when you're dealing with him, he isn't a touchy, feely guy, but his heart truly makes that connection for life. It is hard to not love him. He is one of the greatest artists, and one of the greatest spirits that I have been able to work with in the business, and I have been lucky enough to work with legends. Paul is right at the top.

—Jason Alexander (Actor, Singer, Writer)

Merrily We Roll Along was, from top to bottom, a labor of love. Hal's wife, Judy Prince, had recommended he and Steve work on a show about kids—Hal was a father of two and adored children. As the Prince children grew and matured into their own independent beings, he had been reminiscing to Judy about who they had been, and who they were becoming. One of Hal's favorite plays, 1934's *Merrily We Roll Along*, seemed like the perfect fit to explore these themes. Written by George S. Kaufman and Moss Hart, the play worked its way backward through a man's life, showing an audience member how a jaded and bitter adult had once been an eager and impetuous youth.

Hal took the idea to Steve, who immediately grabbed onto it. Youth, and what happens to youth over a period of time, was a familiar question for him as well. Steve's first show, *West Side Story*, had hit Broadway when he was twenty-five years old, and now at fifty, he had doubled his life experience. They brought on George Furth to write the book, which updated and modernized the original play, and Steve set himself the task of trying to write with the same recklessness he would have utilized when he was twenty-five.

It was an immensely difficult task. Everyone, even geniuses, fall into habits. You don't even notice they've developed until they're already there—little grains of sand slowly pile up, day after day, until suddenly the dune has moved from one shore to the next. To move back in time, undoing the erosion of youth's optimism, is immensely difficult, and Steve labored over it as Hal toyed with doing a reading of the show—getting together a group of kids to read through the updated book, to see if the concept would land. After all, the original play had been a financial failure and had never been revived. By testing the waters, everyone would know what they were getting into and what direction the project would need to take.

They compiled a group of kids from across the city—everyone from high school students to young professional actors came together onstage at the Broadway Theatre, where *Evita* was playing, as the world of the show began to take shape. By having young actors play older, rather than older actors playing young, even the harshest moments of the characters' lives were softened by the memory of the innocent adolescents they had been. You never forgot the child inside each character, and it gave an honesty to the show that was startling. A person cannot be written off as purely mean or nasty when you can see the scared kid beneath the bravado.

Emboldened by what they had seen at the reading, the team moved forward, with two actors coming along. James Weissenbach was given the role of Frank, and Lonny Price the role of Charley. Lonny, a twenty-one-year-old Juilliard dropout and openly earnest twenty-something, had a history with the Prince office. A Sondheim devotee, he had written fan letters to Steve and Hal in his teenage years. Both had written him back, and Hal had offered Lonny a job as an office boy, an opportunity he had leapt at. Lonny had even put his bar mitzvah money into *Pacific Overtures*, becoming one of Hal's thousands of backers.

With Frank and Charley cast, Paul and Joanna Merlin were given the task of finding the rest of the kids needed to fill out the company, including Mary, the third member of the core trio. Paul and Joanna had been a team together since *A Little Night Music*—while casting directors and music directors work together on every musical, their partnership in running auditions was unparalleled. It wasn't uncommon for the two of them to work together to shape an actor, bringing out the shine in them before showing them to Hal. Directors, as a general rule, have a vision going into casting, and Paul and Joanna got good at opening up that vision to alternate ideas.

Casting is an oft-maligned and regularly misunderstood aspect of the process of putting together a piece of theatre. More than just selecting the most talented person in the room, a casting director has to be something close to a fortune-teller, able to see potential success and failure at every turn. Every actor has to be sized up to judge any possible pitfalls, and pairs have to be jostled around until the right chemistry is discovered. A performer could be a perfect fit for the role but have zero chemistry with their costar, who is also a perfect fit, and the show can collapse because of that single unchecked box. Juggling so many balls in the air, it isn't uncommon for casting directors to slip into building a stable of favorite performers, who they know they can trust and who they know play off each other well. These old faithfuls can be called on to save the day, but it can lead to a more homogenous Broadway, with less new blood getting in the front door simply because they're untested.

This was never the case with Joanna. Joanna had been the original Tzeitel in *Fiddler on the Roof*, and she understood just how important opening that door could be to a struggling young actor. With each project, she would start from scratch, tossing out preconceived notions as she let whoever was available present themselves to her. Of course she always had ideas, being immersed in the mix of who was working and auditioning, but she never let those ideas get in the way of a different approach. Paul had learned how to cast from her, sitting to her left behind the table at many a casting session, and when it came time to cast *Merrily We Roll Along*, their approach was matched perfectly to the task.

They needed kids, and lots of them. No one could be too polished or seasoned—they needed fresh performers, straight off the amateur circuits, with a sense of optimism still in their hearts. They had to be naive in the honest way only college kids can be, and they could not have been broken down by the business before coming through their doors. They held open calls and listed casting notices in local newspapers across the tristate area, looking for performers ranging from ages fourteen to twenty. It was a true cattle call, with thousands of kids showing up every day to fight their way onto a daily list that cut off at eight hundred. People traveled from all over to audition for *Merrily*—Hal Prince and Stephen Sondheim might have been friends to Paul, but to the rest of America they had come to define the modern musical theatre. Many of the auditionee's first experiences with theatre had been seeing shows the two men had worked on—*West Side Story*, *Gypsy*, *Cabaret*, and *Damn Yankees* had quickly spread into the suburbs outside of the city, and Lonny Price had even played the Emcee in his high school production of *Cabaret*. For many of these kids, it was a chance to work with their heroes, and they were showing up in droves.

The sign-up sheet for the open calls started at seven in the morning, with kids filing in and out of the room, many on their first big audition. A large number of them didn't even have professional headshots or résumés, and handwritten résumés and old family photos were stapled together in haphazard piles, collecting the early life stories of hundreds of hopefuls. Eventually, more than seven thousand people auditioned for *Merrily*. Paul and Joanna whittled this group down, round by round, finding unpolished talent and promise behind almost every eager face. Among them were Jason Alexander, Tonya Pinkins, Liz Callaway, and Daisy Prince, Hal's daughter. Far from a case of nepotism, she was there of her own accord, and she was under an even more watchful eye than the other "would be" cast members. They put the group through multiple rounds of auditions, parsing down the group until they had reached the final fifty.

On the final day of auditions, they piled into the Minskoff Rehearsal Studios and worked the kids from seven in the morning to seven at night. On each break, they would send Ruth Mitchell out to personally dismiss anyone they were ready to let go of, until finally, Hal rose from behind the table. These kids, ranging from ages sixteen to twenty-five, had made it from the chaos of the first round with Paul and Joanna, to facing down the full audition panel, including Hal, Steve, and book-writer George Furth. Hal walked to the center of the room, hands clasped behind his back in mock contemplation, before looking up with a twinkle in his eye, telling the group that they were the official cast of *Merrily We Roll Along* on Broadway.

Pandemonium erupted. The amount of joy and shock pouring off of the kids was overwhelming. Twenty-one of them would be making their Broadway debut, and many hadn't even graduated college. Two, Abby Pogrebin and Daisy Prince, were still in high school. With the cast in place, and enough youthful energy to power a steamship, everyone bunkered down for seven months while the script and score were finished, with rehearsals set to start in the fall.

The company got close, quickly. It was like a fraternity—everyone went over to each other's apartments, and they would dream about what their world was going to look like once they opened the show. What was it going to be like to be the first performers of songs by Stephen Sondheim, a man many of them had come to see as an unshakable god in the theatre they loved so deeply? Their enthusiasm quickly worked its way through the creative team as well. You couldn't help but love the cast, and you couldn't help but love the material that so honestly reflected who they were. *Merrily* is, at its core, a show about truth, even when it is brutal. Life is rarely as neat and picturesque as some of the musicals Prince and Sondheim had grown up on, and they set out to make a piece that really represented life—to take the lives of three friends and present them fairly, to be judged and accepted in equal turn. No one ever sets out to ruin a friendship, end a marriage, or dissolve a partnership. Just like the shifting sands of habits, the never-ending hourglass of time ticks away at every little decision a person makes in their life. One can never know the ending when they are standing at the beginning, and by playing the show backward, that helplessness was brought to the forefront.

When they entered the six-week rehearsal period, everyone was practically walking on air. They were proud to be there and proud of their work—Sondheim's score, lightly infused with bossa nova like much of his work as a young man, shined alongside Furth's book, and Prince tried out every trick in his arsenal, inventing new methods of approach to keep the show feeling as fresh and new as the company itself. One of these innovations was the removal of traditional costuming from the show. After the costume parade, Hal made the decision to cut all of the fully assembled costumes. Instead, he decided to dress the kids in T-shirts and sweatshirts emblazoned with the name of their characters, with only the graduation gowns surviving from the original costume plots. It gave the show a more youthful energy, and it made it easier to track the kids from scene to scene—with so many bodies onstage, Hal was doing whatever he could to simplify the staging.

The rehearsal room was a flurry of emotions, mostly positive. Jim Walton, the company's oldest member at twenty-five, danced around the show's dance captain, Janie Gleason. Donna Marie Elio, a fresh-faced nineteen-year-old, developed a crush on Paul that he had to gracefully maneuver around. The fast friendships that had formed during the open calls deepened into close friendships, with the entire company eagerly awaiting their eventual opening night. During lunch breaks, the cast would sit around and speculate about what number they would perform on the Tonys, debating the merits of different favorites without ever questioning if they would get that far.

Like any show, *Merrily* had problems, but no one was particularly worried. Everyone was certain that they would work out the kinks, and for the most part, they did. Still, the pressure on Steve and Hal was immense. With a company full of greenhorns, they were the two who had the show firmly on their backs. Paul, as the liaison between the cast and the creative, kept firmly grounded with the kids and their infectious joy, even as he would work with Steve to make adjustments. No one realized how much work was still left to be done until the reaction at previews.

Hal had decided to hold the "out-of-town tryout" in New York, testing their home market. Audiences walked out in droves, with entire rows emptying as the cast watched them leave in the middle of numbers. The reversed time line was simply too confusing for much of the audience and, rather than holding on to take the journey, they left. Paul would look over his shoulder during the show to find the entire front row desolate, when it had been packed at the rise of the curtain. Still, the kids kept their shiny optimism, and everyone committed to streamlining the show to make it as clear as possible to the viewer. The opening night on Broadway was pushed once, and then twice, as entire swaths of the book were rewritten, songs tossed and restructured, and set elements scrapped. Ron Fields, the show's original choreographer, was fired and replaced with Larry Fuller, and James Weissenbach, who had been with the project from the first reading, lost the role of Frank to Jim Walton.

Paul memorizes material quickly, but even he struggled to keep up with the constant flow of music changes. In a departure from pattern, he was forced to keep a score with him in the pit, just to keep track of which measures had been added and which had been cut in the fifteen minutes before the curtain would rise. Paul would have five pages of dense notes that he would quickly list off to the orchestra as the lights would go down, and he would have to drop the pad at his feet and pick up his baton, with no time for the group to absorb the glut of information. Still, they were sure they would make it through the rocky patch and come out unscathed.

There was an old-school MGM air backstage—Mickey and Judy put on a show with the can-do attitude of a Bing Crosby vehicle as the company came together in optimism. Script changes were slid under dressing room doors without warning, actors were being steered into new blocking on the fly, and musical numbers came together powered by hope and chutzpah. Alexander, newly confident in his walking abilities, was as regular a sight backstage as any other member of the creative team, running up and down the aisles with cast members who graciously entertained him when Paul was needed elsewhere. Paul kept everyone smiling and buoyant by scrawling little messages and reminders on a small blackboard to hold up for the cast to read at the curtain call—when an actor forgot a last-minute line change, he would flash up a message telling the offender to call their agent, making a joke of the idea that anyone was at risk of unemployment.

The closing number of Act 1, "Now You Know," was given an entirely new dance break by Larry Fuller, complete with a fresh orchestration, shortly before opening. As the cast rehearsed the new dance during the day, they were performing the old sequence at night, until finally the decision was made to put the new steps into the show. Somehow less than half of the pit got the new orchestrations, and when the time came for the new dance sequence, a clattering cacophony roared out of the pit, the two orchestrations at odds. The cast watched, panicked, as Paul snapped into rescue mode, silencing the orchestra with a slash of the baton as he ordered the kids to keep dancing, with the pianist playing the new orchestrations as loudly as possible while Paul gave a beat to the percussionist to hold the dance steps together. At the same time, Paul barked measure numbers from the old orchestration to the musicians, crafting a new tempo that started in a different place in order to line up with the new dance steps to finish the break on beat in order to finish the last verse of the song. Paul got the company through the debacle mostly unscathed, and the curtain came down on Act 1 with Paul holding up a sign saying that it was time for him to call *his* agent, forcing several of the ensemble members to turn their back on the audience to hide their laughter.

Finally, after an arduous preview period, *Merrily We Roll Along* opened on Broadway on November 16, 1981. The show was clear, it was concise, and above all, it was honest. It reflected the reality of life. Sometimes the best-laid plans and best of intentions just don't work out, and *Merrily* presented that truth in a way that was undeniable. No one was evil, no one was holy. Everyone had a price to pay along the way. It is impossible to make it out of life alive, and *Merrily* dramatized that knowledge in one of the most effective ways ever put on the stage.

At the start of the show, with a house packed to the rafters, the cast sat buzzing with eagerness behind the closed curtain as the audience gave the overture an ovation. The show was eagerly eaten up by the people inside the theatre, and the cast was on cloud nine at the opening-night party. Grateful for Paul's hijinks, and with affection that had turned parental, Donna and Abby bought a bottle of Dom Perignon as an opening-night gift for Paul—it was the most expensive thing they had ever bought, even with the split cost, but they were sure they would be able to afford it by borrowing from their future paychecks in terms of their budget. Unfortunately, it wasn't long until their spun-sugar opening night was dissolved in the salt water of the morning reviews.

To say the reviews were less than ideal would be an understatement. In fact, the *New York Post* was the only major review that leaned positive. Hal and Steve had been on the pedestal for so long, and now the commercial theatre community was itching to pull them down—*Merrily* gave them that opportunity. Many went in expecting to be confused, and got what they came for. Still, no one in the cast thought they would close. The company at large shifted to focusing on the show, and not the outside criticism, as much as it stung. Life moved on.

Unfortunately, *Merrily* wasn't able to move with them. As the company began to settle into their run with a highly devoted fan base cheering them on night after night, the unthinkable came. A closing notice. The cast were suddenly thrust into a world where their little show was ending, and they were pushed through a grief-stricken final performance before many in the company were able to wrap their minds around what was happening. That final show was one of the hardest performances Paul ever had to work through. When "Our Time," the final number of the show, came, everyone in the theatre was in tears. Paul had teared up at the first company sing-through of the song, struck by the sheer hope of the cast, but that hope had been transformed to hopelessness. A company of Icaruses, flying eagerly to their dreams with no reservations, were crashing down to earth with the shattering realization that even the best-laid plans occasionally go to waste.

Merrily We Roll Along closed after sixteen performances on Broadway.

The very next day, eyes swollen and hearts aching, the cast came together one last time to record the cast album. It was an immensely difficult sixteen hours. Recording the album was one of the thorniest moments in Paul's entire career, standing at the podium with the crushing weight of the experience thickening the air. Remarkably, the company came together, finding a final burst of energy to commit the show that meant so much to them to vinyl, giving them a single tangible thing they could cling to as a reminder that it had really happened. The last song they recorded that day, "Good Thing Going," was the song inside the show that launched the career of the characters, and getting through it shredded what little emotional strength was left. And then, with teary goodbyes and cracked dreams, the company said farewell to each other. Many would not speak again for decades.

But life, of course, continued on. Jim Walton and Janie, who had fallen in love during rehearsals, had gotten married the day before closing, after Janie had found out she was pregnant just after opening. Jason Alexander, as one of the slightly older members of the company, at twenty-one, married his girlfriend, Daena, and hit the ground running with auditions. For much of the company, *Merrily* became a wound that would never heal. They had all been so young, and the show had felt so personal, that its ending had felt like a direct attack on who they were as artists and as people. Many of them ended up leaving show business, disenchanted with the harsh realities.

The other, oft-discussed side effect of *Merrily's* failure was the effective termination of the Hal Prince and Stephen Sondheim partnership. The partnership that had begun growing roots in the aisles of the original *South Pacific* had finally begun to wilt, and a decision was made behind closed doors to spend some time apart after working together for more than twenty-five years. Neither had ever intended it to be the end, only a pause, but with each new project, time divided the two friends. Without even realizing it, they had finished the chapter on what has gone down as the greatest partnership between a composer and a producer in the history of the musical theatre.

Merrily, a show about life that had been so full of vitality, was now dead, and it had taken casualties down with it. No one involved with the project could ever keep it out of their heads. Endless stories and questions shifted from person to person, communication turning into a web of who said what over the span of twenty years as an intense love for the show developed among Sondheim fans, thanks to the cast album.

Lonny Price, now a director, eventually approached the company with the idea of a charity reunion. Everyone would be back onstage, doing the show one more time. Remarkably, they all came together, with Paul again holding the baton, smiling up at the people who somehow still looked like teenagers to him. It was an immense success, selling out within days and eliciting reactions from the crowd not unlike the initial crazed audiences of opening night. Emboldened by the response, Lonny decided to go looking for whatever was left of a documentary ABC had started on *Merrily We Roll Along* during preproduction, before the project was abandoned prior to the beginning of rehearsals. Along the way, he had his castmates, now lifelong friends, sit with him and discuss the show and the scars it had left.

The result, *Best Thing That Ever Could Have Happened*, premiered at the New York Film Festival in October of 2016, grabbing immediate buzz. A frank and honest look at a show that had taken on cult status after its explosive end, it received the glowing reviews *Merrily* had always needed, thirty-five years after opening. It was quickly snatched up for distribution and has become one of the most popular and recommended theatre documentaries on the streaming-site Netflix.

Merrily was a show about life that premiered at a time when the last thing anyone wanted to examine was the human condition. It was the start of the Reagan administration, the summer of the Atlanta Child Murders, and the dawn of the AIDS epidemic. People were looking to theatre to escape, and to feel like everything would be alright in the end. At *Merrily*, they got an honest and open examination of how impossible it is to ever predict the end. Life isn't neat, and it isn't tidy. The further you go along, there is more pressure and more things slipping away that get replaced with other little things, without you even realizing. The sand is constantly slipping in the hourglass, and the only way to undo it is to turn over the clock and go back to the beginning.

Chapter Fourteen

Dreamgirls

Gemignani is so different—you could say he is old school, because there is no other Broadway music director like him. They're all gone and the music theater world will be emptier without him.
—Sylvia D'Avanzo (Violin, Concertmaster)

As *Merrily We Roll Along* moved into the Alvin Theatre to begin previews, Paul received a call from Michael Bennett.

Michael and Paul had remained good friends in the years since *Follies*, and Michael had a proposition. He was working on a new show, loosely based on the rise of the Supremes and the Motown label, and he needed a music director. Paul, having been steeped in the jazz and blues world prior to entering musical theatre, was a logical puzzle piece to add to the sonic picture. The only problem—Paul's work on *Merrily We Roll Along* had already begun, and working on two Broadway-bound shows simultaneously was unheard of.

This isn't only due to the time constraints. As music director, you have to deeply invest your time and energy into the shows you work on—when you are distracted or unfocused, the show suffers. You have to be with the show, in every moment, to really live in it and help shape it, especially in the formative stages. Rehearsing a new show and conducting an old one at night is doable, if a bit stressful, but going through dual incubation periods can be a recipe for disaster, splitting your focus on both projects.

Michael must have known it was an impossible question before he called Paul. The time management struggles aside, they both knew how treacherous the situation would be interpersonally. Hal Prince took the business side of shows very seriously, and he would be upset at Paul working outside the office, especially as they were guiding *Merrily* toward opening night. The problem was compounded by Michael's success—*A Chorus Line*, the hottest ticket in town, had opened five years prior, and his follow-up, *Ballroom*, had only had middling success. *Dreamgirls* was his make-or-break effort—the show that would cement him as his own legend or leave him labeled as the creator of *A Chorus Line* for the rest of his life. By helping Michael, Paul would be directly assisting the very competition *Merrily* was to compete against. The situation was fraught.

Paul loved Michael. Less than a decade apart in age, they were ragtag peers, thinking alike in a way that few others in the theatre did. They loved how each other saw the world, and they could get lost in conversations, work related or otherwise. Michael had always treated Paul as a friend and collaborator, from that very first day on *Follies*. With Michael, Paul was never an employee, regardless of who signed the checks. He was something closer to a partner or teammate in the adventure to climb the mountain of whatever idea Michael had set his sights on. Michael had been deeply supportive of Paul even as their careers had diverged, and Paul had always promised to have his back if Michael needed him.

Now, Michael was calling on Paul's loyalty, insisting he needed Paul to untangle the knot of the *Dreamgirls* score as he pulled on every heartstring he could reach, until Paul acquiesced. With a promise from Michael that *Merrily* would come first, and a resolve to help his friend without harming the others, Paul agreed, with the caveat that his judgment be trusted—he had no energy to fight to defend his choices, and Michael would need to trust Paul's instinct. Michael agreed.

The two set out on their undercover mission with the best of intentions. In the mornings, before rehearsal for *Merrily* had been called, Paul would leave the Gemignani home in New Jersey to go to Michael's apartment to meet with Henry Krieger, the composer. Michael and Henry had most of the script cobbled together, and about thirty-five songs, with no set order for the wide swath of diegetic numbers performed by the "Dreams" throughout the evening. Paul would sit with the two men, going through every song one by one, to find the right fit for each character arc, keeping and discarding material as the themes of the show began to become clear: a power struggle between the original, unpredictable lead singer and the new, malleable beauty with the radio-friendly voice; men, and the dynamics that emerge when women begin to equal them in power; racism and colorism in the music industry, and in the world at large. Hunched over a table, the three men slowly stitched together the score before Paul would make a mad dash for rehearsals of *Merrily We Roll Along* at the Alvin Theatre.

Michael, a pioneer of the musical workshop in a world where shows previously had not seen full casts and stagings prior to preparing for out-of-town engagements, had already compiled a cast for the workshop of *Dreamgirls*, giving Paul a bit more breathing room. *Merrily* reached its painful opening night and closed twelve days later. This failure, effectively ending the Sondheim/Prince collaboration, left Paul adrift. The sadness of a show closing is always akin to a death in the family, but *Merrily* was particularly difficult to swallow.

Paul knew that to reveal he and Michael's covert work would be another blow, having seen the pain *Merrily*'s critical failure had caused, and in an effort to protect Hal and Steve, Paul made the decision to keep his early work on *Dreamgirls* hidden from view, supporting his friends as best he could as he walked the tightrope.

Dreamgirls entered the workshop stage, and Paul did all eight of the workshops, polishing the show until the time came to send it for an out-of-town tryout in Boston. Hal called, needing Paul back at *Evita*, and Paul immediately agreed, calling on the "Hal first" agreement he and Michael had made at the very start. He and Michael decided to hire Yolanda Segovia, a young conductor who had made her debut the previous fall in a show called *Perfectly Frank*, a revue of Frank Loesser's songs, and who had played the keyboard and assisted on *Dancin'*, Bob Fosse's concept revue in response to the success of *A Chorus Line*. She would receive the title of music director, taking over the production when Paul returned to *Evita*. Yolanda was more than competent, and she settled into the show nicely. As a final gesture, Paul hired the rhythm section, all but completing the preengagement work of a music director before handing it over and returning to the Prince office as though nothing had happened.

Paul was in the middle of work on a musical adaptation of *A Doll's House* by Ibsen (retitled *A Doll's Life*) for the Prince office when Michael came by to see him backstage.

A Doll's Life just wasn't working. When Michael met Paul at the stage door after the show, the pair didn't mince words. They discussed the show in detail, trying to figure out a miraculous fix before finally coming to the conclusion that it was hopeless. They were powerless to help fix the fallow streak the Prince office had fallen into. Enter one of Michael's bright ideas.

If *A Doll's Life* was to close, through no fault of Paul's, then surely the Prince office would have no objection to Paul finding outside work until Hal had his next show ready. Michael could move Yolanda to Los Angeles with the touring company of *Dreamgirls* and bring Paul home, giving him stable work and a chance to take part in the now hit show he had helped to develop. Paul conducted *Dreamgirls* for the majority of 1983, with the Prince Offices' blessing.

As the years went on, Paul and Michael began to consider new adventures together, with most of their focus going to an adaptation of the film *Love Me or Leave Me*, with Mandy Patinkin and Ann-Margret in talks to star and Quincy Jones on board to orchestrate. Michael had wrangled a book writer and planned to use the original film soundtrack, leaving room to call in Paul when the project got on its feet. They had just begun the process when, out of the blue, Michael disappeared.

It wasn't unlike Michael to go on independent quests into the unknown, but never without a way to reach him. Michael had come to see Paul in *Smile*, the pair preparing to pull Paul from yet another flop, and had suddenly vanished. After waiting months for Michael to resurface, Paul went to Bob Avian, Michael's dear friend and producing partner, and implored him to hand over Michael's new contact information, calling upon every friendly interaction they had ever had to convince Bob to trust him, promising to protect Michael's privacy.

Bob gave it to him, and when Paul reached Michael in Tucson, Arizona, the end was near. It was 1986, and Michael Bennett had AIDS-related lymphoma. People had been dying around Paul, but he had never considered that this might be what Michael was hiding. Michael was untouchable. He was too good, too smart, too brilliant to be dimmed so early. He and Paul had a long phone conversation, tinged with deep melancholy for a future slipping through their fingers, and two days later, Michael was dead. Michael Bennett, shining star of the American theatre, died at age forty-four in Arizona, far from any of his friends and family in New York, save his partner, Gene Pruit, and friend Bob Herr. He left a portion of his estate to search for a cure to the epidemic and was cremated, with his ashes distributed among friends and family.

A memorial service was held two months after Michael's death at the Shubert Theatre, where *A Chorus Line* was continuing to play to sold-out crowds. The theatre overflowed with mourners, a palpable sadness laying over the theatre as friends worked through their grief and gratitude for Michael, and for so many others who were being ripped away with little warning.

John Breglio, theatrical attorney, shared a story from Michael's final year, when Michael first showed him the cast recording of *Sunday in the Park with George*. Michael wept when they reached the show's penultimate song, "Move On." It was the only time John had ever seen Michael cry. And Steve Sondheim, clutching his composer's copy, walked onstage, sat at the piano, and played that song, pushing through tears to complete the song before letting out a shaky "Goodbye, Michael" and turning to face the blackness at the back of the stage, shadowed far from where the stage lights could reach.

Michael wasn't all they were saying goodbye to that night. Michael, and so many others, had been ripped from the community, leaving an entire generation of theatremakers as fragile as cheesecloth. The trauma of it all, of waking up every morning to find a different friend dead, had wormed its way into everyone's hearts, leaving a gaping wound that would never truly heal. With Michael, the community had the opportunity to come together in a moment of catharsis, to celebrate the man who had meant so much to so many. But for every Michael there were a hundred others, wasting away before they even had the opportunity to become who they could be. The optimistic, tight-knit, collaboration-driven world Paul had first stumbled upon in *Cabaret* was changing, morphing into something else in the face of so much tragedy. And for better or for worse, there was no undoing the damage.

CHAPTER FIFTEEN

The Rink

I can thank Paul for being one of those really important people in my life, who taught me that you can have a life and still be in the business, and dedicated to the business. You can still have humor and relation-ships, and all of that, while still being an artist.
—CHITA RIVERA (DANCER, ACTOR, SINGER)

WITH THE PRINCE OFFICE STRUGGLING UNDER THE BURDEN OF A string of financial failures, and Steve squirrelled away, working privately, Paul went back to his foundation. John Kander and Fred Ebb were put-ting together a revival of *Zorba* with the original film's stars, Anthony Quinn and Lila Kedrova, and they needed someone who knew the show to pull it all together. Paul came on board, revisiting his first gig as a music director, and breathed fresh life into the show before handing it over to Randolph Mauldin, who had assisted Jim Coleman on the *Swee-ney Todd* tour. As it began a respectable run at the Broadway Theatre, Paul stepped further into the Kander and Ebb fold.

John and Fred had been working on a new show, far from the stylized veneer audiences had come to expect from the authors of *Cabaret* and *Chicago*. Located in a dilapidated roller rink on an abandoned boardwalk, a mother and daughter worked through their differences and memories in tandem, coming together to realize how alike they had grown to be. It had been initially conceived as an intimate two-person show and prepared for an Off Broadway run, before bigger ideas filtered into the room. New York was hungry for hope, and *The Rink*'s toe tapping story of community and connection appeared to fit that demand. The team shifted gears, expanding the cast from two to nine, and Paul began the task of filling the theatre with a score that had been designed for up-close enjoyment.

Two of the Kander and Ebb stalwarts, Chita Rivera and Liza Minnelli, were brought on to star as the mother-and-daughter duo. A small chorus consisting of six men and a child actress were hired to play the rest of the parts in the piece, including dancers Rob Marshall and Scott Ellis. Rehearsals were a lovely affair, with magic and roller-skating lessons happening in tandem to dance and music rehearsals. Paul and Chita were happy to be reunited after having toured *Zorba* together, and their friendship picked up as if no time had elapsed. Liza, while a legitimate star by this time, was still a theatre creature at heart, and she fit in eagerly with the rest of the company. She and Chita had been circling each other for years, and Liza had been a last-minute stand-in for Gwen Verdon in *Chicago*, in an oft-mythologized move to give Verdon time to recover from a vocal cord injury. Now, with the opportunity to finally work together in earnest, they dove in eagerly. Both women were at the top of their game, and the show shined around them—quite literally.

The set and lighting design that formed around the show was flashy in its simplicity. With only a trunk and chairs moving on and off between scenes, the core set was transformed into various eras of the roller rink, and colorful light shows were punctuated by Liza's song, "Colored Lights." The cast would roller-skate circles around each other in the increasingly harebrained title track, and pure happiness leapt out from every corner. A. J. Antoon, the director, understood exactly what the piece needed, and he provided it masterfully.

The show sold a solid advance before they had even exited rehearsals on the strength of Chita and Liza's names, with the title of the actual show the same size as their credits on the marquee. The theatrical community was abuzz at the idea of Liza and Kander and Ebb's new collaboration—while the Studio 54 heyday and Andy Warhol craze had dimmed to a memory, Liza's celebrity still shined as a symbol of glamorous excess.

Behind rehearsal doors, Liza was just another music-loving girl, eager to make friends with the same interests. Paul and Liza would tuck into a tiny two-person table at the deli across the street from the rehearsal studio and share favorite songs and music anecdotes in between bites of sandwiches, spending their lunch break debating different recordings of popular songs. Liza was a verifiable encyclopedia for pop and show music, and she could rattle off the release dates, songwriters, and alternate recordings of any Frank Sinatra record that would come over the deli's radio.

Back in the rehearsal studio, Chita was setting the standard for excellence. A glorious talent, her skills were superseded only by her work ethic, and everyone in the room couldn't help but climb to get near her level of dedication. Choreographer Graciela Daniele was more than up to the challenge. Paul had first met Graciela on *Follies*, where she was the sensual tango dancer who served as Michael Bennett's dance captain. With a particularly keen eye for the female form and how it could move through space, she was the perfect pick to choreograph numbers for Liza and Chita, both of whom were more than up to the task.

Chita is a dancer at heart, and Graciela choreographed beautiful sequences for her, with the boys backing her up. While choreographing one such scene, the idea of utilizing one of the empty trunks from the back of the set sparked inspiration. There was a place in the back of the trunk for a performer to crawl in and out of, and Graciela experimented with hiding one of the men inside, eventually landing on young Scott Ellis, who could most comfortably contort himself inside before making his surprising entrance. They ran the number over and over, refining it section by section, when a devilish prank came to Paul and Graciela's minds. It was fifteen minutes to lunch, and they decided to run the number one more time. Scott crawled into the trunk, they spun him around a few times, simulating the number, and the cast packed up and left for lunch as Scott patiently waited for the number to restart. Eventually he got wise to the ruse and extracted himself, running after the giggling group as he hollered.

Of all the men in the show, Jason Alexander was the most prominent, as the only male performer with a stand-alone song. With *Merrily*

We Roll Along in the rearview mirror, Paul had been eager to work with Jason again. Jason, like Liza, was a true creature of the theatre, and he was a member of a dying breed of performer—the true character actor. Born to breathe life into offbeat characters, he shimmered when given the space to play, and Paul was more than happy to give him room. His song "Marry Me" was the most difficult ballad in the entire show, and Paul would work with him one on one to polish the piece into the jewel that it was. Jason has a voice that requires almost no tinkering—it fits exactly who Jason is as an actor, and no color or tone adjustments are necessary to match music to the music maker. His voice soared through the piece, and it wasn't long before people began to take notice of the talent skating around the rink eight times a week.

In a flash, they had reached opening night. Crowds went wild for Chita and Liza, and everyone in the company was ready to celebrate at the Roxy, one of the hottest roller discos in New York City. Graciela always dressed to the nines, wearing the odd fashions that dancers can pull off with a safety pin and a prayer, but she had turned the dial up to eleven for the celebration. Dripping in diamonds and her favorite white fur coat, she had ducked out of the show to grab a bite to eat before the party. When Paul turned the corner out of the theatre, he was greeted by the sight of Graciela prostrate on a stretcher, her diamonds clutched in her hand as the flashing lights from an ambulance surrounded her. She had gone to the deli across the street from the theatre and ordered a shrimp cocktail to celebrate—the shrimp had gone off, and so bad was her food poisoning that she had to go to the hospital to weather the storm. Her husband, Jules Fisher, who was the lighting designer for the show, went with her, and both missed the jubilant party. All of Liza's friends showed up and showed out to support her, including Warhol and Elizabeth Taylor, and the party proved an immense success, minus Graciela and Jules.

Unfortunately, the reviews were less successful. Much like Sondheim and Prince, Kander and Ebb had come to represent a very specific type of theatre to the average theatregoer—audiences expected sex, and they expected discontent. While *The Rink* ended on a bittersweet note, the family-centered story line left viewers off-kilter, and theatre critics were less than kind. Still, the advance was enough for the show to push through the initial dip following the reviews, and they found an audience among Liza and Chita's devotees. Chita, as usual, kept up morale and the company continued on.

A few months into the run, Paul, Chita, and Liza did a benefit for the American Musical and Dramatic Academy, a private conservatory in New York. While others were involved, doing one-off songs, half of the first act was a sizable chunk of Chita's nightclub act, and half of the second act was Liza's. They had rehearsed everything during the day, with the show running at night, and Chita had decided to close with "All That Jazz" from *Chicago*, which she had rechoreographed into a three person number—her and two male dancers. Chita had walked Paul through what she needed—he would be situated behind her with the orchestra, and when she turned towards him and made a come-hither gesture, it would be a sign that she was going to go faster. Unfortunately, Paul took that note to mean that whenever she made that motion, she needed him to pick up speed with her.

The piece played as normal for the first half of the song, until she reached the bridge—Chita made the gesture once, and Paul sped the orchestra up by a few clicks. Again, another couple beats faster. With each motion, Paul would pull the orchestra up, until they were positively flying. Chita kept up with him, sprinting through the number without missing a step, and when they walked offstage, she practically collapsed with laughter. Paul had nearly danced her off her feet, and through gasping laughs the pair realized the miscommunication. Thankfully, Liza's set didn't feature any extended dance breaks, and such a mistake was not repeated.

Chita won the Tony Award for Best Actress in a Musical, beating out Liza, as well as Bernadette Peters from *Sunday in the Park with George*. It was Chita's first win after four nominations, and spirits were high backstage. One month later, Liza left the show in order to enter the Betty Ford Center, and Stockard Channing was brought in to replace her.

Now, Stockard is a very fine actress. But she and Liza could not have been more different. Whereas Liza came from the light and bubbly world of the musical comedy, Stockard was a classically trained actress who had her feet firmly planted on the ground. The character of Angel had been so clearly written with Liza in mind that Stockard was forced to grapple with molding herself into someone she simply was not. She got there, and was quite good, but it was never as natural as Liza.

After one month with Stockard as Angel, *The Rink* posted its closing notice. With the loss of half of its megawatt star power, and with the mixed reviews lingering in audience members' minds, the decision was made to close the show before it had a chance to deeply struggle. Kander and Ebb considered *The Rink* to be the most fully realized of their intentions as a composing team, and it has gone on to be a hidden gem of their catalog. Liza would not return to Broadway for another decade, and she never originated another role.

CHAPTER SIXTEEN

Sunday in the Park with George

The reason Gemignani is a legend in the musical theater is because he approaches the work dramatically first and then musically. He wants to understand the story we are telling and how music intersects with the dialogue. He strives to understand the intentions of the writers and director before he works with the actors in rehearsal and later the orchestra in the theater, to help bring the two together: connecting what is going on in the pit with what is going on up onstage. As he once mentioned to me—and I am paraphrasing here—the musicians are in a dark pit where they have no visual connection with the stage. Because of the intensity of the lights onstage, the actors are staring into darkness unable to see the audience. The conductor is the person who brings these two worlds together to tell our story. And Paul is masterful at that. Actors and musicians know he is there for them. He is always present in performance and he is fierce. If an actor or a musician is marking a performance, Paul will wake them up and demand their total attention. He can be a demanding taskmaster, which is exactly the kind of collaborator a composer, lyricist, or director wants both in the rehearsal room and especially when at the podium during a performance.

—JAMES LAPINE (WRITER, DIRECTOR)

A FEW MONTHS BEFORE THE END OF *THE RINK*, PAUL RECEIVED A PHONE call from Stephen Sondheim—he had a new concept, from his least traditional source material yet. Steve had announced his intention to quit the musical theatre after the pain of *Merrily We Roll Along*, but director and book writer James Lapine had convinced him to return to the fold. The pair had studied a postcard of George Seurat's masterwork *A Sunday Afternoon on the Island of La Grand Jatte*, and had been consumed by it. They had been drawn to who they imagined Seurat to be, and what resulted was a mostly fictionalized narrative of Seurat's life surrounding the piece, and his theoretical descendants.

Paul knew who Seurat was, but he had never seen *Sunday Afternoon*, which was, in 1982, mostly remember by the general public in stylized topiary gardens in Middle America. Still, Paul was eager to step back into Steve's orbit. Hal gave him the go ahead, as shows were being postponed and restructured left and right at the Prince office, and Paul signed on for his sixth major Sondheim project.

Sunday was to have an untraditional journey—they did a reading similar to *Merrily We Roll Along* and were invited by the artistic director of Playwrights Horizons, André Bishop, to try out in their space rather than going out of town. There they pulled together what was to be the show's first act, detailing the love and loss of George Seurat and his imagined muse, the woman in the foreground of the painting who they had named Dot in reference to Seurat's pointillism. Lapine, fresh off a show called *March of the Falsettos*, brought orchestrator Michael Starobin to the project, and he, Paul, and pianist Paul Ford became the trio that created the original soundscape.

Casting was a sticky subject—the audience had to empathize deeply with both George and Dot, without being too swept away from the central themes of the story. With an unfamiliar story line, they knew they would need recognizable names leading the company in order to secure funding. For George they brought on Mandy Patinkin, who had become a rising star in Hollywood due to his appearances in *Yentl* and *Ragtime* after winning the Tony for Che in *Evita*. He had the immense intensity that George needed—a sense of dedication and drive that almost seemed to overwhelm him when he disappeared into his work, much like the character of George himself. And for Dot they uncovered Bernadette Peters, who had up to this point been shackled to her Kewpie doll image.

The role of Dot gave her the opportunity to finally be recognized by the artistic community as a woman of formidable acting talent, and when she played against Mandy, the chemistry was electric.

Dot is one of the more deceptively difficult roles in the Sondheim canon. Straddling the line between innocent ingenue and all-knowing sphinx, she is the audience's main contact point. George may be the title character, but he is by nature aloof and unknowable, so married to his art that it swiftly turns to obsession. In contrast, Dot is fiercely human, openly loving and jealous and curious in equal turn. As she is the focal point of the painting, she is the focal point of the musical, and in finding Bernadette, they had found the person capable of making Dot feel effervescent and effortless, when in reality she is the glue holding the plot together.

With their two leads settled, the rest of the cast fell into place as they headed into rehearsals. The first act was shaped as themes of connection and community came to the forefront alongside the initial focus of art and inspiration. The rehearsal space had similar themes—everyone was eager to work and brought their best to the table. One of the greatest aspects of working with Sondheim is his ability to elicit a response from his collaborators—in working with him, you discover creative inspiration that elevates the both of you. *Sunday* was a constant flow of this inspiration, from all sides and from all parties.

The song "Color and Light," which served as George's first artistic soliloquy, was proving troublesome in the room. Mandy delivered a flurry of colorful lyrics, each of which he punctuated with a stab of his paintbrush—while the piano underscored these stabs, there was something missing in the effect. Grabbing a handful of options from his percussion setup, Paul discovered that if he muffled a triangle to prevent it from reverberating, he could strike it in equal time to Mandy's gestures, punctuating his motion with the blunted metallic sound. It was just sharp enough to capture the ear of the listener, without overpowering or distracting from Mandy. Paul was in the best position to follow Mandy, and so playing the triangle became a part of his daily track, both as the percussionist at Playwrights Horizons, and later on as the conductor when the production transferred to a larger venue.

"The Day Off," commonly known as "The Dog Song," was a similar collaboration. Originally written for a man and a woman, Mandy had decided he wanted to do all of the voices involved, exhibiting all of the different inspirational narratives racing through George's mind. He and Paul played with it, finding the right voice for each character, while ensuring that Mandy could safely switch between the voices. Once they had found it consistently, they presented it to Steve, who initially thought it was a practical joke. They sat in the room and auditioned voice after voice for the different dogs, debating the intellectual value of each before deciding on a rough and rumbly growl and a high and piercing yip. George's animist anthem became one of the comedic highlights of the show.

One day, Paul, Mandy, and Steve went to the West Bank Café across the street from Playwrights Horizons. They had a piano in the back for live entertainment and open mic nights, and Steve had a song he wanted Mandy to learn for the show that night. Deeply nervous, Steve sat down and played "Finishing the Hat" in its entirety. By the time he was done, he had sweat through his shirt and the two other men were openly weeping. He had managed to capture a piece of the ephemeral nature of being an artist, and it was deeply effective. Mandy pasted the words to the song in the back of his sketch pad, and he half read along as he presented it to the public for the first time as they were equally overwhelmed by the piece. "Finishing the Hat" has gone on to be one of the most, if not *the* most, lauded songs in Sondheim's career.

With George's soliloquies under control, much of Paul's focus went to the chorus of the piece—with fourteen members, all of whom played multiple parts, finding a balance of sound and vocal coloring was key. Some of the score was composed to be grand and choral, in a style usually aided by hundreds of vocalists. To achieve a similar effect, Paul altered the vocal lineup by having the tenors sing the soprano line and the sopranos sing the tenor—in their respective octaves of course. By putting the tenors at the top of the chord, it gave songs a greater weight when it hit the ear, without changing anything that was actually in the score.

The original company of *Sunday* had an interesting variance of vocal makeup—the two Celeste's were true operatic sopranos, with clear trilling voices reminiscent of songbirds, in contrast to the Boatman, who had a gruff bass baritone voice. Much of musical theatre prizes the male tenor voice, but the song "Sunday" needed all of the vocal colors, with the bass baritone as a grounding force. Whereas pop-based scores can get away with tenor- and mezzo soprano–dominated companies, Steve had composed *Sunday* to be something close to a modern operetta in scope. With some clever arrangements from Michael Starobin, they were able to make a sixteen-person company and a three-piece orchestra sound either royal and grand or intimate and introspective as needed.

They opened in July of 1983 with the majority of the first act in place as they continued to build the second act behind the scenes. The final days were a flurry of learning material and adding it before an audience, as songs were added, rewritten, or scrapped in order to clarify the increasingly complicated philosophy that was working its way into the piece. The second act, which follows George's great-grandson, was only partially brought before the audience three days before the end of the run. The company worked as a unit to bring the show to fruition, and it made immense leaps forward. Audiences who saw the first and last performance would have been able to see both the childhood and the young adulthood of a show—watching it grow and shape in increasingly interesting ways.

They were hopeful for a swift transfer uptown, but none materialized for nearly a year. Unable to wait, they lost several members of the company to new work, including Kelsey Grammer, Mary Elizabeth Mastrantonio, and Christine Baranski, who left to work on *Cheers*, *Scarface*, and Broadway's *The Real Thing* respectively. Bernadette and Mandy made the decision to stick it out, and after some gentle prodding, *Sunday* was picked up by the Shubert Organization.

With the second act still in flux, they moved into the Booth Theatre, a flurry of changes and adjustments happening on all sides. Early in Act 2, there was to be a "Chromolume sequence" showing the artistic efforts of the second George. Steve had made the decision not to compose its orchestral backing, instead handing a series of themes to Michael Starobin to pull together into a piece of electronic music to then be elevated by the use of lasers and projection mapping, two technical elements that had never been used on Broadway before. What resulted was a sweeping piece of electronica that folded the main melodies of Act 1's songs into the synthesizers that had become en vogue in popular music of the 1980s. At equal times familiar and foreign, it was a rather accurate reflection of George himself—complex and layered behind an air of inhuman indifference.

Starobin had utilized the synthesizer throughout the scores orchestration, using it to bulk up the three-piece pit with more colors and tones. When the pit was increased to eleven pieces on Broadway, it remained a key part of the musicals soundscape. When given the assignment of creating the Chromolume, which was defined by the characters as "flashy but empty," Michael turned from using the synthesizer as an instrument, to using it as a tool. Yes, it was playing the same themes that previously had been played on strings, but when rendered through the too-exact pitch of multiple synthesizers, it was given the cold and jolting aura that it needed. It was impressive, but unaffecting, a masterpiece of context-specific composition and orchestration.

Synthesizers littered the pit, with Ted Sperling hired to play multiple analog synthesizers throughout the show in addition to the one played by Paul Ford to bulk up the Chromolume. Analog synthesizers, unlike a more modern digital synthesizer, require tuning just like any other instrument, as it can drift out of tune from continued use. In the pit immediately before Chromolume, Paul would take great pleasure in sneaking a hand over to Paul Ford's synthesizer and pressing the tune button, which would silently take over the machine for twenty seconds, leaving a now tense Paul Ford prone over the machine, waiting for it to unlock so he could begin the sequence with only seconds to spare.

The pit of *Sunday* was cramped, and the percussion setup had to be modified to accommodate the eleven players. The bass drum, normally the largest aspect of a drum kit, was sliced in half and hung on the side of the pit to be hand struck, conserving space by sacrificing the use of the foot pedal. Bob Ayers, the percussionist, also had to make room for a bevy of pots and pans that he would play throughout the piece as alternative percussion instruments, in particular during the Boatman's sequences. Where Tunick orchestrated like one of the great German composers of the classical age, Starobin approached with the inventiveness of youth, inverting what an audience expected to pour out of a traditional Broadway pit orchestra. Even with the size limitations, he worked a large number of different musical instruments into the score by having the players multitask. In addition to Bob's kitchen cacophony and Paul Ford's synthesizer that stretched next to his keyboard, he had the violinists switch to glockenspiel, chimes, and cymbals for the final song, giving the illusion of a more philharmonic-style sound. When Starobin won the Drama Desk Award for Outstanding Orchestrations, he nailed the award to the door of the pit to watch over the company for the rest of the run.

Sunday opened to mixed reviews, with many praising the first act while being confused by the second. Frank Rich at the *New York Times*, however, chose to champion the piece, while acknowledging its few faulty moments. By the community at large, it was considered an artistic triumph, and it redeemed Sondheim in the eyes of those who had thought he had lost touch with the failure of *Merrily We Roll Along*. Frank Rich's column, which was published barely a month before the Tony Awards, did not have much effect on Tony voters, but its reverberation was felt throughout the artistic community at large. Suddenly they were playing to packed houses, even with the loss of eight of their ten Tony nominations, until one year after opening, when the unexpected happened.

Sunday in the Park with George won the Pulitzer Prize for Drama.

No one in the company had dared hope for such an honor, as musicals were rarely honored—only four musicals had ever achieved it prior to *Sunday*'s win, with the most recent being *A Chorus Line* a decade before *Sunday*'s debut. *Sunday* was the only musical to ever be nominated without having already won the Tony Award for Best Musical (aside from *Of Thee I Sing*, which predated the Tony Awards), and their victory was a shock. Sondheim, James Lapine, and Bernadette Peters were greeted with the news outside of the theatre, and photographers snapped pictures as the trio shouted for joy before rushing inside the theatre to have an impromptu celebration.

Shortly after winning the Pulitzer, Hal Prince pulled Paul back into the fold, sending him off to music-direct the show *Grind*. It would be the last show Paul would work for the Prince office.

Chapter Seventeen

Into the Woods

He's jovial but firm. It's a very good personality to have around on a show. You want somebody that's artistic and dependable whose personality is made for such an intimate collaboration.
—Hal Prince (Director, Producer), *The New York Times*

Paul was in Baltimore working on *Smile* with Marvin Hamlisch when he received a phone call from Sondheim. His new show, *Into the Woods*, was suddenly going into rehearsal. They were going to have an out-of-town tryout at the Old Globe Theatre in San Diego, and Steve needed Paul there.

No one had thought *Into the Woods* was anywhere near being picked up when Paul had begun work on *Smile*—they had done a tiny reading for potential backers months beforehand and had expected the show to gestate for a little while longer, as most Sondheim pieces had at least a yearlong development period. Steve had given Paul his blessing to work on *Smile*, believing that the waiting period would easily leave room for him to work on a different project. Instead, Jujamcyn Theatres had unexpectedly picked them up and needed the show ready for the coming season, leaving the creative team with an extremely condensed turnaround time. This put Paul in a very tight position.

After assuring Steve that he would make it work, he hung up and called Marvin. Paul would guide *Smile* through the technical and preview period, all the while rehearsing *Into the Woods* during the day. The *Woods* company would head to San Diego for their technical rehearsals as Paul opened *Smile* on Broadway, and he would hand the production over to a new conductor, who he would find for Marvin himself. Marvin agreed, knowing that pitting *Smile* against Steve was a nonstarter, and Paul began a marathon.

Both of the shows Paul was balancing were in heavy flux. With adjustments coming left and right to *Smile*, he had to keep them straight and up to snuff as he steered the production toward opening night, while filling his head with fairy tales and practical stage magic in the *Into the Woods* rehearsal room. Balancing the two shows, which could not have been more different stylistically, was a maze that Paul managed to work his way through until opening night of *Smile*. He attended to the company, full of shining and hopeful faces, and went straight for home after the curtain, forgoing the opening-night party in favor of packing a suitcase and getting on the red-eye flight to San Diego, where the *Woods* company had already met.

After a five-hour flight, Paul had just enough time for a one-hour nap before hauling himself to the Old Globe, ready to conduct a now orchestrated score that he had not yet set eyes on. It is to Paul and Jonathan Tunick's credit that he was able to read through the orchestrations with few errors, as he was able to trust that Tunick had accurately assigned everything, without leaving Paul any traps to navigate through bleary eyes.

Having reached the finish line, Paul happily joined the *Woods* company as they swiftly got the show on its feet and before an audience. Then he received a phone call from Hal Prince.

Paul technically worked for the Prince office. While he was not under an exclusive contract, it had been expected that he would work whatever shows Hal needed him on. A show that had been on and off in development for over a year, *Roza*, was finally coming to Broadway, and Hal immediately began rattling off start dates. He had given Paul permission to go and do *Smile*, but now that they were open he knew Paul could hand the show over to a new conductor and come to start rehearsing *Roza*.

This wasn't new for the Prince office—Hal would announce a production, and everyone would clear their schedule only for it to be delayed, and he would call out of the blue needing you before the end of the week when things suddenly clicked. On other shows, that wasn't a problem— Paul had always made it clear that he would go if Steve and Hal needed him, and the industry at large respected the bond the three men had. But now it was Hal asking Paul to leave Steve.

Now, Paul was not a child. Far from it—he was over fifty now, with an established career. But to Hal, Paul had always been the San Franciscan upstart Harold Hastings had given a chance on *Cabaret*. Hal had been there from the beginning, and he had handed Paul his career when he brought him on to replace Harold in *A Little Night Music*. The pair had become close friends, and Paul had even accompanied the Prince family on vacation, their professional partnership turning personal. Time and again he had brought Paul with him, gainfully employing Paul for more than twenty years. And now when Hal needed him, Paul was on the other side of the country.

Hal had had a rough go of things following the financial failure of *Merrily We Roll Along*—with five back-to-back flops, the office was in a tight position. They needed a hit, and soon. Hal saw light on the horizon—Andrew Lloyd Webber, who he had previously collaborated with on *Evita*, had written a new show for his second wife, Sarah Brightman, and had brought Hal to the West End to direct it. *The Phantom of the Opera* was a hit in England, making plenty of money for its lead producer, Cameron Mackintosh. If it transferred to Broadway, Hal would again direct the piece, and it would potentially break the stigma that had begun to attach itself to Prince. He had started preproduction on the transfer, and Paul had been told he would take over as music director from David Caddick, who had handled musical responsibilities in London.

Hal had always valued loyalty above everything else. He took care of his own and expected them to do the same for him. When *Merrily We Roll Along* had closed, he had gotten auditions for many of the company, helping them find work in anything else he had going on. Donna Marie Elio, the young and eager woman Paul had befriended in the company, was brought in to audition for *Evita*, for one of the Eva understudies— Paul said she could sing it, and Hal had immediately signed her on, knowing that he could trust Paul to make the call. He had trusted Paul to always be there, ready to tell him what he needed to hear to make a solid production. And now, Paul wasn't there.

Paul knew the ramifications of his refusing Hal, but he was powerless to abandon Steve. Paul was loyal to Hal, deeply, and had he been working on any other show, it would have not even been a question. But there was only one person in Paul's career that came before Hal—Steve. This had, of course, never been a problem before. Hal and Steve had always been a package deal, and Paul had been more than happy to stand between them, eagerly helping each other. Had one of them called, he had always bent over backward to get out of other commitments to join them. But now that Steve and Hal had separated, Paul was caught in the middle. Neither had Paul in permanent contract, leaving Paul to make the agonizing decision.

He knew that if he left Steve in San Diego in the middle of tryouts with no music director, Steve would see it as a betrayal. And he knew that if he stayed in San Diego and left Hal without a music director for *Roza*, that would also be seen as a betrayal. No matter what he did, someone was going to get hurt. Where Steve and Hal had been able to peacefully part ways, there was nothing peaceful to this rack that Paul was tied to, pulling him apart, both emotionally and professionally. Paul suggested to Hal that the man who had played piano in the workshops for *Roza*, Louis St. Louis, would be a good music director, and Hal hung up on him.

Paul and Hal would not have a meaningful conversation for the rest of Hal Prince's life.

This wasn't for a lack of trying on Paul's part—they would see each other at parties and benefits in the years following and would be cordial, but Hal treated Paul like an acquaintance rather than a close collaborator and friend of two decades. He had frozen Paul out, leaving Paul to watch from the outside as David Caddick was brought over to conduct *The Phantom of the Opera*, which has gone on to be the longest-running musical in Broadway history. Paul found out in the press release that he had been replaced—Hal had not sent him any communication letting him know he had effectively been let go by the office. Instead, it was to be inferred.

Paul wrote Hal a letter after seeing the press release, trying to make amends. This wasn't a moment of Paul choosing Steve's friendship over Hal's—on the contrary, letting Hal down felt awful. But Steve was Paul's musical soul. To abandon him would be to abandon everything Paul loved about the musical theatre—the only person who could have ever swayed him from Steve's side was Leonard Bernstein, and Paul would have quit the business entirely had that sort of situation come up. Paul sent the letter, and received no reply—the iron door had been shut. Paul had made his choice, and now Hal was making his. Paul had wanted his freedom to work on the projects he chose, and Hal had given him that freedom, with the cost being that from that day forward, Prince productions were off-limits to him. The man who had once brought Paul along on family vacations now regarded him with the distance of a casual acquaintance.

While Paul had many regrets over how the situation with Hal was handled, he never regretted standing by Steve, and by *Into the Woods*. They had a wonderful run in San Diego, and the company became very close-knit, sharing lunch together on the lawn outside the theatre as they enjoyed the California sunshine. From there they moved straight to the Martin Beck Theatre, where Jujamcyn was hard at work to make the show the family-friendly splash of the season. With *Cats* and *Starlight Express* splitting the audience, they knew they had an opportunity to sweep in as the hot new show, and they took every promotional opportunity, including a massive inflatable boot hanging over the marquee.

Designed by Ann Slavit, a sculptor known for her inflatable vinyl concoctions, the forty-two-foot-tall green boot, complete with spikes, stretched over the marquee, as though the giant was climbing down from the roof to wreak havoc. No one in the company had been forewarned of this decision, and Paul first saw it as he walked toward the theatre, with a number of people planted on the sidewalk and staring at the structure that had gone up overnight. It was whimsical and fantastical and funny— exactly what the show needed. The giant it portrayed was the catalyst for much of the second act but was never actually seen—now whenever anyone asked where the giant was, they could simply point up.

Into the Woods garnered a very different audience than Sondheim's previous shows—where he had always spoken to a particularly adult sensibility, children came to *Into the Woods* in droves, eating up the easily digestible morals of the piece in a similar method to any of Aesop's Fables. But even with the children's fan base, the show was far from a "kids show." Adults could get something very different out of the piece, with parallels and warnings woven into it. A child watching could get a completely different lesson out of a song than the adult next to them, and both lessons were masterfully constructed.

Paul had learned a lesson on *Into the Woods* too. No matter how complex or mired a situation might seem, the only way out is through, and the only way through is by being true to your heart. Your gut knows the way, and you have to trust it implicitly. If Paul had made the smart business decision and followed Hal, he never would have had the joy of standing in the Martin Beck and feeling the waves of exuberance coming off of a theatre filled with children whose lives may be changed by seeing their first show. If he had followed his brain and not his gut, he would've been miserable, working on a show he didn't much like out of obligation rather than an eagerness to collaborate.

Into the Woods competed directly against *Phantom of the Opera* in its season. But even as *Phantom* soared, Paul didn't regret his judgment for a second. David Caddick might have been able to buy a vacation home off of royalties on the show, but Paul had Steve's friendship intact, as well as his own integrity. When he went home every night, he was able to rest knowing he had followed the right path for himself. It might not have been the most glamorous, but it was the thing that brought him more pleasure than anything else in the world.

What is in your heart and soul, and what you believe as an individual all alone in your bedroom is the most important advice to follow. Once you are honest with yourself, you can truly begin to fly.

CHAPTER EIGHTEEN

Jerome Robbins' Broadway

Paul illuminates the orchestra. When you have respect from people, you get what you need, whether you get it like Jerome Robbins got it, or the way Paul Gemignani got it. Jerry was the man we feared and Paul was the man with whom we felt protected. You could just look at him, and one would calm down.
—ROBERT LA FOSSE (DANCER, CHOREOGRAPHER)

INTO THE WOODS WAS WELL INTO ITS RUN WHEN PAUL WAS CALLED TO Jerome Robbins' home for an informal interview. Robbins, who had previously worked with Sondheim on *West Side Story*, *Gypsy*, and *A Funny Thing Happened on the Way to the Forum*, had a fresh idea. An anthology show, tracing his career as a choreographer and director in a way that was much more refined than the standard tribute. With twenty-nine original Broadway productions to his name, he certainly had enough material to concoct a thirtieth. He had been away from Broadway for more than a decade, founding the New York City Ballet alongside George Balanchine, and was finally ready to return to the boards, albeit by reproducing his previous work rather than creating a completely new production.

Paul was a natural fit for this kind of a concept—his work on Sondheim tributes over the years, ranging from the one-night-only *Sondheim: A Musical Tribute* to the longer-running *Side by Side by Sondheim*, proved that he both understood the revue format and could handle navigating through sharply shifting styles without being thrown. Robbins had called

Sondheim before scheduling the interview with Paul and had both his recommendation and his blessing to bring Paul on for the idea. It was going to be a difficult job—dance revues had all but disappeared from Broadway after the 1960s, and Bob Fosse's *Dancin'* had seemed to be an outlier rather than an establishment of a new form, as nearly a decade had passed with no follow-up productions. Never one to run from a challenge, Paul signed on.

It was to be an extremely extended process—Paul stayed on with *Into the Woods*, working nights while rehearsing *Jerome Robbins' Broadway* during the day. This double function continued for nearly eight months as Robbins worked to articulate exactly what he wanted his legacy project to look like.

Dance shows take a lot of time to pull together—where an actor can learn a new scene and get it on its feet in decent shape in under a day, dancers have to get movement into their bodies, which takes an immense amount of repetition. For a show such as *Jerome Robbins' Broadway*, casting dancers who were already familiar with Robbins' style and articulation could speed up the process slightly, but that required an exhaustive casting process. The dance calls were seemingly endless. Performers were brought in from throughout the country, with Robbins personally selecting those he trusted to execute his vision. Some, including Robert La Fosse, were former principal dancers from the New York City Ballet who deeply understood Robbins's more classically based technique that was on display in such shows as *On the Town* and *West Side Story*. Others were from the theatre dance world, with many dancers coming directly from the infamous flop *Carrie*, including Scott Wise, Mary Ann Lamb, and Charlotte d'Amboise, whose father, Jacques, had danced alongside Jerome when both men were young. They auditioned dancers for months, with many performers not getting official word as to if they had gotten the job until months after their fifth dance callback.

The principal vocalists fell into place somewhat easier—Robbins loved storytellers, and with a wealth of wonderful actors available to him, he selected Jason Alexander, Faith Prince, and Debbie Shapiro to fit in among the cavalcade of dancers. Jason and Debbie had both worked in a leading capacity on Broadway before, and both with Paul—Jason having done *Merrily We Roll Along* and *The Rink*, and Debbie *Zorba*. Faith Prince was functionally untested when she was brought aboard. With no New York theatre credits to her name, no national tours, and only a small handful of college productions on her résumé, Robbins saw something in her that he decided to follow.

Faith and Debbie's positions in the show were understood from the outset, acting as the vocalists and leading players throughout different songs in the show, standing in for the original leading ladies. Jason's was far more nebulous—Robbins did not know how to pull together all of the different productions into a cohesive night, and he hand-selected Jason to write the glue that held everything together. Following *The Rink*, Jason had appeared in Neil Simon's *Broadway Bound*, where he had made a name for himself as a joke writer in the cast with his tongue-in-cheek-newsletter *Broadway Blown*, where he recorded and editorialized line flubs from week to week. Manny Azenberg, the producer of *Broadway Bound*, had loved the quips and had hired Jason to write the script for an award show that Manny wanted to put together, with every person in the company winning an award of some kind. When Manny had come on board as the producer for *Jerome Robbins' Broadway*, he had immediately suggested Jason to Jerry as the person who could give the show a through line—but there was a problem. Jason had no interest in being in the show.

Jason turned down multiple audition requests, knowing that the project was going to be a dance show through and through. While he had dance training, he had no intention of putting his dance skills against members of the New York City Ballet in the audition room. Finally, he relented, coming to a meeting with a very perturbed Robbins.

"Why the fuck am I having so much trouble getting you to audition for my show?"

"With all due respect, sir, I don't really want to be in your show."

Jerry blanched as Jason explained his concerns; he was an actor, and a show driven by dance didn't seem to make any sense for him—Jason wasn't going to play Tony in *West Side Story* or dance Gabey in *On the Town*, and he had long since aged out of playing one of the brothers in *Peter Pan*. He didn't see where he could possibly fit and had rejected the auditions in an effort to keep from wasting anyone's time, including his own.

What Jason hadn't realized was that Jerry wanted him specifically because he wasn't like any of the other career dancers that were coming into auditions. The show needed a chameleon of an actor to jump in and out of the leading male roles, while also acting as a pseudo-narrator—Jason was exactly who Jerry needed to play Tevye in *Fiddler on the Roof* and Pseudolus in *A Funny Thing Happened on the Way to the Forum*, and he had the writing chops to write his own track as the narrator.

They struck a deal—if by opening night, Jason wasn't happy in the show, he could leave, no questions asked. But Jerry needed him in the rehearsal room and up to opening night to create his own track, even if he chose to immediately vacate it. Jason agreed to the terms, and to being both the actor and writer.

After many long months of grueling auditions, the company finally entered rehearsals with a cast of sixty-two members, doubling the thirty-one performing in *Les Miserables*, then the largest cast on Broadway. Such a large cast meant a huge investment financially for their salaries alone, with constantly changing sets and costumes added on top to separate each production Jerry was restaging. There was immense pressure on Robbins to both produce his own legacy and to make it profitable—where most tributes are created by acolytes of the person they are uplifting, Jerry was making his own, and he knew that if he stumbled, it would directly affect the way he was going to be remembered.

Shouldering that burden made Robbins more curt than was normal. He had always been known for being a taskmaster—trained under strict dance teachers from childhood, he often presented the image of obsessive perfectionism, and he expected the same of his dancers. It wasn't uncommon for him to fume when a concept was not clicking, as he had difficulty communicating movement through words. They rehearsed for twenty weeks before first going out of town, more than triple the usual six-week rehearsal period. Within that period of time, entire numbers and performers were scrapped and moved around. Dancers were expected to know every single track in the show, and Jerry would pull someone from the sidelines to replace a lead dancer in a number at the last second.

If the new replacement stumbled, it would set Robbins off, leaving the company to wait for him to reconquer his temper so they could continue. In many ways, Robbins would have been happiest had he been able to clone himself sixty times—he knew exactly how he wanted a sequence to be danced, and he would crack under the frustration of not being able to get into his dancers' heads to show them what he saw in his.

With his non-dancers, he was much kinder. He would come into rehearsals early to stage numbers with Jason, Faith, and Debbie, helping them find their own sense of movement with the guiding hand of an understanding teacher. He knew they were not professional dancers and did not penalize them for their stumbling blocks in learning his choreography, an allowance he did not allow the rest of the dancing company. Jason had tap training, and the number "I Still Get Jealous" from *High Button Shoes* was brought into the show to allow him and Faith to perform a soft-shoe routine, and Jerry took care to personalize each of their tracks to match what they were capable of in terms of dance technique. At the start of each rehearsal the company would split into three groups for a dance warm-up, with his top-level dancers from the New York City Ballet warming up with him, the rest of the dancing company warming up with Cynthia Onrubia, one of the dance assistants, as another dance assistant, Jerry Mitchell, warmed up the non-dancing company. By separating out the groups, everyone got the personalized attention they needed, and none of the non-dancers were spooked from trying to keep up with the career dancers.

Robbins was a true genius of movement. However hard he may have been to work with, his talents outweighed much of the struggle behind the scenes. Dancers would gripe and complain at his methods but could not deny that at the end of the process they were better performers. At the end of every rehearsal, when the dancers would be worn down and worn out, Jerry would have everyone dance the *West Side Story* Suite, one of the most intensely difficult sequences in the show. As the dancers would strain to pull the number from their bodies, cursing under the exhaustion, their bodies got stronger, and their stamina increased. What had felt impossible at the first rehearsal began to be doable in the room, and by the time they reached the theatre, the number was flying at the end of Act 1, with the dancers able to pour their energy into the piece since they had grown accustomed to presenting it when they were scraping the bottom of the barrel for energy.

The show was exhausting on all sides. Every single number in the show was the "big number" from its original production—if you are doing a production of *The King and I*, dancers can conserve their energy for the "Small House of Uncle Thomas" ballet, knowing that that is their most strenuous fifteen minutes of the show. But in *Jerome Robbins' Broadway*, every number was the most strenuous fifteen minutes of a show. It was unrelenting and unending, and you had to be in incredible shape to maintain the energy required.

One sequence toward the end of Act 1, the Charleston from *Billion Dollar Baby*, featured Susann Fletcher in a dramatically difficult role as The Timid Girl. Starting as a straightlaced technique-driven dancer, by the end of the number she had to dance with such overwhelming abandon that it seemed to have no actual thought, her feet wildly spurring her on throughout the six-minute sequence. In order to support such movement, Paul had to conduct the orchestra at the very edge of the tempo—rather than working under the beat, he had to be directly on top of it, in order to help Susann ride the wave of the music. The music had to capture her, pushing her ever so slightly forward as to make it possible for her to really soar through the sequence—if either of them fell behind, the magic would be lost. None of the dancers in the sequence ever dropped their heels during the Charleston—it was a high-octane Charleston step on steroids, with heels swinging and toes tapping at such a speed as to spellbind the audience.

With Paul pulling from every trick in his arsenal, he was able to capture this effect in the Charleston and the other numbers in the show—unlike a traditional book musical, there were no book scenes to relax and breathe through. Like the dancers, his feet were to the fire, and by the end of the night, he would have to peel from the podium to crawl home before doing it all again the next day. At the end of a run-through, Robbins would gather the entire company onstage to deliver notes, preferring for all information to be public rather than giving notes behind closed doors from person to person. Paul only ever received one note, day after day—the tempo for "America" in *West Side Story* wasn't right. One day Jerry would need it a few clicks faster, the next a few clicks slower. No matter what Paul did, he could never find the pocket Jerry was aiming for, and after receiving the same note every day for almost a year, he simply stopped adjusting it, instead playing it by his own ear and the visual of the dancers in front of him, since Jerry could never seem to make up his mind as to where he wanted the number to sit.

"America" wasn't the only thing Jerry couldn't make a final decision on—Jason's track was full of introductions to different songs as the narrator, and every couple of weeks Jerry would change his mind as to how he wanted the shows introduced, leaving Jason to rewrite his track multiple times, until they finally settled on Jason entering before numbers as a character from the show, to introduce the show—for example, he appeared as a dock worker at the Brooklyn Navy Yard to introduce *On the Town*. For a legacy piece, Jerry wanted very little fanfare about his contributions in the introductions—instead, he wanted Jason to provide context, explaining where certain numbers fell in the show in order to make their original narrative function make sense.

As Jason sped through constant rewrites, the rehearsal doors were left open for any of Jerry's previous collaborators to come in and check on their material—Stephen Sondheim came in regularly to watch the *Forum*, *Gypsy*, and *West Side Story* material, and Jule Styne would occasionally come along to see how "Gotta Get a Gimmick" was going. Mary Martin came by to support the new *Peter Pan*, Charlotte d'Amboise, and even sang "Never Never Land" to the company. Original cast members from *High Button Shoes*, *Fiddler on the Roof*, and *On the Town* came to reminisce, and such members of the classical ballet world as Mikhail Baryshnikov came to see the magic Jerry was re-creating. Yuriko, the original Eliza in the Small House of Uncle Thomas sequence in *The King and I* who had been the original production's dance captain, returned to teach the choreography to her own daughter, Susan Kikuchi, who performed as Eliza and was the dance captain for *Jerome Robbins' Broadway*.

At the final company rehearsal before bringing in the orchestra, Leonard Bernstein and Mary Martin came to watch the complete run-through. They stayed through notes as Paul stood off to the side, with the cast in a tight half circle surrounding Jerry. When he gave the note that "America" was a hair slow, Paul nodded, brushing it off as he had for the previous month of rehearsals. Suddenly, Bernstein appeared behind him, breathing the words "you'll never get it right" into Paul's ear as Paul desperately tried to hold in his laughter. Jerry had given Bernstein a similar note while working on *West Side Story* originally, and he had not made his mind up on the tempo in the thirty years that had passed.

The company had a costume parade shortly before going to Purchase, New York, for their out-of-town tryout. Irene Sharaff, legendary costume designer of the original productions of *The King and I*, *West Side Story*, and *Funny Girl*, had created stunningly beautiful hand-painted costumes for the company that were wearable art. Each of the girls had a beautiful pink silk flapper dress for the *Billion Dollar Baby* sequences, with hand-painted musical notes and piano keys that were completely unique to each performer, quite literally draping the dancers in measures of music. Having gone to Hollywood in the 1960s, Irene's sense of style had become immensely influential in the glamorous fashions of the United States, and she had worked to create many wonderful pieces for dancers across the industry. When the dancers gracefully swept through the costume parade, presenting her work, Robbins lost his cool. At almost eighty years old, Irene sat still, occasionally puffing her cigarette in its elongated holder as Robbins berated her, cutting almost every costume she had created to match every dancer's personal energy. Each costume had fit like a glove, both physically and emotionally, with many of the dancers feeling the most beautiful they had ever felt in their lives. But that was precisely the problem.

Irene's costumes were overshadowing Robbins' vision. This was to be his legacy project, and he couldn't let her stunning work take precedence over his. When the dancers moved in her costumes, you watched how the fabric stretched and floated rather than how the dancers articulated the shapes Robbins had spent months refining. The dancers looked their best and were polished until they gleamed in their original gowns, but Jerry wanted them to look like poor and tattered dreamers from the Bronx. The dresses were cut, and the dancers were put in significantly more plain costumes that Irene preemptively prepared, having predicted

Jerry's outburst. Due to the costs associated with storing and preserving the costumes, in addition to the tax rates applied to non-destroyed assets, Irene's original silk dresses were burned, alongside thousands of theatrical costumes that were discarded before the advent of costume preservation throughout the industry. No photographs of the hand-painted flapper dresses are believed to exist.

Following their out-of-town tryout, Robbins completely upended the running order and expanded the amount of *Fiddler on the Roof* in the piece, with three numbers inserted into the end of Act 2 that were story and not dance focused. Ten more weeks of additional rehearsal was added to the schedule in order to accommodate these changes. This seemed like a complete nonstarter to the company—the show had played gangbusters during their weekend out of town, and suddenly reworking it to include a quietly sentimental moment like "Sunrise Sunset" felt like a stunted landing. But of course, Jerry knew when something was missing from his creative vision. *Jerome Robbins' Broadway* had been a dance show through and through, and by adding *Fiddler*, it memorialized his work as a director as well as his work as a choreographer. With the finale of *On the Town* now serving as the entire show's finale, the piece ended on a sweetly melancholic note, rather than an energetic explosion. It was a risk—normally you want to end the show with a big and flashy number to send the audience home impressed. Instead, Robbins had pulled it back, presenting things simply to let the quality of the material speak for itself, rather than dressing it all up in bells and whistles. The company went to work reinventing the second act as they moved closer to their opening night, with tensions running high.

During technical rehearsals, a number of other last-minute changes were made. As Equity deputy, Jason had been the contact point between the company and the union, and he had struggled to decide when he had to report Jerry's more caustic behavior as crossing the line. One of the agreements they had come to during rehearsals was that every member of the company would receive a bio in the program—originally the producers had pushed for only the twelve leading performers to be given bio space, but the company had fought back and gotten everyone space to write a few lines. During tech, the final proofs of the programs had come in. Two of the younger members of the company had submitted improper bios, with one making a political statement and the other soliciting for an agent within their bio. Instead of having the production's stage manager, Beverley Randolph, ask the two cast members to change their bios, Jerry made the flash decision to cut the bios back to the original twelve as punishment to the entire company.

The cast immediately began to rumble, and Jason took a seat next to Paul as he tried to figure out how he would explain to Jerry that he could not do that. Jason knew it was likely to be yet another fight between him and Jerry, and he turned to Paul as a friend for advice on how to get Jerry alone at the end of rehearsals to bring it up. The pair were whispering when suddenly, from six rows behind them, they heard Jerry call Jason out, ticked off. Jason did his best to calm the situation, telling him they would talk about it later, but Jerry pushed him, ready for a fight as Paul stood between them. With no other options, Jason explained the situation to Jerry, which only infuriated Robbins more. The company had all stopped to watch the exchange as Jerry began yelling, until finally Jason threatened to pull his own bio from the program and vowed to tell any interviewer what Jerry had done if he didn't stand down and print a bio for everyone in the company.

This was no empty threat. Jason knew the power he held in the show—as the leading actor he was one of the first people audience members would look for in the program, and reviewers were sure to notice his absence. His promise to tell anyone who asked him why he had refused a bio had serious weight, as the negative press it would garner had the potential to cast a shadow over the entire production.

Furious, Jerry refused to back down and attempted to shut Jason down one more time.

"Go fuck yourself!"

"No sir, you can go fuck yourself."

The company was thunderstruck as Jason met Jerry with just as much force. It was as if a bomb had gone off in the theatre. Everyone watched, mouths agape, as Jason stormed out, leaving Jerry alone in the center of the explosion. The entire design team, the producing team, the Shubert Organization, and the majority of the company had watched Jason stand up to Jerry in a way no one working on the project had ever had the guts to. Shell-shocked, Paul stood to the side of the blast crater, desperately trying to make sense of what had just happened. He and Jerry had disagreed before, but no one had ever cursed back at Jerry—if you were in the unfortunate position of being on the other end of Robbins' wrath, you had been expected to take it until he calmed down. No one yelled back at Jerry. No one.

Upstairs, Jason had started packing up his dressing room, positive that he had fired himself with the stunt. He and Robbins had struck a deal at the start of the production, and Jason had reached the limit of the amount of abuse he could endure—Jerry was a genius, yes, but he was a deeply tortured one, and Jason did not have the emotional bandwidth to tolerate the constant lashing out. He was halfway through figuring out how to explain to his wife what he had done when Beverley came over the PA and called for the entire *Fiddler* cast to come onstage to begin teching the number. Jason knew that included him as Tevye, and he quietly went down the stairs, expecting to be formally fired, but when he walked onstage, Jerry wouldn't even look at him. They set up the entire number that way, with Jerry acting as though Jason was not in the room. At the end of the night, confused, Jason went to Paul to ask if he had been fired. Equally baffled, Paul shrugged.

The next day, Jerry called a full company meeting to declare that he had decided to keep the company's bios, and that they all had to approve their bios one by one with Beverley. Jason had won the battle. As the rest of the company filed over to Beverley to confirm their mostly normal sentences, Jason pulled Jerry aside to thank him for backing down, and to apologize for cursing. Jerry dryly accepted the apology and refused to acknowledge the fight any further.

Thankfully, the show was able to run smoothly into previews following the uproar during tech. The theatre was packed from the get-go, with thousands of Robbins' devotees appearing to show their love for the man who had created so many seminal moments in musical theatre history. During an early preview, Debbie Shapiro caught a glimpse of Leonard Bernstein conducting the *West Side Story* Suite a few rows behind Paul, his arms fully outstretched and eyes closed as he relived his own glory days. Before the opening-night curtain, Jerry went to visit Jason with tears rolling down his face. Concerned, Jason went to him, assuring him that the show was in great shape and that the audience was sure to continue loving it as they had during previews. With a small smile, Jerry explained.

"I know, but no one understands how much I don't want this to end."

For all of the fights and fears, Jerry had deeply treasured the time the company had spent in the rehearsal studio. After so many years away from Broadway, he had finally come home and had been able to relive, in some small way, the period of work that had come to define his legacy for all time. The theatre had changed drastically since he had first stepped foot onstage in 1938 as a member of the ensemble of *Great Lady. Jerome Robbins' Broadway* represented the turning of the generational tide—Jerry was going out with one giant burst of light, with the sixty-two performers in the show holding the keys to how he would be remembered. For all of his pain and antagonism, Jerry had never wanted to be a monster. His temper had haunted him his entire career, but in spite of his worst behavior the company had come together to make something beautiful. And now, he faced his final big Broadway opening night. It wasn't only the rehearsal process for *Jerome Robbins' Broadway* that was ending—it was the end of Jerome Robbins the man on Broadway. He wasn't crying out of worry that the show wasn't going to succeed. He was crying out of recognition that after fifty years, his journey on Broadway was complete.

When the curtain rose at the Imperial Theatre, it was to much fanfare. In an industry that was struggling under the immense loss of the AIDS crisis, *Jerome Robbins' Broadway* was a welcome reminder of the golden age of Broadway. For many people in the community, the show that had stoked their love of musical theatre was a Robbins show, and now numbers that had been thought lost to time were suddenly alive again, exactly as Robbins had intended them.

They became one of the hottest tickets of the season and won six Tony Awards, including a Best Actor statuette for Jason Alexander, and Best Musical. When the Drama Desk Awards came around, Paul received a phone call telling him to attend the ceremony itself. Paul had never been one for award shows and tended to skip them if he wasn't involved in a performance that was happening, but they pressed him to come for one key reason—they were giving him the Drama Desk Special Award. Their equivalent of a lifetime achievement award, it is an annual prize given to people who have had a significant impact on the New York theatre scene.

Paul was surprised for several reasons—for one, he associated lifetime achievement awards with people who had retired, and he was nowhere near slowing down. The idea of receiving an award for his work had never come up before—music directors were, across the board, not recognized by any of the main theatrical award ceremonies. The Tony Award for Best Conductor and Musical Director had been discontinued in 1964, before Paul had ever come to New York, and he had swallowed the fact that the only public recognition he would get would be if Sondheim won for Best Score, when he would mention his music director and orchestrator by name in his speech. The Drama Desk Special Award was the first significant tip of the hat that Paul had received from the Broadway establishment at large, and he proudly accepted it beside Jerome Robbins, who also received a Special Award for his imprint on the theatre.

Robbins' legacy had officially been cemented as legendary, and the company prepared for a long, exhausting run. The production stage manager, Beverley Randolph, would purchase a massive bottle of ibuprofen at the start of each week, and by Wednesday it would be half empty, with every member of the company in a significant amount of pain from start to finish. Under significant physical stress, the company still had an immense amount of fun.

Mary Ann Lamb, one of the dancers in the company, shared a dressing room with her dear friend Charlotte D'Amboise (daughter of legendary dancer Jacques D'Amboise), who was one of the principal dancers. Both ardent dog lovers, they adopted a German Wirehaired Pointer puppy as a surprise for one of the light operators who had lost his wife during the production. Named Blue, the puppy was immensely affectionate and bonded with Mary in the short period before he was given to his owner, where he quickly grew into a two-foot-tall frame, complete with distinguished beard and expressive golden eyes. When the time came for Mary to leave *Jerome Robbins' Broadway*, she pleaded with

Blue's owner to sneak him into the theatre so she could see him—he acquiesced when Mary promised to hide him away in her and Charlotte's dressing room on the upper floor of the theatre, far from where anyone could disturb Blue.

By the end of Act 1 of the sweltering summer matinee, he had gotten into a box of chocolates the girls had stashed and eaten a lipstick out of Mary's makeup bag, his agitation ramping up, when the unthinkable happened. Another dancer tried to sneak into Mary and Charlotte's room to borrow a lipstick (something she had done before without issue), and Blue peeled out of the dressing room at full speed, forcing her to the side as he rocketed through the stairwell, where Mary had just taken her place as Louise for *Gypsy's* rousing burlesque number "Gotta Get a Gimmick."

Terrence Mann, who had replaced Jason Alexander as the production's pseudo-narrator, was standing in the wings with a large illuminated book in his hands, preparing for the *Peter Pan* sequence (starring Charlotte) that was set to follow the burlesque routine. Suddenly, his legs were forced apart as Blue burrowed through him in order to make it onstage, where he could hear Mary's voice. Shocked to suddenly be astride a large, wiry dog that had seemingly appeared from the ether, he did not understand what was happening until it was too late to do anything but watch in horror. The company watched with a mixture of panic and hilarity as Blue trotted on, looking at the girls and the audience, before making direct eye contact with Paul, who was in hysterics in the pit. Blue stood stock-still at the center of the stage, staring down Paul, as Faith Prince, Debbie Shapiro, and Susann Fletcher, who played the three strippers teaching Louise the ropes, struggled to continue on with the scene through their tears of laughter as Mary desperately tried to corral Blue through sharply pleading cries to sit and not wander farther onstage. Mary tried to cover her body mic as she called to him, to little avail as her frenzied commands echoed through the theatre, and the audience joined Paul and the girls in an overwhelming fit of laughter.

Blue's owner, who was helpless as he operated one of the spotlights from the back of the balcony, trained the spotlight directly on Blue as the stagehands' headsets picked up a cacophony of confusion, punctuated by one repeated message.

"Oh my god, Blue's on Broadway."

As waves of laughter poured forth from the audience, Beverley Randolph recognized that the situation was unsalvageable and called down the curtain, with most of the company doubled over in laughter as she hauled Mary to her feet and instructed her to do whatever it took to get the dog out of the theatre before her next number; Charlotte and the rest of the *Peter Pan* company was pushed onstage, desperately trying to stifle their laughter. Faced with a massive, slightly rambunctious dog who had gotten a taste for stardom, Mary grabbed Blue by the collar and sprinted across the street to McHale's Bar, a legendary working-class establishment frequented by stagehands, where she burst through the doors in full costume, hair aflutter, with Blue lolling next to her as if on a great adventure. With the fervor of a woman on the brink, she begged the bartender, Ken, to hide Blue behind the bar for her until the end of the show, when she could secret him back to his owner before Beverley had the chance to put two and two together on how the dog had ended up at the theatre in the first place. Ken agreed (both out of compassion and confused concern), and Mary sprinted back across the street, narrowly making it back for her next number.

After the show, rumors abounded as to where in the hell the dog had come from. Some thought that it was a stray that had snuck in through the cracked stage door the company had opened to get fresh air backstage. Others theorized that it could be somehow connected to Robbins himself, as a test of the stage management's ability to expect the unexpected. Beverley cornered Charlotte and Mary, having pinpointed that the dog somehow recognized the two of them, and put the pair through the ringer—since it was Mary's last performance anyway, there wasn't much that could be done to her beyond a stern verbal admonishment, but Charlotte was sharply warned to not allow any more animals to "mysteriously appear" in her dressing room. They decided to publicly acknowledge the stray-dog theory, and the full sequence of events was kept secret for decades, with no one wanting to own up to being responsible—finally, nearly thirty years later, the dancer who had gone to borrow the lipstick confessed to Mary what had happened, and the pieces were put together. When Actors Equity found out what had happened, union rules were amended to make it a contract violation to bring a dog backstage who was not appearing in the show as a performer (and all animals have to have an assigned handler backstage at all times).

While Mary's exit from the production was particularly melodramatic, dancers came in and out of the company regularly, as the wear and tear on their bodies caused them to need to leave the production quicker than other shows. When Robert La Fosse made the decision to leave, Cleve Asbury was brought in to replace him. Cleve had been one of Robbins' *West Side Story* boys during the 1980 Broadway revival, and he quickly assimilated into the company's tight-knit atmosphere. Donna Marie Elio, Paul's dear friend since *Merrily We Roll Along*, had been cast as Debbie Shapiro's understudy, and she began to watch Cleve from wings, dancing with a ferocity that was undeniable, even in the throngs of movement surrounding him during group numbers. Soon he and Donna were finding little moments to spend together onstage, flirting and falling in love before Paul's eyes.

Robbins would come in to check on the show every Saturday before the company's day off on Sunday. Of course, everyone wished he would come any other day, since they were all beat down and exhausted by the end of the week. Paul and drummer Mike Berkowitz had a long-running gag where one of the two would greet Jerry when he arrived at the theatre with a $5 bill in their pocket. They would press it into his hand, urging him to go and catch a movie instead, which he would laugh off, although he always kept the $5.

Near the end of the run of *Jerome Robbins' Broadway*, Cleve proposed. Donna knew she wanted Paul to walk her down the aisle—her own father was not in the picture, and Paul had been one of the most influential paternal figures in her life, ever since *Merrily We Roll Along*. Paul immediately said yes, and Donna and Cleve were married in California on February 22, 1991, with Paul accompanying her down the aisle before he took over the national tour of *Jerome Robbins' Broadway*.

While the show had been exhausting on all levels, it had also been equally thrilling. When the conductor of the touring company called, needing to unexpectedly exit, Paul returned, working with the dancers across the country until the time came for his next project—*Crazy for You*.

Chapter Nineteen
Crazy for You

It was December of 1989 and I bought a cheap front-row ticket to see Jerome Robbins' Broadway *at the Imperial Theater. I was so excited. Little did I know that in addition to loving the Robbins choreography and the cast of amazing dancers, I would be mesmerized by the conductor in the orchestra pit. Here was a conductor who was into a ten-month run of this show, and he was conducting like it was opening night. You could tell how much he loved it by watching his body respond to the music. I marveled at how he was in complete command of the whole orchestra. At one moment, I saw him point to his eyes with his two fingers and then point to his trumpet player to make sure the musician was following his conducting. When the dancers bumped their way through "You Gotta Have a Gimmick," so did this conductor. He swayed and danced with the rhythm as he flicked his baton and made his fellow musicians smile. I was so happy to be sitting in the front row, so close to this powerful artist. At the end of the show, I looked up his name in the Playbill—Paul Gemignani. I even said it out loud, "Paul Gemignani." I thought how lucky I would be if I ever got the chance to work with this incredible musical director. I made a wish on my program that night that someday it would happen.*
> —Susan Stroman (Choreographer, Director)

Crazy for You was a show in a similar vein to Jerome Robbins' *Broadway.* Dance focused, it took the music of George and Ira Gershwin and updated the plot of one of their seminal hits, *Girl Crazy*, to create a fresh show with a classic feel. With an updated book by Ken Ludwig, whose *Lend Me a Tenor* had been hailed as one of the great modern farces, it took what had originally been a meager plot and made a meal out of stolen identities, accidental love triangles, and the gulf between small town and city life.

Of course, it was also good business sense. In the United States, music copyright expires ninety-five years after it has been published. But should a song be a part of a copyrighted production, an estate is able to maintain copyright over the performance use of a piece. By creating *Crazy for You*, the Gershwin estate was able to take some of their biggest hits, including "I've Got Rhythm" from the original *Girl Crazy*, and prevent their release into the public domain.

Mike Ockrent, whose *Me and My Girl* revival had proved a sensation, had been brought on to direct, and during a lunch meeting he laid the production out to Paul. A show driven by dance, with the structure of Gershwin songs to hold together a traditional musical comedy plot. Paul had been home from the tour of *Jerome Robbins' Broadway* for a short time and was already itching for the next job—he and his wife had separated, with Paul living apart from the family whenever he wasn't visiting Alexander. The strife at home had always been easier to swallow when working, and when Ockrent asked him to join the creative team as music director, it was a no brainer.

They needed a choreographer. A number of options had been suggested to Ockrent, and as he rattled off names to Paul, one stuck out—Susan Stroman. A member of the Kander and Ebb family, she had choreographed a production of *A Little Night Music* at City Opera with Scott Ellis, now a director, before creating a revue entitled *And the World Goes 'Round*. It was a hit Off Broadway, with her choreography shining in the re-creations and reinventions of classic Kander and Ebb numbers, many of which Liza Minnelli had made her career off of. Liza brought her on to choreograph her sit-down engagement at Radio City Music Hall, and Stroman had been nominated for an Emmy for her work. Susan and Paul had been circling each other for some time, and he immediately singled her out to Ockrent, knowing that she would be able to handle the levels of ballet, tap, and traditional showgirl choreography necessary for the piece.

Creating *Crazy for You* was not unlike creating an entirely new show—rather than putting a show back on its feet, as is the function of many revivals, they were starting from near scratch. With George and Ira long buried, Paul was the ultimate head of the music department and acted the role of the composer in negotiations of song selections and placement when they deviated from Mike's original layout. They would move things around, finding the right spot for puzzle pieces as Mike would help Ken swiftly write a book around shifted songs. The four became quite close, with late nights and early mornings all around as they created the first "new" Gershwin musical since 1935, save a similar attempt at reinvention by Tommy Tune in 1983 with *My One and Only*.

Once they had their marching orders, they set to casting. Finding the classic Broadway showgirls proved to be a nightmare. In an echo of *Jerome Robbins' Broadway*, they had to have endless dance calls to find girls who both looked and danced the part. They had to make immensely difficult tap movements seem effortless, while maintaining an old Hollywood air of glamor, even as Stroman put them through their paces. Thankfully, unlike *Jerome Robbins' Broadway*, they needed to find only nine women, and their search proved fruitful.

Their leads, Polly and Bobby, came together in a similar fashion. Jodi Benson, who Paul had worked with on *Smile*, had become a hot commodity after voicing Ariel in Disney's *The Little Mermaid*. Now three years after release, she was returning to Broadway with star billing to play the tomboy turned hopeless romantic Polly. Harry Groener, who had been a replacement for George in *Sunday in the Park with George*, was the perfect Bobby, able to act the fool without ever losing his sense of charisma. Bruce Adler, a beloved Borscht Belt comedian, was brought on to play Bobby's accidental shadow Bela Zangler, and the rest of the supporting players quickly filled out with up-and-coming talents. The Manhattan Rhythm Kings were brought on as a unit to play the tight harmony-singing cowboys Mingo, Moose, and Sam, and the company was off and running.

As with most dance shows, rehearsals were a matter of repetition as the creative team worked behind the scenes to parse down and perfect the piece. They had no interest in including a hit just to have it in the show, and certain sequences were scrapped, including a lengthy "Stairway to Paradise" sequence, in favor of more emotionally resonant moments. They had mostly found their rhythm when they went to Washington, D.C., for their early tryout, and when they finished rehearsals the Friday before their travel day, all seemed well. The next morning, Paul received a phone call instructing him to come to an emergency meeting in one of the train cars once they had all left the station together. There was only one small problem: Paul had opted out of taking the train ride with the rest of the company and had already left for DC in his car, leaving Stroman and Ockrent to meet him at the theatre that night.

Mike had decided to scrap the entire second act. It wasn't landing how he wanted, and he knew they could do better. In the middle of technical rehearsals for the tryout they were suddenly writing a completely new second act, with Paul and Stro working as quickly as possible to rehearse the company so they could tech numbers that hadn't existed a day before. The second act that continued with the show was written in approximately a week, under the influence of a significant amount of caffeine, adrenaline, and gumption.

The second number in the second act, "What Causes That," was a particular beast. A lesser-known song from 1928's *Treasure Girl*, they had repurposed it to act as a shared lament between Bobby and Bela, with the two characters mirroring each other in extended comedic sequences as each loses track of his own identity. They gave Bruce close to free rein to ad-lib, and he and Harry would go for it every night, screwing around and messing with each other in ways that made every single performance completely different in timing. A moment that might take fifteen seconds one night would take forty the next, and Paul had to be on the edge of his seat watching them both to keep the orchestra on track with them, even as they would have him laughing so hard it was hard for him to see.

While in DC the company celebrated Christmas together with a production-wide Secret Santa, with what was supposed to be a secret draw. Paul pulled the name of one of the showgirls, and soon the seven company members who had gotten the other girls came together to coordinate their surprises. The showgirls spent the overwhelming majority of the show in sync with each other, presenting a united front, and the men thought it was only fitting that their Christmas surprises link together as well. Knowing them to be good sports, they went to a Victoria's Secret that had recently opened in town and selected matching lounge sets for the girls, with every girl getting their own corresponding color in the rainbow. The girls went wild trying to figure out how their surprises had been coordinated, questioning everyone backstage as they tried to figure out the trick. The gifters swore each other to secrecy, and no one squealed for the entirety of the show's run.

New York embraced the show with open arms. Perhaps Frank Rich, then chief critic of the *The New York Times*, put it best.

When future historians try to find the exact moment at which Broadway finally rose up to grab the musical back from the British, they just may conclude that the revolution began last night. The shot was fired at the Shubert Theater, where a riotously entertaining show called Crazy for You *uncorked the American musical's classic blend of music, laughter, dancing, sentiment and showmanship with a freshness and confidence rarely seen during the* Cats *decade . . .* Crazy for You *scrapes away decades of cabaret and jazz and variety-show interpretations to reclaim the Gershwins' standards, in all their glorious youth, for the dynamism of the stage.*

The efforts of Paul, dance arranger Peter Howard, and orchestrator William Brohn to create a score that returned to the original Gershwin style was not the only moment of dynamic identity in the piece. The show had an immensely strong visual identity—Stro had created immediately recognizable moments of dance, including an extended sequence where the showgirls would become upright basses through the help of a well-placed length of rope. The image, fittingly in the number "Slap That Bass," became one of the calling cards of the show, and almost every review of the piece mentioned the moment as a highlight, alongside the taptastic closer of Act 1, "I've Got Rhythm." Unlike other productions cobbled together from a composer's back catalog, *Crazy for You* felt intentional, mainly because it was. It was a labor of love from the entire creative team.

Love of work wasn't the only thing that had been percolating back-stage. Mike was married with two children, but over the months of intimate work on the show, he had fallen in love with Stro. His wit and her sense of joy blended perfectly, and he began divorce proceedings as the show launched sit-down productions across the globe, capturing the excitement around the piece with sit-downs in Tokyo, London, Melbourne, and Toronto. Paul was on a plane more often than not as he supervised the different companies, as well as maintaining the New York flagship. Some, like Tokyo, had been mostly uneventful restagings of the show, while others, like London, had struggled with some technical fits and starts (a stunt in the first number of the show, "I Can't Be Bothered Now," involved all of the showgirls appearing out of a car fully coiffed and dancing. This element had proved troublesome on the West End, and it gave the team more grief than it ever had in New York). But no matter where they went, the show's music and story played gangbusters. They hadn't just created a new Gershwin musical—they had created a new Gershwin hit.

While in Melbourne, putting together a limited engagement of *Crazy for You* for the Victorian Arts Centre, Paul called his mother, Margaret. Ever since moving to New York, Paul had called home every six weeks or so to check in. They were brief phone calls, but Paul had kept up the ritual in an effort to maintain some kind of family ties, even though he had functionally exited their world, and his world was a perennial mystery to them. In order to save his parents the long-distance charge, Paul was always the one to reach out from whatever corner of the world he happened to be in. He was prepared for the usual routine of his mother running him through the health of various family members, but her response to his location surprised him.

"You know that's where my father was born."

Paul paused. His mother had always said her side of the family was Irish, and she had practically hung her hat on it. When Paul asked for clarification, she repeated herself, saying that her father had been born in Melbourne before eventually immigrating to Wales, and then the United

States. For Paul's entire life, his mother had given him an incorrect family history, likely due to her still associating Australia with being a penal colony, and therefore less respectable than the rest of the family's history. She continued on, chuckling, as if she hadn't just dropped a huge piece of information, leaving Paul dumbfounded until the end of the phone call. He had accidentally ended up in his family's homeland without having any knowledge of it. Shaking off the revelation, he quickly put together the engagement and headed back to North America, with the decision made to not question his mother further on what else she may have mixed up during his childhood.

Stro had moved on to choreographing Hal Prince's revival of *Show Boat*, which was in Toronto having its out-of-town tryout as Paul and the rest of the creative team were putting together the Toronto company of *Crazy for You*. This was exceptionally rare—when sit-down productions are produced of Broadway hits, the original creative team is usually tossed to the winds, with only one or two people keeping tabs on restagings. So deep was their shared love for one another that the *Crazy for You* team moved as a unit, coming together every time a new production was put on its feet.

Stro's longtime assistant, Chris Peterson, invited Paul to see one of the performances of the new *Show Boat* with him after rehearsal one night and handed Paul the program to look through until the end of rehearsal. Paul flipped through the bill, looking for any familiar names with half interest until coming to the headshots page. There, gazing straight at him, was Derin Altay. For the first time in more than a decade, they were working in the same city, only a few blocks away from each other.

Paul nearly threw up. He had shut Derin out of his mind, focusing on work and parenting with his full might, but had never been able to completely banish her from his dreams, where she had always remained on the wispy outskirts of his subconscious. Now she was so close it felt he might be torn apart from the strain of continuing to stay away. Unable to go to the show that night, he went home from rehearsal and drove himself insane, with hundreds of potential scenarios playing out as he tried to wrap his mind around what this meant. Derin was married now, and he had promised himself when she had called him with the news of her engagement that he would do whatever it took to let her be happy. After being apart for so long, he had no idea if seeing him would bring her any kind of happiness. Still, when Chris asked him to come with him the next week, Paul agreed.

The moment he entered the theatre he was a goner. As the song "Can't Help Lovin Dat Man" echoed through the room, he was immediately brought back to taking Derin through the song at her first *Evita* audition, when she had overwhelmed his senses. Sitting there, he knew he couldn't just watch and leave. He had to at least serve the ball into her court, letting her know he was there and letting her make the decision if they would speak face-to-face. The next day he had two dozen long-stem cream roses sent to her dressing room, much to the curious delight of her castmates who knew her husband wasn't the type to shower her with surprise floral arrangements. Tucked in the blooms was a card, identifying Paul and asking her to a drink after the show, which Derin promptly hid from view. Much to Paul's surprise, she called, and they agreed to meet at the King Edward Hotel bar.

The moment Derin set eyes on Paul, it all came flooding back. Every laugh, every smile, every kind word. And every cold hard night that had passed since that pivotal phone call. Her marriage had not been a happy one, and when Paul asked her how she was doing, she was blunt, letting her frustration out as he laughed at her candor. One drink soon multiplied, and they spent the night catching up in that hotel bar as every barrier they had put up crumbled. From that point forward, they promised to do whatever it took to walk forward into the future together, regardless of the past's pain.

CHAPTER TWENTY

Passion

*Paul always brings his humanity into every room. Paul is gregarious
and private, hilarious and deeply serious about what he does. He can
be improvisational and exacting, jolly and soulful. He is a brilliant
guiding force who is also a true collaborator. He always wants to get
the work to the best and most wonderfully expressed place possible.*
          —DONNA MURPHY (ACTOR, SINGER)

PASSION HAS THE DISTINCTION OF BEING ONE OF THE ONLY SHOWS
Sondheim himself conceived. In 1983 he had seen a film called *Passione
d'Amore*, by Ettore Scola, and had been immediately taken with the love
bordering on obsession that surrounded the main character of Fosca, and
he had left the movie theater with the songs already forming in his mind.
He called up James Lapine to once again collaborate, and the decision
was made to present a night of one acts, with *Passion* played opposite an
adaptation of Sam Fussell's memoir *Muscle*, which dealt with the obsessive nature of perfection.

When Steve called Paul, it was in the very early stages—with the
opening number and a few other selections, Sondheim sketched out the
scope of the piece for Paul, handing him a rough script. Paul had also
seen the film on which it was based, and he had been equally enamored
with Valeria D'Obici as Fosca. There was something in her desperation
that was entrancing, and the team quickly got to work trying to reinvig-
orate the story into a theatrical experience.

It didn't take long for them to realize that *Passion* was outgrowing the double-bill format. The piece was so psychologically complex that jolting the audience to a modern setting simply didn't make dramatic sense. *Muscle* was shelved, and *Passion* began to flourish into an entire evening of theatre, sans intermission. By omitting the intermission they kept the audience firmly in the piece, with no moment of reprieve—it became all-encompassing, as the film had, and audiences would simply have to hold on for the length of the ride.

Passion rises and falls on the strength of Fosca. A sickly woman of unfortunate countenance, she was simultaneously the hero and the villain of the piece. One had to be equally dazzled and disgusted by her, without the role ever feeling put on—she was an incredibly bright character who bordered on Machiavellian at times, and the viewer had to fall in love with her alongside Giorgio, without the curve of the emotion feeling forced. It required an actress of immense skill and dedication to pull off properly.

Enter André Bishop and Donna Murphy. André had left Playwrights Horizons in the years between *Sunday in the Park with George* and *Passion*, and he had gone to Lincoln Center Theatre, taking over as the artistic director in 1992. He had worked out an arrangement with Sondheim and Lapine to workshop their new project at Lincoln Center, giving them a home in Midtown to uncover the piece. At the same time, Michael John LaChiusa's musical *Hello Again* was making its Off Broadway debut at the Mitzi E. Newhouse Theater, also in Lincoln Center Plaza. Graciela Daniele had choreographed the episodic piece, with a cast full of rising actors, including Donna Murphy, who had made a splash replacing Betty Buckley in *The Mystery of Edwin Drood*.

Donna received a call from her agent in the middle of *Hello Again*'s workshop process telling her that she had an audition for the new Sondheim-Lapine project the very next day. With the character description of "18th-century consumptive neurotic," the sheet music for "I Read," Fosca's first song, and a small handful of scenes, she was given less than twenty-four hours to bring Fosca to life. Donna was immediately drawn to the complexity of the role but made the decision to turn down the audition, knowing she could not do Fosca justice with such a tight turnaround time. When the team came up empty-handed after the first day of Fosca auditions, they called Donna once more, this time giving her multiple days' notice to immerse herself in the role before coming in.

The Donna Murphy who walked into the audition room was a far cry from the woman they had been watching enter and exit the stage door every night at *Hello Again*. Clear of makeup, with unwashed hair and loosely kept clothes, she sat herself in front of the panel and transformed into Fosca before their eyes. Without the aid of makeup or costuming, she captured the sheer loneliness and desperation that grounded Fosca, and by the end of "I Read," they knew they had found their linchpin.

The second corner of the show's love triangle fell into place similarly. Clara, the bright and shining married woman who holds Giorgio's heart at the beginning of the piece, had to be equal parts loving and logical, with the ability to portray civility in contrast to Fosca's more animalistic qualities. When Marin Mazzie entered the picture, any other potential Clara was immediately out of the question. Marin, who had been a young and pleasant girl as a replacement Rapunzel in *Into the Woods*, had grown into a vibrant and vivacious woman. Paul had barely recognized her when she had walked into the room, newly blonde and made up to the nines. The contrast to Donna's Fosca was perfect, and Marin's glittering soprano made the show's opening number, "Happiness," sparkle in a way that simply cannot be taught. Jere Shea was brought in to play Giorgio after an extended hunt to find the correct energy to match Donna and Marin. Many performers were brought in to test the material, but Jere finally came out on top after his chemistry won over Lapine.

In comparison to the core trio, the surrounding characters were simple to cast. The soldiers were filled out with actors of gravitas, and the show was crafted around the guidance of the trio's interpretations. They moved into rehearsals in a tiny corner theatre at Lincoln Center that was unavailable to the public, and the newly assembled company embarked on a grueling rehearsal process.

Passion is a deeply complex score. Individual songs have to be understood more like a Shakespearean sonnet than a traditional song—the rhythm of the lyrics governed the entire piece, and much like iambic pentameter, a beat could not be dropped or altered without the entire flow warping. Fosca in particular was complex, with entrances often difficult to navigate, and with intellectually dense lyrics that could twist the tongue if not fully understood. Donna put in the time, and she tackled every challenge Sondheim sent her way. Rehearsals were tense and emotionally draining, with every member of the company leaving it all on the line in order to find exactly how far they needed to go.

One of the difficulties with finding that place was the schedule everyone was working under. Lapine did not like to stage sequences independent of the songs that came before and after scenes, knowing that it would result in a less cohesive flow to the piece, but Sondheim did not have a full score ready to present. It was immensely tricky subject matter for him to pin down, and rather than rush through the process to present a product, he took his time to get it right, although it often resulted in the cast not being able to rehearse anymore because they had reached a point in the show that had not yet been written. Both Steve and James put immense pressure on themselves to get *Passion* right, writing and rewriting furiously, and the company did whatever they could to support them as they slowly brought the ship to harbor.

The soldiers began to fill the role of reprieve in the piece, contrasting with the psychological turmoil of the core trio. Paul worked closely with them, and he wrote the drum music for them throughout the piece, which was to be played in mock military style. Paul had always done vocal arrangements for Steve's shows, and folding in the percussion was simply another wrinkle of his job as music director in his eyes—Steve had enough on his plate, and Paul was happy to complete the nonconsequential drum beats, even as Paul was fighting behind the scenes to cut back on the extraneous comedy moments. He was loyal to the darker underpinnings of the piece, which began with the first drumroll as the curtain rose.

The first scene in *Passion* had been written before they had entered rehearsal—entitled "Happiness," Clara and Giorgio are in bed, with the opening chord musicalizing Clara's orgasm. It is a startlingly intimate moment, with the lyrics of the piece deconstructing just how disorienting vulnerability can be with a partner. Love is not a wholly pleasant thing when it takes over a person, mind, body and soul, and "Happiness" uses the physical vulnerability of the nude actors to uncover their psychological nudity. They rehearsed that opening number with strict privacy for weeks, with only Jere and Marin in the room with James, Paul, and Paul Ford at the piano. Steve would make occasional appearances to check on how the material was landing, but it became a gem of collaboration between the five as they found the right tone, both in terms of performance and vocals, to set the stage for the rest of the piece.

Marin was in a particularly vulnerable state. While Jere had a modesty covering, she was nude under the sheet that loosely covered them. Paul made a point of keeping her smiling through rehearsals, and the two became close, with Marin trusting Paul both as a collaborator and a confidant. Her body had completely transformed through her twenties, and she was still settling into herself. In Paul she had someone who was always ready with a wink and a nod, who kept the energy backstage from ever becoming so dense it could choke.

When they moved into the Plymouth Theatre and prepared for audiences, a small changing room was assembled for Marin on the first floor. The dressing rooms at the Plymouth were above the stage, and rather than having Marin wandering backstage nude, the changing room made it possible for her to get ready in her dressing room before donning a robe and going down to the changing room to wait for her entrance. Her changing room was near the door Paul took to enter the orchestra pit, and every so often Paul would knock on the door and play at coming in, eliciting laughter from Marin that ensured she never got too into her head about the exposure.

Unfortunately, Marin's was not the only laughter that could be heard throughout the early previews. When Fosca collapses in a seizure halfway through the piece, audiences jeered at her, with at least one person yelling out "Die Fosca Die!" Donna had been made up to be as visually unappealing as possible in order to underline the mental aspects of love rather than the physical, but her makeup had made her a source of mockery for the audience rather than a source of pity. She would be prostrate on the ground, quivering as the audience applauded her suffering. People came to the show expecting something similar to *Into the Woods*—many of the young fans Sondheim had accrued were now teenagers, and many of them acted out during the piece, standing up during random songs, shouting non sequiturs in reaction to poignant moments, and generally being disrespectful in the name of making a scene.

It was intensely frustrating for the entire company. They had labored over creating an immensely complicated piece, and people were writing it off without even trying to engage with it deeply. On particularly tense nights, Paul would grab a handful of Ricola cough drops to stick to his face in a similar fashion to Donna's wart prosthetics, mirroring his curtain call behavior during *Merrily We Roll Along*, to give the company something to laugh and smile at even as the audience left early.

In spite of the rude behavior, *Passion* came out on top. Critics were intrigued by the piece, and much of the audience reaction was seen as a sign that the piece was right on the money—they were uncomfortable with the realities being presented to them and acted out in an attempt to deny the truth. *Passion* won the Tony Award for Best Musical, as well as Best Book and Score, and Donna took home the Best Actress award, her first.

Passion has the distinction of being the shortest-running musical to ever win the Tony Award for Best Musical, and the production was filmed shortly after they closed in January of 1995. At closing, Paul returned to *Crazy for You* as the rest of the team scattered to the wind.

CHAPTER TWENTY-ONE

Fun for the Whole Family

Paul Gemignani is a true legend in our world of musical theater. The dynamism of his conducting creates an absolutely palpable tremor of passion and power in any group of musicians and actors he leads in performance.

—ALAN MENKEN (COMPOSER)

PAUL HAD SAFELY RETURNED TO *CRAZY FOR YOU* WHEN MIKE OCKRENT gave him a call. He and Susan Stroman had begun work on an adaptation of Charles Dickens' *A Christmas Carol* with Alan Menken and Lynn Ahrens, and they wanted Paul on the team as music director. A seasonal production, they would run for a few weeks during the holiday season, and then everyone would return to their normal lives, with Alan returning to his work on the Disney Renaissance and Lynn returning to her writing partner, Stephen Flaherty.

Paul signed on immediately. He had missed Mike and Stro, and the creative environment they had created together, but the idea of *A Christmas Carol* as a musical would have grabbed him regardless of the team. As a child the Alastair Sim film had been consistent viewing every Christmas, and now as a father he had continued the tradition with Alexander. He loved the story, and when he went to Lynn's apartment to read through the script and hear snippets of the score, he was hooked.

They knew it had to be big—big in scale, big in scope, and especially big in audience. When a show has as short of a shelf life as a holiday production, it is key to get into the biggest space the production can fill in order to make back the investment a large-scale musical requires—instead of having months to pay back investors, they had only weeks, which meant a 600-seat theatre wouldn't cut it. Instead, they picked the Paramount Theatre at Madison Square Garden, with room for more than 5,600 audience members at every performance. It was a massive space, but Mike had an idea up his sleeve to make it feel engagingly intimate.

The Paramount had originally been a grand movie house during the golden age of cinema, and it had a steeply raked seating area with no balcony overhang. Audience members entered through doors at the top of the space and would walk down to their seats, with large aisles on either side allowing for the immense amount of foot traffic. In these aisles, Mike had a series of shops installed, selling little nutcrackers, candies, and souvenirs. Each shop was made up to match the set onstage and was manned with salespeople working in character to make its audience members feel that they had stumbled into Victorian London before the show began.

Children would pour into the space with their parents, their voices echoing over one another to create so loud an atmosphere that it was ear-splitting. The moment Paul would raise his hand and start the overture, the space would go silent. It was as if someone had muted the audience, only to turn the rapture up to eleven after every number, which would be applauded and cheered for at the top of their lungs. The demand for tickets skyrocketed, and they were soon faced with the question of how many performances they could do per week without killing the performers.

That first year they settled on four performances every day, starting at nine in the morning and going into the evening, with every audience member home in time for bedtime. The show itself was an hour and a half, and the company would have ninety minutes to regroup and pull themselves back together again to bound out once more. It was incredibly grueling, and by the end of the day dancers were having to crawl back home, their bodies on the brink of collapse. But even in the face of such immense exhaustion, there was an end in sight, which kept everyone firing on full cylinders—they had less than two months to make more than half a million kids' Christmas dreams come true, and they helped each other up to make it through the marathon.

The set was beautiful, but immensely dangerous for the performers. Much like on *Sweeney*, if a person wasn't paying attention, things could go sideways very quickly. Paul was stationed in a very narrow pit and could only watch the stage in hopes that everyone was aware and ready to move at a moment's notice. "Link by Link," Jacob Marley's big number, had the majority of the company flying through the air on wires, narrowly avoiding each other as they would swing back and forth, with people ascending and descending from the ceiling. It was immensely lucky that they never had any in-air collisions, although it came too close for comfort regularly.

Animals had been inserted into the show to add layers of realism to the picture of London being portrayed, namely a large horse who would come trotting out pulling a cart as the audience would erupt with appreciation. The horse would walk straight at Paul, their eyes locked, and it would only stop when the tip of his hooves touched the edge of the stage, barely not stepping onto the musicians. Thankfully the horse never overestimated, but Paul would stare him down just the same.

During weekday performances, Paul would conduct the first two performances of *A Christmas Carol* before rushing over to *Crazy for You* to do the evening performance—on matinee days at *Crazy for You*, he would do the 9:00 a.m. performance of *A Christmas Carol* before going to the Shubert Theatre and handing *A Christmas Carol* over to his assistant, Mark Mitchell. Paul had never had a dedicated associate conductor before, but the sprinting strain of maintaining multiple shows at once made their partnership a necessity. He spent most of the holiday season bounding around Midtown Manhattan before getting Christmas Day off to spend with Alexander, and then one final push to bring the show to its closing date of New Year's Eve. They sold out every single performance of that holiday season, with more than 720,000 people seeing *A Christmas Carol* in six weeks.

So great was the success that the decision was made to make *A Christmas Carol* an annual event (the schedule was adjusted to three performances on weekdays and four on Saturday and Sunday, resulting in twenty performances a week instead of the first year's twenty-four, three times the normal Broadway production schedule). They played to sold-out crowds year after year, with new crops of kids appearing with open hearts ready for the particular joy they had cultivated. Several years into the run, Derin brought her eight-year-old-son, August, to see the show, and it was in the middle of the debris following a performance that Paul first met the boy who would one day be his stepson.

For nine years *A Christmas Carol* delighted audiences, proving an immense success and setting the stage for the holiday extravaganzas that would follow in its footsteps. Two years into its annual run (and shortly after the closing of *Crazy for You* after 1,622 performances), Mike called Paul with a new idea for a family-friendly romp. *Big*, the 1988 comedic fantasy movie starring Tom Hanks, was getting the musical treatment by David Shire and Richard Maltby Jr. With no rumblings from Sondheim about any projects on the horizon, Paul had functionally become a part of a trio, with Ockrent, Stroman, and Gemignani becoming the go-to group for joyous musical theatre that the whole family could enjoy. They leapt into *Big* feet first, ready to explore a more modern setting than Victorian London or Jazz Age Nevada, but ended up being thrashed on every side.

Big the Musical, as in the movie, involves scenes in the Manhattan F.A.O. Schwarz store when the suddenly adult Josh begins working for the toy company due to his ability to "see what the child sees." Naturally, F.A.O. Schwarz was contracted by the company to provide the toys involved in the show—hundreds of teddy bears, toy cars, dolls, and every type of toy were required, and by having a corporate sponsor they could get the props they needed for the production.

Unfortunately, the New York theatre scene didn't see it this way. The team was accused of selling out, and the show was labeled as a commercial for F.A.O. Schwarz before anyone had even seen it. The community treated it like a complete corporate cash cow of a production due to the sponsorship and acted like it was entirely a toy commercial, with rumors spiraling. Of course, this couldn't have been further from the truth— F.A.O. Schwarz had zero producing input, and it simply provided the toys requested in exchange for having their name listed in the program. This wasn't some new development—companies have provided items for productions since the dawn of time, with entire characters costumed by designer labels in exchange for program credit during the golden age of Broadway. But in 1996, Broadway was extremely wary of corporate involvement in theatre, as Disney cleared out and reshaped Times Square in order to bring in *Beauty and the Beast*. Everyone was wary of the amount of money being poured into shows, and *Big* was hit with the full force of the backlash.

Big was a good show. It wasn't *Hamlet*, but it had no intention of being a piece of serious art—it was a happy musical comedy about a thirteen-year-old boy waking up in an adult body. The performances were solid, the score catchy, and the families who came to see it left smiling. The company shut out the vitriol outside and went to work, with a strong tourist audience offsetting the blacklist they had received from the theatre community.

The show opened with Josh yelling up at his best friend Billy, asking him to come out to play. Stro had choreographed a moment where Billy would drop a baseball bat down to Josh, where it would hit a rubber garbage can and land straight in Josh's hand. This moment usually flowed easily, but one night the aim was off, and the baseball bat hit the stage floor, where it ricocheted straight out at Paul in the pit. With barely even a second to think, Paul plucked it straight out of the sky and threw it back onto the stage as the audience applauded, with the drummer sitting next to him staring at him in shock. He had very narrowly avoided a concussion, and had he been looking down at his score instead of watching the action onstage, he would've had the top of his skull cracked open.

The next day he went to the team and told them that if anything else ever came into the pit, he would be keeping it—no more Hail Mary's, he couldn't risk getting clocked by a flying toy. They agreed, and by the end of the run Paul had a great big collection of stuffed animals and rubber balls and toy trucks to distribute to kids during Christmas, including a remote control–operated truck that he gave to Alexander after it drove off the stage and into Paul's lap.

Big made it through the summer season before losing every award it had been nominated for, the theatre community at large making their stance clear. They closed in October of 1996, without enough money to get them to the holiday rush. It broke Mike's heart—he was a straight-shooting man, with an honest heart and a willingness to try, and the fact that the community so thoroughly shut them down was a deep blow. Mike and Stro had gotten married on New Year's Day 1996, and they retreated back together, waiting for the animosity to die down so the trio could reunite on a new project. They came together for *A Christmas Carol* each year, and Mike helped Alan Menken bring *King David* to Broadway for a two-week run before the unthinkable happened.

Mike Ockrent was diagnosed with leukemia shortly after he, Stro, and Paul began work on an adaptation of Mel Brooks' 1967 film *The Producers*. They had met with Brooks and had begun preproduction when Mike suddenly took ill, leaving Paul to pick up the pieces and keep their touring projects afloat as Stro stayed with Mike through the cancer treatments. Once again, Paul was losing a best friend and favorite collaborator—he and Mike had become close, spending time together in and out of work, and the entire situation echoed Michael Bennett a decade prior.

Paul had always been a bit of a loner, but for good reason—those he let himself get close to tended to die on him. His closest childhood friend, Johnny Seaborn, had died at age ten when he and his father's fishing boat had been cut in half by a tanker next to the Golden Gate Bridge. Paul's father's best friend had also died suddenly, and Paul had worn the dead man's winter coat for a season, stewing in the memories until the family could afford to buy him a new one. With Hal Hastings dead, Michael Bennett gone, and Mike Ockrent on the swift decline, Paul was left alone, careful not to get too close to anyone else for fear they meet the same fate. The only exceptions to his isolation were Alexander, Derin, Stro, and Sondheim.

Paul was empty-handed when he received a call from Scott Ellis, now a member of the Roundabout Theatre Company. He was working on an adaptation of *1776* and needed a music director.

Chapter Twenty-Two

1776

Paul is truly the actor's conductor. He gets his face out of the book and knows what is going on around him. He throws away the page so he can be involved in the process. He is an acute listener. It is a living art for him.

—Mark Mitchell (Pianist, Conductor,
Paul's longtime associate)

The Roundabout Theatre Company is one of the leading non-profit theatre companies in Manhattan, with Lincoln Center Theatre, Second Stage Theatre, and the Manhattan Theatre Club serving as its Broadway competition. Nonprofit theatre is, by nature, designed to elevate art that isn't necessarily the most profitable for producers. In the late 1990s, as Disney swept in and exploded the financial sector of Broadway, non-profits became the home of classic revivals and reimaginings, maintaining a more open-minded programming list than producers who were jockeying to adapt big-budget Hollywood productions into stage adaptations.

In the years since *The Rink*, Scott Ellis had shifted his focus from performing to directing, with a hit revival of *She Loves Me* under his belt in addition to the revue *And the World Goes 'Round*, which he had created with Susan Stroman. *1776* was going to be a big step for the Roundabout—*She Loves Me* had been their first musical, and the classic *1776* required a hearty cast, a large orchestra, and a significant investment to do properly. When Scott called Paul, it was with the knowledge that there was no one better equipped to pull off the production—Paul's ability to be inventive in the face of a challenge was invaluable in making musicals a more robust part of Roundabout's programming.

The original *1776* had been a big and broad production, orchestrated for thirty-five—the Roundabout was able to provide Paul with eight musicians. Brian Besterman, who had designed the electronic music for *Big*, provided the new orchestrations, which were pared down to suit the Criterion Center Stage Right space that Roundabout called home during the 1990s. The show was transformed from a monolith to an intimate piece, with the cast of twenty-seven men capturing the five hundred-seat theatre in a way that swept up the audience into the piece itself.

1776 is, at its core, a play with music. It opens with a rousing number, "Sit Down John," before entering into a twenty-five-minute book scene. Once this giant pause ends, the songs come more rapidly, but the plot is deeply tethered to the book rather than the songs, which elaborate character more than they do circumstance. Because of this, you simply must cast performers who are strong actors. Scott had gathered a cast of immense talent, including Brent Spiner, Pat Hingle, and Tom Alderedge, and new dressing rooms had been built at the Criterion in order to accommodate them. In particular Gregg Edellman, who played Edward Rutledge, shone with his Act 2 showstopper "Molasses to Rum," which detailed the Atlantic Slave Trade that funded the majority of the early United States. This cast was deeply effective, and the production became a hot ticket, with old fans of the show coming out of the woodwork to join people who were discovering the classic for the first time.

Paul had left the conducting duties to Mark Mitchell, as he was playing piano in the pit and there had been no need to lose space in the pit for a dedicated conductor. The space was small enough that Mark could conduct from the bench, and when the show transferred to Broadway at the Uris Theatre, Paul gave Mark the show, even as Besterman's orchestrations were scrapped in favor of a return to the original Eddie Sauter orchestrations in the larger space.

Something of the intimacy they had found at the Criterion was lost in the transfer—rather than a near immersive piece, it became more presentational, because there is simply no way to be intimately involved in a 1,900-seat theatre without having the Founding Fathers wandering out into the audience a la *Cats*. Regardless, the production played to healthy crowds, with complex plots centered on identity, responsibility, and fatherhood intertwining.

The same themes had taken hold of Paul's home life as his son, Alexander, graduated from high school and left New Jersey for the University of Michigan to study trumpet. It was not uncommon for Paul to linger backstage with the company of *1776*, discussing whatever exciting thing Alex had called home about—he was, as always, the child of the theatre, even when he was not physically present.

Alex had always been an imaginative child—his childhood had been Rockwellian, growing up in the town of Tenafly, New Jersey. A large tree was the centerpiece of their front lawn, and he would spend hours creating magical worlds under the coverage of the lowest hanging branches that swept the ground, creating natural arches and doorways to childhood realms. He was swift to make friends and soon joined a childhood baseball team, becoming a proficient catcher as he played with the idea of becoming a professional baseball player.

Paul's father, Ezio, loved baseball. He had encouraged Paul to engage in athletics as a child, to little avail, but Alex took to it immediately, with a sense of competitive camaraderie that Paul had never fully subscribed to. Alex and Ezio became especially close, with memories of fishing in puddles and trading specially coded letters punctuating his childhood. With time, Paul bought a condo for Margaret and Ezio so that they could be closer to Alex in their retirement—Paul's sister, Marie, had raised her children in California prior to Ezio stepping down as a schoolmaster, and Alex was the only grandchild they could dote on from infancy.

When Alex wasn't adventuring around the neighborhood, he would be in the city with his father, watching shows with the unending curiosity that only a child can effortlessly maintain. *Into the Woods* swiftly became a favorite, and he could regularly be found sitting next to his father in the pit or standing next to David Gotwald at the soundboard. When the giant's voice would crackle through the mammoth speakers at the back of the house, Alex would climb on top to feel the rumble rattle through his bones. He became so frequent a visitor backstage that on Valentine's Day

1988, he received a surprise valentine from Bernadette Peters, who had first met him as a burbling toddler during *Sunday in the Park with George*. Alex first picked up the trumpet in fifth grade, and he had written an arrangement of the title song to *The Phantom of the Opera* for their little elementary school brass band at only age ten. By junior high he had Mr. Schnieder, whose crazy temper and devotion to music immediately swept Alex away, alongside his own sons, who became Alex's close friends. He took every music class available to him, including Music Appreciation, Band, Wind Ensemble, and Percussion Ensemble. Like his father before him, he couldn't get enough of the intangible connection that happens when musicians play together, and he was soon spending as much time in the band room as he was on the baseball diamond.

His freshman-year baseball coach was a miserable man who took his anger out on the children, and Paul eventually pulled Alex off the team after seeing him cry following a harsh dressing-down from the coach—what had been a fun and fruitful game for Alex and his friends had turned into a wretched time, and Paul refused to watch his son grow to hate something he had previously loved. With a baseball career no longer in the cards, Alex begged his way onto the runcrew for the school's production of *The Wizard of Oz*, where he guarded the dog playing Toto and operated the Oz head.

Alex had always known about the life of a pit musician, having come in and out of pits since before he could form memory. As he became more serious about the trumpet and began considering it as a career, Paul would hire trumpet players from the pit of whatever show he was working on to tutor Alex in addition to his litany of classes. He would stand next to his father on the podium during *Jerome Robbins' Broadway* and survey the scene, seeing the musicians and the performance in tandem as his father delicately blended the two.

Paul had never pressured Alex to go into theatre—what had always been paramount to Paul was that Alex be happy. Regardless of pressures, Alex had been born with one foot firmly in the world of theatre music, and this love had only grown with each score he uncovered. *Jerome Robbins' Broadway* was a master class in all theatre music could be, and *Passion* had sealed the deal for Alex on opening night, when he had immediately fallen in love with Marin Mazzie and the deep complexities of the show.

When Paul moved out of the house, his and Alexander's relationship had strengthened. His scheduled time with Alexander made their connection far more stable, and the structure lent itself to their time together being precious. In the period following *Passion*, as the divorce was finalized, Paul took Alexander to Maryland to sail. They went through an official sailing school and spent the week together as Paul showed Alex the literal ropes. For three days they sailed with a couple from Canada and a grizzled old captain, having the time of their lives as Paul shared his most precious of childhood hobbies.

While driving back from Annapolis, Alex nagged Paul endlessly to be allowed to drive the car—having just gotten his learner's permit, he could barely contain himself at the idea of driving Paul's BMW. After much cajoling, Paul agreed to switch with him at the New Jersey border, so that Alex could finish the journey home. Alex remained focused, with a light foot and a clear eye, and the pair were nearly home when a car slammed into them from behind at a stoplight.

With Alex shell-shocked, Paul put the car into park and stormed after the pale-faced driver behind them, filling out every inch of his brawny six-foot frame as a nearby cop intervened, assuring Alexander that he had done absolutely nothing wrong. The Gemignani family has an unfortunate tendency toward car crashes where they are not responsible—when Paul was in high school, he had been sideswiped while driving his first car, only moments after driving it off the lot (a scam artist had intentionally driven into the car, predicting that Paul wouldn't have his insurance set up yet. The case had ended up going to court, where Paul had been proven innocent). The lead-footed lummox in Alex's case was dealt with in a similarly quick fashion, and the pair returned home, slightly rattled but no worse for wear. Less than a year later, Alex was left to handle a much more serious crash alone.

Paul had bought him a shiny black Jeep for his seventeenth birthday—while driving home from a friend's house, a speeding car clipped him out of nowhere, tipping the Jeep over on its side and rolling Alex down the curved suburban road as the car sped off, leaving him for dead.

When the Jeep came to a rest on its left side, Alex was able to climb out of the shattered back window with only a bruise on his knee and cuts on his hands from the glass. He wandered in a daze, unable to focus from the shock, until a neighbor pulled him out of the line of traffic and sat him on a curb while the police called Paul. August, Derin's son, would have a similar crash the first time he drove, continuing the evil eye on Gemignani men and their first cars.

By the end of his time in high school, Alex was confident in his love for music, and in his understanding of the daily life of a musician. After watching his father and his musicians, day in and day out, he had a better understanding than most of what it really took to accomplish such a life, and he devoted himself to it. When he told his father that he wanted to go to school for trumpet, Paul immediately supported him as he left New Jersey for the University of Michigan.

During his first year of college however, Alex reached an impasse. He knew what it really took to be a great trumpet player and also knew how high his own expectations were—he had no interest in being a medium-quality player, and as he observed his peers, he realized that the effort it would take to rise to their standards wasn't worth the reward at the end. He was doing well in his classes, but he simply wasn't happy. The definable destination of an instrumentalist overwhelmed him—the idea that the best life could have in store for him was being a principal trumpeter at a place like the New York Philharmonic did not motivate him in the way he knew it should—even the idea of becoming a legend like Winton Marsalis held little interest when compared to the freedom of choice he had seen his father experience.

He missed the adventure and the curiosity of his childhood, uncovering new twists and turns in every story he concocted for himself. He and Paul had always been near twins in sensibility, and comfort in unpredictability had been passed down as readily as their shared build and smile. Paul had rejected similar attempts to pen him into a recognizable career path from the start when he had rejected Ezio's attempts to guide him toward a career as a music teacher. The lack of planned stability provided by a life of jazz gigs and touring had enamored Paul immediately, and he had maintained a similar curiosity when he had entered the world of theatre—every show was different, and he never stayed with a production long enough to become bored. Now, when faced with a set life, with a pre-trodden path and expectations, Alex decided to take the same left turn, before playing the trumpet could become something he resented in the same way baseball had been warped.

After a period of reflection, Alex settled on auditioning for the school's brand-new musical theatre program—he had always enjoyed acting in school productions (including a memorable turn as The Baker in *Into the Woods*) and knew he possessed a voice that was at least on pitch. He loved the University of Michigan, and when he called his parents to explain his plan, it was with the intention of staying there no matter what.

At first, there was pushback—a bachelor of fine arts in musical theatre was a very new concept, and his parents were worried that by getting this degree, he would be shortchanging himself in other areas—why not get a degree in acting or in singing, instead of half doing them both? Alex stuck to his guns, and in the end, Paul supported him. Luckily, it turned out that Alex had sidestepped into one of the most prolific training programs of musical theatre performers in the history of the artform.

When Alex entered the musical theatre program, he soared. With proper training, a voice rich with depth emerged, and his commitment to the stories he told made him an immediately intriguing actor. When he would call home to Paul, telling stories of happiness and hope, it was an overwhelming comfort to Paul.

All he had ever wanted for his son was for him to freely pursue his happiness, and Alex had found his in record time. As *1776* came to a close, and the stories of the Founding Fathers were packed away, Paul's own fatherhood came to the forefront. The little boy who had hidden behind his father's legs was no longer a child. After years of fighting with himself in the name of being the best possible father, Paul had made it to the finish line.

There are only two creatures of value on this earth: those with a commitment and those who require the commitment of others.
—John Adams, *1776*

CHAPTER TWENTY-THREE

High Society

Paul has a nose for theater—his instincts steer him towards spontaneity and strong choices. He understands the difference between a theatrical choice and a purely musical choice, and he brings this understanding to both the actors on the stage and the musicians in the pit. He holds the focus of these two sets of performers, and they trust him to always be there with that difficult mixture of control and collaboration. He doesn't conduct a succession of songs—he conducts the play and shapes the music to the drama. I can count on one hand the people who have taught me what musical theater consists of—and Paul is one of them.

—MICHAEL STAROBIN (ORCHESTRATOR,
COMPOSER, MUSIC DIRECTOR)

HIGH SOCIETY WAS A BIT OF AN ODD DUCK. BASED ON THE 1956 MUSICAL film starring Frank Sinatra, Bing Crosby, Grace Kelly, and Louis Armstrong, it borrowed from the original play *The Philadelphia Story* and took several songs from Cole Porter's other musicals to fill out the score. Following *Crazy for You*, an interest in reviving the music and stories of the pre-1960 musical theatre had bloomed, alongside an increasing demand for the familiar and comforting. As the jukebox musical began to take hold alongside the influx of nostalgia-focused pieces, producers vied for any well-worn property they could get their hands on.

Dodger Properties had sprung up as a producing partnership in the late 1970s, with *Pump Boys and Dinettes* and *Big River* proving successful prior to their involvement on the original *Into the Woods*. Michael David, one of the producing partners, had met Lauren Mitchell, who had played the stepsister Lucinda, and they had fallen in love, with Mitchell leaving the world of performing to join the world of producing.

When Mitchell called Paul about *High Society*, it was a no-brainer. He needed a job following the closure of *1776*, and he had always liked the original film, as well as Cole Porter's music. It was the kind of project a music director could have a lot of influence on—much of the music in the original film had been put together in a rather slapdash manner, and by taking on the project he had the opportunity to shine up a Porter classic much as he had a Gershwin. Unfortunately, Paul was not given the opportunity to shape as much as he wished.

Christopher Renshaw, the British opera director who had been hired to guide *High Society* to Broadway, was a disaster waiting to happen. A loosely functioning alcoholic, he frequently showed up to team meetings and rehearsals under the influence and would leave long before any constructive work was completed. Much of the actual work of directing fell onto Lar Lubovitch, the show's choreographer, who was left to patch cracks Renshaw didn't care to address.

A good musical can survive many things, but *High Society* had been on shaky ground before Renshaw had even been hired. While it had that classic Porter flair, it had never been one of his megahits, and the original film had been overshadowed by its competition, having premiered the same year as film adaptations of *The King and I, Anything Goes*, and *Carousel*. While Porter is a familiar name to audiences today, it is almost entirely for two stage musicals—*Kiss Me, Kate* and the aforementioned *Anything Goes*. His later film work had been only modestly successful when first released, and *High Society* required a deft hand to elevate it. The careful steadiness the show needed was not something Renshaw was capable of providing.

Still, Paul and Lubovitch stuck it out, hoping that things would turn around in rehearsals. They put together a stellar cast, including Melissa Errico, Randy Graff, Marc Kudisch, and a young Anna Kendrick in her

Broadway debut, and headed into rehearsals. Much of the piece was disjointed, with logical fallacies and loose plot threads only exacerbated by Renshaw's meddling. Paul was able to pull the company together vocally, interpolating Porter hits such as "Just One of Those Things" into the score to increase its heft, and Lubovitch choreographed deft classical sequences to create an elegant aura around the show. Melissa Errico, who played the leading role of Tracy Samantha Lord, shined, with her warm soprano soaring on the traditional Porter melodies, but the undisputed discovery of the show was twelve-year-old Anna Kendrick, playing Dinah Lord, Tracy's grumpy younger sister with a talent for deceit.

Child actors are typically a mixed bag—often overcoached, or undertrained, it can be extremely difficult to produce a performer of equal talent and imagination who is able to withstand the rigor of a Broadway schedule. Anna leapt to the challenge, squeezing out laughs and smiles with a comedic timing of someone twice her age, and she gave the show a charm that it so desperately needed in order to be seen as something other than antiquated.

Unfortunately, Anna's charm and Melissa's talent were not enough to overcome the storm brewing behind the scenes. They made it to a tryout in San Francisco, where it landed flatly with audiences, and the team began work on a significant number of changes to improve the piece before New York. Lubovitch was hastily filling in cracks as Renshaw retreated further and further from the process until one day, shortly after the company had returned to New York, he disappeared.

This was the final straw. While Renshaw had hardly been reliable, he had never been untraceable before. They eventually found him across the city the next day, but the damage had been done, and he was removed from the project, with Des McAnuff brought in to completely redirect the show in two weeks. With him, he brought Wayne Cilento, his preferred choreographer, leaving Lar Lubovitch out of a job alongside Renshaw.

Paul was not informed of any of this until he walked into the theatre one day to find Lar and Renshaw gone. The injustice of the situation infuriated him—Lar had been holding together the entire production, and no one had even bothered to give Lar a phone call when he had been unceremoniously replaced. No one had contacted Paul regarding the changes, and Paul was expected to just go along with it as if everything was normal. In the musical theatre, the only people above the music director in the creative team are the director, the choreographer, and the composer—with Cole Porter dead, and Renshaw and Lubovitch thrown out the door, Paul's head was on the chopping block next.

Paul had never quit a job in his entire career. Regardless of how bad it got, he had always stuck it out, his sense of duty toward the music overshadowing any personal slights behind the scenes. *High Society* tested that resolve. He prepared to leave, refusing to take part in the coup happening, until the cast came to the forefront of his mind.

The cast couldn't leave. While Paul had built up a large enough legacy to break contracts, none of the actors could break free without severe career ramifications. If he, as the last leader of the original production, were to abandon ship, they would have no one left to cling to as they desperately learned McAnuff's new staging in an attempt to save the show. With the thought of the cast's stricken faces upon being told of Lar's removal, he swallowed the disrespect and stayed on as McAnuff quickly dictated a new production and Cilento replaced Lar's original choreography.

When *High Society* opened, it was to little fanfare. The show was swiftly labeled as tacky, outdated, and periodically robotic, with any heart it had once possessed having been beaten out by the chaos backstage. Still, the show was nominated for two Tonys, losing both, and managed to hold on until the end of August to go quietly into the night, a mostly forgotten footnote in the careers of every person who participated.

Paul had learned an immensely valuable lesson—you don't have to just say yes to a project because you need a project. Needing a job is rarely the reason to say yes, provided you have things squared away financially. Paul had become enthralled with the constant flow of work and had forgotten how not to be busy. *High Society* was the wake-up call Paul needed to look around and see that he was in a position to step back and work only on shows he actually wanted to work on. You have to really think about the direction you want your career to take, and you cannot approach everything with the open eyes of a green beginner forever.

So, Paul stepped back. He and Derin moved in together, and he took up the mantle of helping to raise her son, August, a bright and charming boy in need of a more stable father figure. The pair immediately took to each other, with Paul's strength serving as the support system Augie had been searching for—in Paul he found a person who deeply, altruistically cared for his welfare and development. Any question he might have was worth taking to Paul, and their relationship blossomed as the family settled into a comfortable and loving rhythm. That is, until Michael Blakemore called, with a new opportunity to do Cole Porter justice—the first major revival of *Kiss Me, Kate*.

Chapter Twenty-Four

Kiss Me, Kate 1999

When he's in the pit and you're onstage, he is breathing with you. We feel each other. The passion, the way his body moves, the expressiveness, it's in him. It's inspiring.
—Marin Mazzie (Actor, Singer), *The New York Times*

Kiss Me, Kate has the kind of pedigree most musicals can only dream of—the first winner of the Tony Award for Best Musical, it had played to raucous crowds for more than one thousand performances when first staged in 1948, and it had been inspired by the marital strife of legendary team Alfred Lunt and Lynn Fontanne during their 1935 production of *The Taming of the Shrew*. Porter's career had been on the downswing during World War II, when his refined sensibility had ceased to amuse audiences, and *Kiss Me, Kate* had elevated him to icon status, with the score filled to the brim with some of his most beloved songs. In 1998, the original 1948 cast recording had been inducted into the Grammy Hall of Fame as one of the most important show albums of all time, cementing the legacy of the piece on its fiftieth anniversary.

Kiss Me, Kate had never been revived after its original engagement, outside of a weeklong encore the year after it had shuttered on Broadway. Its original production had been so sublime that few had wanted to touch its memory, and it had lived on for generations through its significantly altered film and a succession of televised adaptations. Paul and Mike Ockrent had attempted a revival once before, starring Kevin Kline and

Mary Elizabeth Mastrantonio, but the Porter estate had refused to allow for edits to the show's original book, which stalled the project. Now, Michael Blakemore had decided to take on the challenge.

When Robin Wagner, scenic designer, called Paul, it was a thrilling moment. Paul had always loved *Kiss Me, Kate*, and its rich instrumentation and romantic grandeur had swept him away similarly to how *South Pacific* had captured him as a child. Blakemore had been on the list of Paul's dream collaborators since he had stepped into the musical theatre with *City of Angels*, and the combination of the score and the team convinced Paul to return to the fold, the sting of *High Society* in the rearview mirror.

Kiss Me, Kate hinges almost entirely on the actors playing Lilli and Fred, the quarreling lovers. The entire romantic core of the piece relies on their chemistry being an overpowering, and at times overwhelming, thing. They have to be drawn to each other in a fashion that is undeniable, and the chemistry between the two actors has to be palpable at the back of the house. They found their pair in Brian Stokes Mitchell and Marin Mazzie.

Paul was thrilled to be back with Marin, and the two picked up their friendship immediately. She and Mitchell had performed together in *Ragtime* the year prior and had an easy chemistry that proved perfect onstage. Brian Stokes Mitchell has the kind of voice that immediately captures a listener in its rich tone. It demands respect from the first note and, combined with Marin's instrument, gave life to some of Porter's most beautiful love songs. The rest of the company quickly filled in around the neutron star of Mazzie and Mitchell, with Michael Berresse and Amy Spanger coming on as the contrasting couple Bill and Lois, who exemplified toxic romance to a tee.

John Guare, esteemed playwright, was brought on by the team to essentially rewrite the book. Many of the contemporary references contained in the extended scenes had aged like milk, and several of the scenes that were meant to underline Lilli and Fred's passion had begun to appear abusive to a contemporary viewer. The Porter estate is a notoriously difficult estate to work with—when a writer or composer of significant output dies, their work is handed over to an estate to manage in their absence. Some estates, such as the Rodgers and Hammerstein Organization, are open and willing to explore reinterpretations of the creators' original works in an attempt to keep the canon fresh. Unfortunately, the Porter estate had a completely different view—to them, the original production of *Kiss Me, Kate* was sacrosanct, and they heavily objected to any attempts to make the piece more palatable to a new audience.

One of the most powerful skills Paul has in his arsenal is his ability to be liked. This likability has always helped him make friends with the right people, and in the case of *Kiss Me, Kate*, it came in handy. Rather than approaching the estate with a bullish determination, Michael, John, and Paul came to them at their level, explaining every single change they wanted to make in a way that made the estate feel like they were in control, rather than having the control of the piece ripped away from them. Piece by piece they took them through measures of music they wanted to shorten, lyrics they wanted to adjust, and book sequences that needed replacing. Their diplomacy paid off, and they walked away with permission to make almost every change they had requested.

Paul brought on Don Sebesky to do the new orchestrations as they began retooling the show around the score. To put it plainly, Don is a genius. A jazz musician, he orchestrated like a symphonic composer, but with a freedom of movement and style that is rarely found. To read one of his scores was to glimpse into the world of classical genius, with overcomplicated staffs and smudged ink betraying the speed with which the composer's mind produced intricate melody. For an orchestrator to have the skills required to reorchestrate a piece with such fresh abandon is rare, and Paul was eager to take on the challenge of collaborating with such a talent.

They headed into rehearsals confident and settled into a community rhythm that quickly became a family atmosphere. Kathleen Marshall, the show's choreographer, had hired some of the most talented dancers Paul had ever worked with, and he learned an immense amount from how Michael turned dancers into actors. The play within a play of *Kiss Me, Kate* proved difficult, as most high-caliber dancers of the musical theatre are not also classically trained Shakespearean actors. Blakemore had them rehearse the Shakespearean scenes as if they were their own play, devoid of the context of *Kiss Me, Kate*. He transformed the performers into pseudo Royal Shakespeare Company members before Paul's eyes, with Blakemore exhibiting the same skill at turning non-actors into actors that Paul had to turn non-singers into singers.

The company became very close, with groups going out for meals after rehearsals almost every day. They made the decision to forgo an out-of-town tryout and went straight into dress rehearsals in the Martin Beck Theatre. One scene, about halfway through the first act, gave the team trouble, as certain technical elements were not quite meshing. They ran the scene over and over, with Marin kicking a stool in time. With each successive restart of the scene, Marin would kick the stool just a little bit harder, until it was skidding to a stop just inches from the lip of the stage. Concerned, and with the memory of *Big*'s flying props nestled in his mind, Paul requested a net be installed over the pit on the off chance that one day, during a performance, the stool might come flying out too far. Kathleen and Michael agreed, and a net was ordered, but by the time the final rehearsals had come around, the net had not yet been installed. During the final dress rehearsal, the second woodwind player, Eric Weidman, was knocked nearly unconscious by the stool, splitting open his skull.

Dominic Derasse, one of the trumpeters in the pit, had EMT training, and he kept Eric stable until an ambulance arrived to rush Eric to the hospital to receive ten stitches. Marin and Stokes were stunned, having never been aware onstage that the stool was anywhere near being a dangerous projectile. After checking on the rest of the pit to make sure no one else had been hurt in the aftermath, Paul pulled the creative team aside, furious. Paul is immensely protective of his musicians, and he made it abundantly clear that there would be no repeat of the traumatic incident. The next day Paul got his net, and the stool's trajectory was significantly pulled back.

The revival of *Kiss Me, Kate* was a bona fide hit. Nominated for twelve Tony Awards and ten Drama Desk Awards, Marin was regularly trotted out to do press events, appearing on *The Today Show*, *The Early Show*, and the *Rosie O'Donnell Show*. Paul accompanied her to almost all

Wedding photo of Ezio Paul Gemignani and Margaret Helen Lewis.
COURTESY OF PAUL GEMIGNANI

Paul, playing the drums with the Purple Onion trio.
COURTESY OF PAUL GEMIGNANI

San Francisco's Purple Onion jazz club.
COURTESY OF PAUL GEMIGNANI

Choreographing *Follies*, with Paul Gemignani, John Berkman, Graciela Daniele, Michael Bennett, and Bob Avian.
COURTESY OF ESTATE OF BILL YOSCARY

Paul and Elizabeth Taylor on the set of *A Little Night Music*.
COURTESY OF PAUL GEMIGNANI

The *On the Twentieth Century* family (L-R Kevin Kline, Madeline Kahn, Cy Coleman, Betty Comden, Adolph Green, John Cullum, Imogene Coca, Paul Gemignani).
PHOTO BY MARTHA SWOPE ©THE NEW YORK PUBLIC LIBRARY FOR THE PERFORMING ARTS

Two peas in a pod.
COURTESY OF ALEXANDER
GEMIGNANI

Kurt Peterson, Victoria
Mallory, and Paul.
COURTESY OF KURT PETERSON

Do you see what I see?
COURTESY OF ALEXANDER
GEMIGNANI

Paul, Tom Sheppard, Stephen Sondheim, and Hal Prince.
COURTESY OF PAUL GEMIGNANI

Recording the *Sunday in the Park with George* cast recording.
COURTESY OF PETER CUNNINGHAM

The dream team—Paul Gemignani, Jonathan Tunick, and Stephen Sondheim.
COURTESY OF PAUL GEMIGNANI

Conducting the cast recording of *Jerome Robbins' Broadway*.
PHOTO BY MARTHA SWOPE ©THE NEW YORK PUBLIC LIBRARY FOR THE PERFORMING ARTS

All smiles with Paul, Jerome Robbins, Leonard Bernstein, Scott Wise, and Scott Frankel during *Jerome Robbins' Broadway* rehearsals.
PHOTO BY MARTHA SWOPE ©THE NEW YORK PUBLIC LIBRARY FOR THE PERFORMING ARTS

Patience is a virtue.
COURTESY OF ALEXANDER
GEMIGNANI

Paul and Beverley
Randolph, his favorite
stage manager and dear
friend.
COURTESY OF SCOTT TAYLOR
ROLLISON

The apple doesn't fall
very far from the tree.
COURTESY OF PAUL
GEMIGNANI

Paul and Donna Marie at her
wedding.
COURTESY OF DONNA MARIE
ASBURY

Christmas at *Crazy for You* (L-R Paul Gemignani, Chris Peterson, Susan Stroman,
Mike Ockrent, Steve Zweigbaum).
COURTESY OF PAUL GEMIGNANI

Paul and Derin's private wedding ceremony.
COURTESY OF PAUL GEMIGNANI

Paul with the Broadway on Broadway Orchestra.
COURTESY OF PAUL GEMIGNANI

Wandering the forest of the 2002 revival of *Into the Woods* with the stage management team (L-R, Paul Gemignani, Beverley Randolph, Scott Taylor Rollison, Lisa Dawn Cave).

William Ivey Long costumed everyone involved in *The Frogs* for company photographs—Paul made a pretty convincing Vitellius.

Paul's stepson, Augie, and the family dogs, Toni and Bennent.
COURTESY OF PAUL GEMIGNANI

Like father, like son.
PHOTO BY BRIAN HATTON

Goofing around after a performance at Carnegie Hall.
COURTESY OF PAUL GEMIGNANI

The legacy lives on—Paul's grand-
daughter, Olive, holding a photo of
Paul conducting *Pacific Overtures*.
COURTESY OF ALEXANDER GEMIGNANI

of these outings, with special arrangements of songs created in order to suit these press events.

There are a number of ways to approach press performances—oftentimes it isn't economical to bring the entire orchestra to a soundstage, and so a recorded track will be made for actors to perform to, or new arrangements using only the piano will be created for the express purpose of being able to be taken around town. In the case of the *Rosie O'Donnell Show*, Paul and Don created a beautiful arrangement of "So in Love" set to a new three-piece orchestra of piano, viola, and bass, and Marin and Stokes performed it for the one and only time on air, to much fanfare by the audience.

These press events are all a part of the job as music director—while they are often more utilitarian than creative, a music director should keep a tight eye on how the music of the show is presented to the public, as it is going to be their main impression until the release of the cast recording. These press events not only sell tickets to New York audiences, but to viewers across the country. More people saw the pared-down arrangement of "So in Love" on the *Rosie O'Donnell Show* than ever saw the real version inside the Martin Beck Theatre, and much of the revival's glowing reputation can be traced to how high quality their public presentations were at all times.

During the preproduction of *Kiss Me, Kate* in 1998, Derin and Paul had purchased a home in New Jersey together and settled into a comfortable life with her son, August. In 2000, shortly after opening *Kiss Me, Kate*, they were married.

Neither wanted to go through the pageantry of a large wedding after their respective divorces, so Paul had worked out an agreement with Gerald Schoenfeld of the Shubert Organization to let them get married where their story had begun—in her star dressing room at the Broadway Theatre. Unfortunately, renovations had destroyed Derin's original dressing room from her time in *Evita*, and they pivoted to the ground-floor lounge, nestled in a corner with only a judge and Paul's lawyer as witnesses and an acquaintance of Derin's filming. After twenty years, Derin and Paul were married as privately as possible, on Valentine's Day.

Eighteen months after *Kiss Me, Kate* had opened on Broadway, a second production was set for London's West End, with Marin reprising her role as Lilli Vanessi. When a production has a West End transfer, it is traditional for an entirely new music department to be hired in Britain, with the original music director acting as a supervisor. Instead, the producers made the unorthodox decision of having Paul music-direct and conduct the London production, taking them through rehearsals and the opening weeks until he felt comfortable handing it over to the British conductor. Paul handed the flagship New York production to his associate and traveled to London with Marin in September 2001, pulling the production together when tragedy struck.

Paul stood in a cramped guard's office watching the television as the World Trade Center collapsed. He and Kathleen Marshall, the show's choreographer, immediately called off rehearsals and sent everyone home to their hotel rooms and apartments in London as they tried to parse out what everything meant. Paul, Marin, Kathleen, and a handful of other American company members bundled off to an Indian restaurant to keep their eyes on the news as the sun set around them, drinking and holding each other as they tried desperately to reach loved ones back in New York. Thankfully Paul was able to get a hold of Derin and August almost immediately, but others in the company had more difficulty, and they supported each other wholly through the terror.

Three days later Paul was on a plane back to New York to salvage what was left of the *Kiss Me, Kate* company. When a plane flies into JFK airport from across the Atlantic, the plane takes a looping route that goes directly over Manhattan before landing. From Paul's window, the smoke and crumbling hole where the Twin Towers had been was clearly visible, and ash and rubble littered the city as he made his way to the Martin Beck Theatre.

Roger Berlind, the production's main producer, was ready to close the show. While Broadway itself had only been closed for two days in response to the attack—the doors had been reopened on September 13—air advisories warned against exposure to the debris that filled the air. While a precious few had put on a brave face and gone to the theatre as if nothing had changed, audience rates had dwindled deeply below what was needed to keep any show running. Tourism seemed to be a functionally dead industry, and few could see a way forward with no audiences.

The cast and the orchestra of *Kiss Me, Kate* came together in an unprecedented move and presented an offer to Roger in order to save the show. They would all take a steep pay cut to keep the doors open, making it possible to make pure profit off of any seats that did end up being sold. Remarkably, Roger agreed. He knew how badly the company needed the theatre to cling to as their stabilizing force through the sudden upheaval—in 1975, he had lost his wife and three of his four children during the crash of Eastern Air Lines Flight 66, and he had turned to producing theatre the following year as a community in which to find solace.

On September 23, at what had been announced to be the final performance, Roger walked onstage before the overture with the closing notice in hand. He held it aloft, before ripping it down the middle.

"The show will go on!"

The cast gave up 25 percent of their pay and donated an additional 25 percent to buy tickets to the show for rescue workers—anything to get people back in the theatre. With one another to rely on, the company worked until audiences began to trickle back in. After a month of steady sales, Roger paid every member of the cast and orchestra back.

The coalition formed by the various union members of *Kiss Me, Kate* became COBUG, the Coalition of Broadway Unions and Guilds. Consisting of thirteen separate unions and guilds, the organization serves as a joint representative for everyone it takes to produce a Broadway show. When tragedy strikes, there is now a protocol and leadership in place, giving a collective voice to make a united front possible across the industry.

Kiss Me, Kate ran until the end of 2001, when it crossed the threshold of 909 performances, making it one of the longest-running revivals in Broadway history. Shortly thereafter, August enlisted in the Navy, in search of the discipline promised by a military career, in addition to the financial freedom veteran status would give him to pursue his education. A somewhat lackluster high school student, he scored remarkably high on the Navy's mathematical exam and, after two years of training, became a nuclear reactor operator aboard the aircraft carrier USS *Theodore Roosevelt*. Together, Paul and Derin sent him to the sea, as memories of Paul's own time in the military reverberated against his subconscious. After fifty years, and in spite of Ezio's Army-first initiative, Paul had a sailor for a son.

CHAPTER TWENTY-FIVE

Assassins

*When I work with Paul, I feel that I have the greatest creative part-
ner. He brings his immense skill, impeccable taste, and years of experience to the table, so that wherever you want to go as a director, you
have this incredible support system behind you. His only goal is to be
in service to the piece itself. You couldn't ask for a better collaborator.*
— JOE MANTELLO (DIRECTOR, ACTOR)

THE 1990S WERE AN ODD DECADE FOR MUSICAL THEATRE. WITH THE
ever-increasing power of Disney Theatricals casting a heavy shadow, projects had been taken on and scrapped in equal measure as the community
came together during the onslaught of the AIDS crisis. Many sought a
new method of making theatre, with a more modern approach than the
standard style of Broadway's golden age.

It was at the dawn of this new environment in 1989 that Sondheim
had called Paul with a new show idea—a concept musical following nine
assassins of the president of the United States. John Weidman, the book
writer of *Pacific Overtures*, had returned to the fold as James Lapine had
focused on turning *March of the Falsettos* into a larger piece, now entitled
Falsettos. It was to be a revue-style show, with distinct musical styles for
every assassin that would interweave to create a rich tapestry of material
exploring the dark psychology of these would-be killers.

Steve played two songs for Paul as he explained the concept—"The
Ballad of Booth," to be performed by the piece's narrator, the Balladeer,

alongside John Wilkes Booth, and "The Gun Song," a group number among the assassins. Of the forty would-be assassins known to the general public, they had selected ten, consisting of:

John Wilkes Booth, killer of Abraham Lincoln;

Charles Guiteau, killer of James A. Garfield;

Leon Czolgosz, killer of William McKinley;

Giuseppe Zangara, failed killer of Franklin Delano Roosevelt;

John Schrank, failed killer of Theodore Roosevelt;

Lynette Fromme, failed killer of Gerald Ford;

Sara Jane Moore, failed killer of Gerald Ford;

John Hinckley Jr., failed killer of Ronald Reagan;

Samuel Byck, failed killer of Richard Nixon; and

Lee Harvey Oswald, killer of John Fitzgerald Kennedy.

Some of their selections were obvious—a piece discussing the assassination of US presidents had no choice but to include John Wilkes Booth, the first successful assassin, and arguably the most famous. Others were obscure—Samuel Byck had been intercepted in his plan before he could commandeer a plane to crash into the White House, becoming a footnote in history books. The one thing every assassin had in common, outside of their obvious common thread, was their unbridled belief in their actions, be they politically motivated or spurred on by delusions. They were immensely complex people, who all had come to the same conclusion to solve their disparate problems—killing the president of the United States would somehow right a wrong they felt had been leveled against them.

Except for Lee Harvey Oswald.

Paul had been studying for his final exams on November 22, 1963, when he heard the apartment building erupt with noise from the neighboring apartments. Instinctively he turned on the television, and he watched the immediate aftermath of the assassination of John F. Kennedy from his small apartment in San Francisco as the entire country was thrown into mourning. With Oswald, there was no explanation. No treatise, no note, and no confession before his own death two days later. Almost thirty years later, the country was still wrestling with the collective flashbulb memory, and *Assassins* had the potential to finally lead a portion of the public to come to terms with the scar that had been inflicted upon the country time and again.

A cast was compiled in order to hold a reading of the material in 1989, including Victor Garber as John Wilkes Booth, Christine Baranski as Sara Jane Moore, Jonathan Hadary as Charles Guiteau, Nathan Lane as Samuel Byck, Christopher Durang as John Schrank, and Swoosie Kurtz as Lynette Fromme. The material proved to have legs, with John Weidman turning out swathes of entertainingly dense scenes that left the viewer with no option but to empathize with a character they had entered the theatre expecting to loathe. Nathan Lane, fresh off of his breakout turn in *The Lisbon Traviata*, turned a Santa suit–clad Samuel Byck into a comedic high point of the piece, contrasting to the rest of the company as the assassin with the smallest musical footprint.

Schrank was cut in rehearsals after a modest Durang correctly identified Byck as the more tonally appropriate comedic relief, but the core of the show was present as they moved forward with a workshop production at Playwrights Horizons, using the same developmental model that had been used for *Sunday in the Park with George*. Unfortunately, the majority of the reading cast did not transfer with it, returning to more substantial contracts that had been put in place long before the reading.

A workshop cast was quickly compiled around Victor Garber and Jonathan Hadary, the two members of the reading to continue on to the workshop. Many were hired off of previous experience, with only a few having to actually "audition" for Paul on account of his having never heard them sing. Patrick Cassidy, son of Shirley Jones and Jack Cassidy, was brought in to play the show's narrative through line, the Balladeer, and William Parry rounded out the non-assassin characters as the Proprietor, a gun salesman who represented the worst inclinations of society throughout the piece. The same music department was again compiled from *Sunday*, with Michael Starobin and Paul Ford coming together with Paul to reform the "Broadway Bar Mitzvah Boys," the tongue-in-cheek name applied to their trio in the corner of the rehearsal room.

Throughout it all, Victor Garber remained the linchpin of the production. A consummate professional, he brought a gravitas to Booth that enveloped the entire company, serving as the steady and sure hand that pulled the first trigger in the line of succession. His refrain, "The Ballad of Booth," was objectively the most difficult vocal piece of the show—it is full of deceptively difficult hairpin turns and requires a strength of voice that can easily wear out a less adept vocalist. It was an immensely intricate role, and Victor was able to uncover moments of ease that set the tone for the entire night that followed his sequence.

In many ways it was fitting that the first pieces Sondheim presented to Paul were "The Ballad of Booth" and "The Gun Song." Although they were the first written, they also proved to be the most difficult to properly pin down (Victor's brilliance aside).

"The Gun Song" is a mammoth task. Tightly constructed harmonically, it requires strongly individual acting from all of the assassins while still providing a moment for them to be perfectly in sync, reaching across time for one of the only moments in the piece. Actors had to pull unconventional harmonies out of thin air, and the number underwent constant repetition to get it into their bodies.

When the workshop opened at Playwrights Horizons it was to much fanfare—they were sold out for the entirety of the run, and, unlike in *Sunday*, they were presenting near the entirety of the show from the moment an audience was brought in. *Assassins* had come together remarkably well, but plans for a swift Broadway transfer came to a bombastic end due to the Gulf War—a show delving into some of the most politically divisive figures in the country's history felt far too fraught, and the project was tabled as a cast album was made, with intentions of picking the project up again in the future.

What had originally been expected to be a pause of one or two years quickly turned into a decade as the US military involvement in Iraq slowly increased, and the remnants of the Cold War turned caustic.

In 2000, Joe Mantello brought a fresh concept for the show to Todd Haimes at the Roundabout Theatre Company. A Tony-nominated actor for his performance in *Angels in America*, Joe had made the pivot to directing shortly after with the play *What's Wrong with This Picture?* He had seen the original workshop production of *Assassins* and was inspired to take on a remounting of the project as his first musical. It was a good transition piece—a hybrid of a play and a musical, it gave him the best of both worlds to work with as he found his footing as a director in the musical theatre. After a two-week workshop to prove the piece could withstand a retelling, Todd agreed, and the Roundabout signed off on a fresh production, set to open in 2001.

Joe immediately went to work on casting the project with fresh and exciting faces—Douglas Sills was hired as John Wilkes Booth, alongside Mary Catherine Garrison as Fromme, Raul Esparza as Giuseppe Zangara, Becky Ann Baker as Sara Jane Moore, John Dossett as Leon Czolgosz, Mario Cantone as Byck, Denis O'Hare as Guiteau, and Neil Patrick Harris as the Balladeer, who was now combined with Lee Harvey Oswald.

A number of people were brought in for the role of John Hinckley Jr., including Alexander Gemignani. Fresh out of college, *Assassins* was his first major audition in New York after receiving his bachelor of fine arts from the University of Michigan. When he came in to audition for Hinckley and the Proprietor, Paul was so nervous that he made the decision to step out of the room, standing just outside so as to listen to Alex through the door.

Alexander soared. Through a closed and windowless door, the Hinckley he had crafted came through, captivating in its earnest simplicity. When Alex walked out, Paul immediately pulled him into a hug, and when Alexander was called back, they made the decision to keep Paul in the room.

Alexander was put through the audition ringer. No one pulled a single punch on behalf of his being Paul's son—if anything, he was scrutinized even more. He had a half-hour callback where they had him present almost every moment Hinckley has in the show—every scene, every vocal line, and Hinckley's core duet, "Unworthy of Your Love." After

Alexander's second callback, the team faced a table with every potential performer's headshot laid out. After making the final decisions on every other character, Joe took a deep breath, and picked up Alexanders headshot, placing it in the yes pile.

He had gotten the job.

Paul requested that he be the one to tell Alexander and called him less than an hour after he had left the rehearsal space where they had held auditions. For seven straight minutes, Alex detailed every moment he had torn apart in his mind, explaining everything he was convinced he had done wrong—second-guessing every choice down to the minutiae. When he finally paused to take an anguished breath, Paul pounced.

"Well, let me tell you something, okay?"

A long pause as Alex waited for his father to explain everything else he had done wrong.

"You got the part."

The phone was deathly silent until Paul's eardrums were nearly shattered by a full-bodied scream echoing through the phone.

Paul had known exactly what his son would do when given time to stew from callback to callback. He also knew that the moment of release after tying himself up in knots would be overwhelmingly cathartic. No matter how much Alex had ripped himself apart as an actor, he had *still gotten the job*. After that, getting any kind of critique in the rehearsal room would be a cakewalk.

Paul was in London with *Kiss Me, Kate* as *Assassins* began ensemble auditions in the fall of 2001. Following the events of 9/11, the plug was almost immediately pulled on the production. With the country thrust into chaos and another war in the Middle East, patriotism and nationalism were at an all-time high, making *Assassins* feel even more divisive than it had in 1991. The show was again put on the back burner, and the team moved on, with Joe Mantello instead directing *Wicked* as his musical theatre directorial debut.

Alex returned to the life of a struggling actor, switching between temping at a legal agency and auditioning for readings as he fit in regional theatre gigs whenever they popped up. In the spring of 2003, he was swept into the Vineyard Theatre production of *Avenue Q* as the first replacement for Brian, where he closed out their run prior to the Broadway transfer. While doing a production of *Zorba* at the Northshore Theatre, he received a call to audition for what was to be the final year of *A Christmas Carol* at Madison Square Garden. He had the right build and voice for Mr. John Smythe, one of Scrooge's fraught debtors, and was soon hired. He was in the middle of preparations to step into the six-week sprint when he received a call from the Roundabout Theatre Company, only three weeks before he was due to begin rehearsals for *A Christmas Carol*.

Enough time had passed that Roundabout was ready to examine the possibility of the *Assassins* revival. They were gathering the cast together again for one night to do a reading, and based on how the material played on that day, they would decide if they were going to go forward with the full revival. This left Alex in a tight bind—with the fast turnaround time required of *A Christmas Carol*, he couldn't miss a single rehearsal. If he didn't do the *Assassins* reading, and they decided to do the production in full, it was almost guaranteed that he would be recast with whoever was brought in for the reading. In the end, he took the leap of faith, withdrew from *A Christmas Carol*, and signed on for the reading of *Assassins*, trusting that the show would come to full fruition.

While most of the creative team was able to hop back in the room, many of the performers had signed with other projects and taken on new jobs over the intervening period that they chose not to leave, which forced the team to recast Booth, Zangara, Czolgosz, and the Proprietor, who had not yet been cast when the show had been suspended (further auditions for the Proprietor had been scheduled for September 12).

Auditioning people for the role of John Wilkes Booth is always difficult. It requires a high level of charisma and fortitude in order to offset the reaction the audience expects to have to the character—often, classically trained actors are the ones who are best at filling the role, as they have been trained to inhabit those larger-than-life characters, including Brutus in *Julius Caesar*. Victor Garber had been trained at the HB Studio, run by legendary acting teachers Herbert Berghof and Uta Hagen, and Douglas Sills, the revival's original Booth, had trained at American Conservatory Theatre, one of the largest nonprofit theatres in the country. But even with his Yale pedigree, Michael Cerveris was nervous walking in.

Michael had grown up on Sondheim—the son of a music professor and a dancer, he had been immersed in the arts from a young age and had oscillated between studying acting and philosophy. The first musical he had ever seen had been a preview of the original production of *Sweeney Todd*, and it was Len Cariou's performance onstage at the Uris that had made him want to do musical theatre. Now, twenty-five years later, with a starring turn in *The Who's Tommy* under his belt and two productions of *Passion* in his recent past, he was walking into a room full of the people whose names he had memorized off of that original *Sweeney Todd* LP, and every other Sondheim record he had devoured.

While Paul was not officially running the audition, it was to him that Michael deferred. He had known Joe for years as an actor and had met Sondheim during the Kennedy Center Production of *Passion*. While the production was ostensibly theirs, it was to Paul that he immediately felt a draw.

Paul is a champion of the auditioner in the room—anything that he can do to make a performer more comfortable will be done, because he knows that you can't get a real sense of a performer when they're uncomfortable. Casting can sometimes feel like predicting the future—you have to tell what a person will feel like in the role after they have had weeks of rehearsals, based on how they approach material after a relatively short period of time. In many cases, the best way to do this is to have performers bring in their own material—when they have selected their own audition songs, they're bound to be more comfortable performing than they would be trying to remember the lyrics to a song they memorized at three in the morning the night before.

In the case of Sondheim, this is doubly true (triply if it is a completely new production). He has become so revered in the musical theatre industry that he has taken on a deific energy, and performers will fall over themselves trying to unlock the material—when presented with a Sondheim song no one has ever heard, it is not uncommon for a performer to drive themselves hoarse from overpractice due to their wish to get it "perfect" the very first time. Both of these issues can be mitigated by having them select their own material, and a good music director can hear what they need to hear even if they aren't singing directly from the score.

Unfortunately, Michael had not had that option. He had been brought in in the middle of the callback process, after Sondheim and John Weidman had requested him. While Michael had heard the original cast recording of *Assassins* beforehand, it had never been one of the major shows on his radar, and when he was asked to bring in "The Ballad of Booth" for the audition, he was starting from scratch. While he trusted his acting abilities, Michael was tense to pass Paul's critique musically. It was a difficult song to tackle, but he dove in with gusto, trusting that the complex vocal shifts would be there if his passion was.

By the end of his audition, Michael all but had the role. His Booth was sinister, with a sharper edge than Victor's—where Victor's original Booth had been levelheaded, focused, and driven to the point of ultimate control, Michael's was raw and on edge, with a barely controlled fervor about him that was unnerving when revealed under the careful exterior. When he made his entrance, you could feel the ions in the air change. Unlike others, he had not attempted any imitation of Victor, or Victor's approach, and had instead invented his own Booth. He was put through an additional callback to confirm the initial impression before being cast alongside James Barbour as Czolgosz and Jeffrey Kuhn as Zangara. Marc Kudisch, fresh off a Tony nomination for *Thoroughly Modern Millie*, was cast as the Proprietor, and the cast moved into rehearsals.

In the original production of *Assassins*, director Jerry Zaks had implemented shades of a carnival to the opening of the piece, with fair games and assorted accoutrement filling out the scene. Mantello had made the decision to maintain that aspect throughout the piece as a unifying theme—with the assassins fading in and out of view between vignettes, a sense of cohesion was critical to making the show feel whole. By uniting the show in a time and a place—a carnival free from linear time—he gave the audience a thread to cling to as they journeyed throughout more than a hundred years of history.

Another unifying addition to the show was the song "Something Just Broke"—originally written for a British production in 1992, it gave a moment of immense emotional catharsis to the show's ensemble, letting them act as ciphers for the American people following the assassination of John F. Kennedy. It was such a strong moment of collective trauma for the entire country that unifying the ensemble in a moment of grief allowed the audience to release some of their lingering pain as well. It served as a stark contrast to the callous behavior of the previous scenes involving the ensemble, and it gave a humanizing angle to the piece that elevated everything around it.

The other substantial change to the show was the unification of the Balladeer and Lee Harvey Oswald—originally written as distinctly separate characters, Joe followed instinct to combine them into one thorough piece—by having Oswald, the only assassin with no known motivation, sing as the narrator before revealing himself, it made his identity even more impactful. In the original production, Oswald had seemingly appeared from thin air, having never been seen before appearing in the bookshop with his rifle. In Mantello's production, he was someone the audience sided with and rooted for until he was corrupted by the influence of the assassins surrounding him. The scene where Booth and the other assassins appear to him, urging him to take the shot, took on a greater weight when the audience had an investment in the character that had been built up over the entire night.

The question was, what do you do with that weight at the end of the scene?

In the set design of the revival, there were timbers of broken-down roller coasters painted in a light color in the background. The initial plan was that after the explosion of Oswald's gunshot, the stage would cut to black, with the Zapruder film of the assassination projected onto the beams as a rudimentary projection screen. When the time came to run the sequence during technical rehearsals, they could not get it to work. The projection either came out blurry and unfocused or as a hard-to-decipher pinkish blob.

Joe was understandably frustrated. The entire production had been building up to the grandeur of the moment when the set would be transformed, and the inability to make it work threw a massive wrench into his entire vision. During a dinner break he met with a close friend, T. Scott Cunningham, and explained the problem. Cunningham urged him to keep with the concept, but to refine it into something more workable—surely there must be something flat and white on the stage somewhere. When Joe returned, he told the projection designer to throw the Zapruder film onto the small white surface of Oswald's white T-shirt, to see if the footage would even show up on a stark white background in such a small scale.

It was chillingly perfect. It was the opposite of the image they had originally been going for, of excess and explosion. Instead, with the crash of the gunshot the focus was pulled tightly inward, with the entire theatre viewing the film no larger than if it had been on the television set that they had first watched the assassination from. It was contained and claustrophobic and overwhelming and emotional—exactly what the moment needed to be. The "Zapruder projection" went on to be one of the most recognizable elements of the revival, and a calling card of the production.

While Joe was working onstage, Paul was standing among junk and debris in the unused opera boxes of the theatre. Long before it was a nightclub, Studio 54 had been an opera house, opening as the Gallo Opera House in 1927. The original orchestra space had been massive, with enough room for nearly a hundred musicians comfortably. Over time, the pit had been closed up and turned into the club's infamous basement VIP lounge before being converted into offices and storage rooms when it had returned to theatrical use. This had not been a problem for *Cabaret*, the first musical to play in the Studio 54 space—with their band on and around the stage, a pit did not make or break their production. That left Paul to figure out where in the world the musicians of *Assassins* were going to be situated.

Ideas had been floated of putting the musicians offstage in the wings, but Paul had immediately rejected that concept—he needed to be able to see his actors, and the musicians needed to be in the room with the people they were playing for. They couldn't reopen the original pit without doing a significant amount of damage, which left Paul to search for alternate solutions. After poking around the space, he found the opera boxes that had been converted into junk storage. They were full of broken lights, scrap curtains, and dust-covered boxes, but their positioning gave Paul a fantastic sight line of the stage. They had four boxes in total to work with, with two on each side stacked vertically. Paul had them clear everything out of the space and began placing musicians.

One of the hidden blessings of Studio 54 is its natural acoustics. The opera house had been constructed with natural amplification in mind, and sound traveled beautifully through the space unmic'd. With consultation from Michael Starobin as orchestrator and Dan Moses Schreier as sound designer, Paul placed the band across from one another in the space, with the percussionist, pianist, and strings on the left with him, and the brass and the woodwinds on the right. Not only could they see the performers onstage, they could all see one another across the orchestra seating, and they were able to communicate in real time visually.

This was critically important in order to accurately produce Michael's new orchestrations. While the original Playwrights Horizons production of *Assassins* had been orchestrated for three players, it had been completely reorchestrated for the cast album, with a full thirty-three-piece orchestra brought in for the recording. In the decade that had passed, Michael had played with different ideas for how the show should sound, and he had been brought back to orchestrate the piece once again to fit Studio 54. What he had landed on was an orchestra consisting of fourteen players—the magic number for the space that left everything balanced and polished without feeling overblown. This required almost every member of the orchestra to play more than one instrument—Dennis Anderson alone played the flute, piccolo, clarinet, soprano saxophone, and harmonica. In fact, the only musicians who weren't doing at least double duty were the pianist, the percussionist, and the French horn player. This minimalist setup with maximalist payoff gave the score an incredibly diverse color, and each character was able to have a defining musical motif without the score feeling disjointed— "Ballad of Booth" was now punctuated by a banjo, "Guiteau" had lilting flutes and pseudo-organ sequences, and so on.

"The Ballad of Guiteau," sung by Charles Guiteau, the assassin of William McKinley, was particularly difficult, both to orchestrate and execute. Of the assassins, he is perhaps the most unhinged—the madman among the madhouse, he sharply moved between concepts, as did his music. He was off to the races from the very beginning, when Denis O'Hare had to pluck his starting note out of thin air, with only a shrill train whistle to tune against. From there Guiteau navigates between somber spirituality, playful hope, startling fury, and bright exuberance, with the orchestra firing on full cylinders by the end as Denis would dance his way to the gallows.

On the night before opening, Michael Cerveris got food poisoning, and ended up having to go to the hospital to be medically rehydrated in order to make it to the theatre. When he arrived, he had to have an emergency steroid shot to make it through the show—due to a handful of historical precedents, he would not be considered the original cast if he did not perform on opening night. He made it through, but his voice was gone when he woke the following morning.

Steroid shots (or cortisone shots) can be a performer's best friend, or their enemy. In drastic emergency situations such as Michael's, they can buy a performer a few hours of renewed strength to power through a situation, but they remove pain, which makes it next to impossible for a performer to judge any damage they may be doing. The pain sensors of the human body are necessary to help us calibrate our own existence—if we move our arm a certain way and it hurts, we know to stop moving it that way. When the pain sensation is removed, our ability to judge physical situations is impaired. While the shot had gotten Michael through the performance, and the reviews were released with flying colors for his performance, they had come with the cost of keeping him out of the show for several days to recover. He had to go on complete vocal rest to repair the damage and had to slowly build back up to the strenuous vocals that Booth required, as his stamina was shredded.

Thankfully, his risk paid off. At the 2004 Tony Awards, *Assassins* received five Tony Awards, including a win for Michael Cerveris as Best Featured Actor, beating Denis O'Hare, who had been nominated in the same category. The revival ran for 101 performances, and it successfully cemented *Assassins* as a key part of the Sondheim canon.

When Sondheim has been asked about *Assassins*, he has readily described it as near perfect and his best written work. Of his entire body of work, it is the one that has most accurately evolved into exactly what he saw in his head when he began work on the piece.

Although it had begun life in 1990, prior to *Passion*, *Assassins* is the most recent full-scale production on which Stephen Sondheim and Paul Gemignani have collaborated. After more than thirty years of consistent collaboration, the time had finally come for both men to slow down.

CHAPTER TWENTY-SIX

Ravinia Festival

Paul is able to read a performer instinctively. He knows where they are on that given night and can sense what is coming. He can find you in thin air, bring an entire orchestra there to meet you, and guide you all back home.
—MICHAEL CERVERIS (ACTOR, SINGER, MUSICIAN)

THE RAVINIA FESTIVAL IS THE OLDEST OUTDOOR MUSIC FESTIVAL IN the United States and has been continually operating since 1905. Outside of a brief hiatus during the Great Depression, the festival has been a mainstay of Midwestern culture, with the original structures still visible through the modern advancements.

Paul was in between projects when he received a call from Lonny Price inviting him to come and work with Ravinia. Now a director, Lonny had made quite the name for himself in the years following *Merrily We Roll Along*—after a respectable performing career On and Off Broadway, with several successful forays into film and television, he had pivoted to directing and had earned a Tony nomination for his work on the book of the musical *A Class Act*. Ravinia had become one of his artistic homes. He had directed several concerts and semi-staged productions for the festival at the turn of the millennium, including a successful production of *Sweeney Todd* starring Patti LuPone and George Hearn, and Ravinia's artistic director, Welz Kaufman, had made the decision to produce an extended Sondheim festival, where they planned to do five Sondheim shows in five years. They were starting with *Passion* and needed a maestro who was up to the task.

Paul signed on and began a multiyear journey with what became the adult artistic equivalent of summer camp.

Over a period of seven years, Paul and Lonny collaborated on productions of *Passion, Sunday in the Park with George, Anyone Can Whistle, Gypsy,* and *Annie Get Your Gun,* all of which involved Patti LuPone. Soon, a core company sprouted around her, with Audra McDonald and Michael Cerveris coming aboard to create the core trio around which the summers were staged. This superstar repertory group became the bedrock that Lonny and Paul pulled from to reinvent and reimagine scores that they both deeply loved—for Lonny, the original cast recording of a show like *Gypsy* was burned into his brain, and Paul had a sentimental attachment that eagerly blossomed into creative inspiration.

The turnaround time on a Ravinia production is lightning fast when compared to the original New York development periods Paul had gone through for many of the shows—with the score and book intact, they had only a few short weeks to get a show up and on its feet, with some of the most incredible talent in the Chicago acting pool filling the stage when a role was not fulfilled by the trio. Lonny had the immensely difficult task of not only bringing the show safely to life, but of doing it with such a deftly dexterous hand as to make it appear almost effortless.

Passion was a particularly difficult beast for the quintet's first grouping. What had originally been a deeply intimate show had to somehow be elevated to the level that it could play to thousands of audience members at a time. Sound travels differently outdoors than it does in a confined space like an enclosed theatre, and both the vocalists and the musicians had to adjust how they approached the score to make it properly audible, even with the aid of microphones. Regardless of the hurdles, the company soared, and as the sun set over the show every night, painting the park in warm tones of ochre and peach, their inner contentment was made manifest.

All shows become a family after a while, but the Ravinia family had the remarkable experience of going through the bond-forging fire of putting on a show over and over, with periods of separation in between.

It was not a sure thing that everyone would be available every summer—one or two people might be working a long-term job in New York and be away for a summer or two, but when the company came together, it was the same as when a child reunites with friends after a school holiday—in the middle of sprinting through memorizing a new script and score, they would be catching up with one another, trading triumphs and heartbreaks in tandem.

Some shows had a more complicated life than others—namely, *Gypsy*. It was the perfect show to do at Ravinia—it was a bombastic musical that had the perfect role for their crown jewel, Patti. The role of Madam Rose had been one that people had been begging her to take on since she had been in her twenties, and Patti had been circling it for years, only to be rebuffed by the show's book writer, Arthur Laurents. A notoriously cantankerous man, he had made the decision to bar Patti from ever being allowed to appear in productions of his work after she had turned down his play *Jolson Sings Again* in 1999. Ravinia, as a semi-staged production, narrowly fit under the metric of Laurents' ban, and Patti was able to appear as Rose in a performance that was immediately lauded as monumental. Though it had been only five years since a revival of *Gypsy* on Broadway starring Bernadette Peters, rumors immediately began swirling of a transfer.

This was huge. *Gypsy* is one of those unusual shows that seems impervious to revival fatigue—there had been a revival every decade since the production opened in 1959, and all had been sell-out hits. Patti was so deeply beloved, and the role fit her so perfectly, that it was sure to be a success. She set to work on repairing the gulf between her and Laurents as Paul and Lonny prepared to take their production back East, when things skidded to a halt.

Laurents would give permission for Patti to play Rose on Broadway with one caveat—he directed the production. Cut Lonny out, and they had a deal.

This was a heavy blow. *Gypsy* could have, and rightfully should have, changed Lonny's career. Although Lonny had directed five productions on Broadway, only one, *A Class Act*, had passed the 100-performances mark, eking out 105. The *Gypsy* that he had put together was fated to be a hit. Had he taken it to New York, it would have been as the conquering son, bringing to fruition a production that thousands had been searching for. Instead, he was being shut out by a man who had been firmly against the idea until he had heard of what Lonny had done at Ravinia.

When Patti called Paul to ask if he would still be coming with the production as music director, the answer was a swift no. That isn't to say he didn't want to do *Gypsy*—he wanted to do *Gypsy* more than almost any musical. To him, *Gypsy* was one of the masterworks of the American theatre, and he had been close with composer Jule Styne up until his death in 1994. The pair had been working on a revival of *Funny Girl* when Styne died, and Paul had been searching for an opportunity to breathe life into his work ever since. Paul had seen Ethel Merman work her way through Rose in the original production's tour, and he had been conducting selections from it for decades at various Sondheim tribute concerts. It was the show that Paul most wanted to conduct on Broadway—the revival that first came to mind when he was asked what he wanted to do next.

However, when the dream of conducting a revival of *Gypsy* came with the price of cutting out Lonny, there was no question. Paul was loyal to Lonny, as he was to any of his closest collaborators. He had known Lonny since he was the teenager running around at the Prince office and had been by his side during one of the most difficult experiences of either of their professional lives in *Merrily We Roll Along*. He and Lonny had maintained a friendship through the decades, and he had treasured working with Lonny time and again as a director, when Paul could clearly see how brilliant the little bar mitzvah investor had become. In many ways, Lonny had become the spiritual successor to Hal Prince, and his endless empathy for everyone it took to create a show was unparalleled in a world where many new directors sought to break free of the Prince model. Lonny was, and is, one of the good guys, and Paul refused to step on him to elevate himself. With one phrase Paul put an end to the tango of undercutting and overstepping, effectively severing himself from ever conducting a revival of *Gypsy*.

"I will not be another knife in Lonny's back. Get yourself another boy."

CHAPTER TWENTY-SEVEN

The Mystery of Edwin Drood

*Paul is my very favorite music director I have ever worked with.
His knowledge and the way he teaches everybody and helps everyone
is admirable. Paul has a great sense of humor. I love working hard,
and Paul does too. The one thing Paul has which I so love in another
human being is his sense of humor. Every time we work together, we
work extraordinarily hard, but we laugh very much. That is very
difficult to forget, because it does not happen too often.*
—GRACIELA DANIELE (DANCER,
CHOREOGRAPHER, DIRECTOR)

WILL CHASE WAS ONE OF THE YOUNG ARTISTS WHO HAD GROWN UP WITH
Paul as an idol. As a percussionist, the original cast recording of *Sweeney
Todd* was his touchstone, and he had dreamt of becoming Paul, and following in his footsteps as the next great conductor/percussionist. He listened
to every recording he could get his hands on, inhaling every move Paul
made as he linked up with composer David Carson at Oberlin, with grand
visions of their partnership entering the same echelon as Paul and Steve's.

For him, there was no greater musical director than Paul, and this
steadfast belief only strengthened as he became an actor and began work
with other up-and-coming music directors. What Paul made look so
simple was immensely difficult, and immensely misunderstood. When
Will received a call from Scott Ellis asking him to play John Jasper in *The
Mystery of Edwin Drood*, it was Paul's participation that sealed the deal.

Following *Assassins*, Roundabout had become Paul's home base in New York, working on four productions back-to-back when Scott approached him about a revival of *The Mystery of Edwin Drood*. Paul had seen the original production of *Drood* in 1985, and he had thought of it rarely—a pastiche of the British music hall style, it was one of a number of European musicals that had taken root in a post–Andrew Lloyd Webber world. The English pantomime tradition is one that is deeply baked into British culture, but that has never taken off across the Atlantic, which makes the premise of the piece a difficult sell to audiences; as a general rule, audiences prefer theatre that they know how to engage with. If the audience does not have that shorthand, you have to work to establish one for them at the top of the show in order to facilitate the best possible experience.

Scott Ellis and the Roundabout solved this problem by putting an emphasis on the music hall characters before they transformed into the characters within *The Mystery of Edwin Drood*. Actors would intermingle with the audience in character, establishing the environment that the external show took place in before the internal show began. This "pre-show" period was invaluable in terms of initiating audience engagement—in the United States, theatre is traditionally thought of as something that is passively enjoyed without the viewer inserting themselves into the action. *Drood* required audiences to engage with the show in a different way, with audience and performer interaction encouraged at every turn. By opening the show with a performer directly talking to an audience member, the audience member is put at ease with that sort of interaction throughout the show.

Of course, this kind of engagement also requires a very specific type of performer. You have to be quick on your feet and ready for anything—in a show with this sort of structure, there can be no such thing as marking or phoning it in—if you lose track of what you're doing, even for a short moment, you can completely unravel. Stephanie J. Block, a luminous leading lady of the highest caliber, was brought on for the title role of Edwin Drood, in addition to Will Chase as John Jasper, Betsy Wolfe as Rosa Bud, Jim Norton as the Chairman, and Andy Karl and

Jessie Mueller as the Landless twins. And, of course, Chita Rivera as the divine Princess Puffer.

Puffer was, in many ways, a different role than Chita had ever played. A haggard opium dealer of ill-repute, she was the most staunchly British character in terms of the writing, with classic British comedy interwoven with classic music hall melodies. It was also a "bits and pieces" role—that is, she appeared and disappeared from the plot, with her actual plot purpose never explained by Dickens himself. Chita dove into unraveling this unique character and produced a completely compelling woman unlike anything else she had played before.

Drood is a somewhat jagged musical. The breadth of the music is immense—one song does not necessarily lead into another, and it is up to the music department to create a cohesive sound to a score that is fully fragmented. The vocals pivot between extremes and are often so densely layered that a performer can easily get lost in the cacophony. And then there are the endings.

The core conceit of *The Mystery of Edwin Drood* is that Charles Dickens never finished the original novel—he died before he solved the mystery, leaving the story up to a multitude of interpretations. The musical solves this conundrum by placing the story within a show inside the piece. By using a British music hall structure, they are able to insert a moment for the audience to vote on who they believe to be the killer. These results are then communicated to the actors offstage, and an ending is presented. The audience is given seven options, and six different endings can happen depending on the voting. (The discrepancy is if they select John Jasper as the killer, as his confession is performed as a fake-out immediately before the reveal. Should the audience select him as the killer, the second most voted killer performs.)

While this interactive element makes the show immensely fun for a viewer, it can be extremely stressful for a performer. Some endings were performed more often than others, which meant that multiple months could pass between opportunities to perform a certain ending. Of course, Chita had the most difficult task in this as well—while the rest of the company would be told the voted killer offstage, giving them several minutes to review lyrics if they had been chosen, Chita was onstage performing her final song. She would have only a few seconds after walking offstage to be informed of the vote by her assistant, all the time praying that she hadn't been selected for any of the ending roles. If a person wasn't voted the killer, they weren't off the hook—it was also up to the audience as to who were the erstwhile lovers and who was the dastardly detective, Datchery.

Over the six-month run of *The Mystery of Edwin Drood*, the most common choice of killer was Betsy Wolfe (and later Erin Dilly) as Rosa Bud, who was selected sixty-one times, almost half of all performances. The most common couple was Princess Puffer and the Deputy, resulting in eighty-year-old Chita Rivera and fourteen-year-old Nicholas Barasch singing the final love ballad together forty-six times, much to their mutual amusement. Peter Benson's Bazzard took on the role of Datchery a whopping ninety-seven times, after lobbying for the role onstage with his song "Never the Luck."

By the end of the run of *Drood*, Paul had come to a long-awaited decision. With Augie and Alexander living their own lives, Derin retired, and Paul's career on the downswing, they sold the house in New Jersey and moved thirty minutes outside of Charleston, South Carolina, at the start of 2013.

The world had changed immensely in the years since Paul had first come to New York. Friendships had been forged and forgotten, shows had come and gone, and in 2013, he was finally given the opportunity to step back. Paul had never gone more than six months without a show between 1973 and 2013 and had been working the equivalent of overtime for two straight decades. He had entered the industry in the middle of an artistic renaissance, and he had been beside Stephen Sondheim through some of the greatest artistic triumphs in the latter half of the twentieth century. His work had influenced countless musicians and theatre aficionados across the world, reaching heights he never could have imagined when he signed on to drum on the tour of *Cabaret*. After giving forty-three years of his life to Broadway, he was ready to step away from the theatre to enjoy life at a more leisurely pace.

CHAPTER TWENTY-EIGHT

She Loves Me

Paul Gemignani is inarguably one of the greatest music directors that Broadway has ever seen. He is a legend. Everyone knows that. What they might not know is that he is one of the funniest, most loving people to ever walk the face of the earth. Paul has lifted me up during difficult times, cracked me up at inappropriate times, and raised the bar on my musicianship. I genuinely love him and feel so grateful to call him a mentor and friend.

—LAURA BENANTI (ACTOR, SINGER)

THREE YEARS AFTER LEAVING NEW YORK, PAUL RECEIVED A PHONE CALL from Scott Ellis.

In 2011, the Roundabout had held a benefit concert of the musical *She Loves Me*, starring Kelli O'Hara, Josh Radnor, and Victor Garber. A charming piece, it had been the first musical produced by Roundabout in 1993, and in 2013, twenty years after the initial revival, they had toyed with the idea of reviving the revival—a complete re-creation, down to set and costume choices. That idea had been scrapped in favor of a more free interpretation, and Scott was finally ready to lift it off the ground, just as Paul began to crave the bustle of work once more.

Three of the benefit cast stayed on—Gavin Creel and Jane Krakowski played the hot and cold lovers Steven Kodaly and Ilona Ritter, and Peter Bartlett brought a particular neurosis to the tightly strung Head Waiter. Kelli O'Hara was involved with a revival of *The King and I*, Josh

Radnor had returned to Hollywood, and Victor Garber was filming three separate television shows, which left the casting field wide open by the time Paul flew back to New York for one last show.

Paul had been toying with the idea of retiring from Broadway appearances for some time before moving to South Carolina—as he had aged, the theatre industry had changed around him. Money had poured in, even as the budget for the music department was slashed on all sides. When he had started working as a music director, pits of more than twenty-five musicians were the standard—now he was lucky to wrangle thirteen pieces. Pits had been filled in or covered over, and musicians were either set onstage or shuttled into rooms outside of the main space, playing to click tracks and unable to really be a part the live action onstage. Prerecorded audio and synthesized instruments had become the name of the game as production wallets had ballooned, with no one willing to risk a potential wrong note when they could press play on a perfect recording.

This was the antithesis of what Paul loved about the theatre. That it was malleable and new every night was the point—if he had wanted to play the exact same thing the exact same way every single night, he would've joined a classical repertory group that did the same three Mozart pieces for a decade. At Roundabout he knew he could maintain some sense of what being a musician had been like in 1971—with his opera box system permanently installed in Studio 54, he could always see his performers, and he had a core group of musicians he could call on to fill the space with a lush musicality that had been lost in many of the other anemic pits.

Paul has always contracted his own musicians—in a Broadway music department, there is usually a music director, a musical contractor (also called an outside contractor), and a house contractor. A musical contractor is almost like a hiring manager—they do not play in the pit and are not there for the day to day, but are instead in charge of hiring and potentially firing musicians for a pit orchestra. If an orchestration calls for two trumpets and a French horn, they will present those three musicians to the music director, having vetted them. Paul has always preferred to take on this job himself, valuing a personal connection with every single musician he collaborates with.

As a contractor, Paul had built a decades-long working relationship with hundreds of musicians, whose skill and dedication he could trust. In the mix he was always sure to add a few fresh and exciting new players, breaking down the door that so often limited who was given a chance to enter a Broadway pit. Musicians such as Suzanne Ornstein, Glenn Dicterow, Sylvia D'Avanzo, John Beal, Nick Cerrato, Paul Pizzuti, Tedd Firth, Karen Dreyfus, Andy Schwartz, Irving Burger, Ron Sell, Les Scott, John Moses, John Campo, Dave and Jack Gale, Eric Weidman, Kathleen Nester, Bruce Eidem, Charles McCracken, Dominic Derasse, Mike Berkowitz, Joe Pasarro, Paul Ford, Dean Plank, Don McGeen, Peter Gordon, Thad Wheeler, Luther Henderson, Nick Archer, George Brown, Jennifer Hoult, and Peter Howard had been his collaborators through multiple projects, and many had begun as the new player whose energy elevated the entire cohort.

In contrast to the work of a music contractor, a house contractor is a musician in the pit who handles the payroll, paperwork, and any union or production negotiations that have to occur. This job is, by nature, something that cannot be subsumed by a music director. Should anyone ever have an issue with Paul, it is the house contractor they would go to, and by completely eliminating the chain of command, he would be doing the team a disservice (of course, passing off the paperwork isn't exactly an unwelcome side effect).

The score of *She Loves Me*, written by Jerry Bock and Sheldon Harnick, is incredibly well written—with a flowing grandeur across the score, it borders on being a chamber music piece, with plenty of moments for a musician to feast. Roger Shell, a cellist Paul had been working with since *Jerome Robbins' Broadway*, had taken on the role of his house contractor, and the pair had pulled together a team of fantastic musicians, headed by concertmistress Sylvia D'Avanzo. The fourteen-piece orchestra included the accordion, the flute, the piccolo, the English horn, the bassoon, and a wonderfully utilized harp, which gave the score a gorgeous classical scope. It was playful and bright, and it danced upon the ear when listened to.

The glorious music was further illuminated by their cast, with Laura Benanti, Zachary Levi, and Byron Jennings brought on as the bickering lovers Amalia and Georg, and their employer, Mr. Maraczek. Paul had adored Laura ever since working with her on the 2002 revival of *Into the Woods*—the musical theatre is an artform that has, since its inception, been motivated by its leading ladies, and Laura was one of the many Paul had admired, with her shimmering soprano voice and clever comedy rivaled only by her gentle kindness and tender heart. She had a gorgeously goofy sensibility that made her a delight to watch and gratifying to work with. Zachary, who was primarily known as a television star, was a fearless performer, with a sense of timing that had the audience in his palm without him even recognizing it had happened. When performers come from filmed mediums to the live theatre, there is often some tension—there are no retakes when the audience is directly in front of you, and that can summon fear in even the most seasoned performer. One of the most fulfilling aspects of Paul's career has been helping performers overcome that self-doubt—to him, it does not make one bit of difference that he has done forty shows and a performer may have done four. If a person is right for the role, and has been cast, then they are in the room for a reason, and they deserve to feel as confident in their own talents as possible. Much of Hollywood operates in such a way to cause a performer to lose that confidence, and Paul has relished reminding performers of their own ability to grow and change and flourish in a theatrical environment.

Jane Krakowski is a comedienne of the highest standard. The role of Ilona Ritter is one that requires a sharp sense of timing, as well as an immense amount of pathos—far from a dumb blonde caricature, she is an openly earnest person who could easily fall into stereotype when handled by the wrong actress and director combination. She is the type of role actress Judy Holliday made her career on in the 1950s, but that had fallen to the wayside as a role handed to any woman who can handle a moderate amount of comedy—between Scott, Paul, and Jane, they gave new life to Ilona and to her turbulent relationship with the charming philander Steven Kodaly, played by the always charming Gavin Creel.

When they opened, it was to swift admiration. With *Fiddler on the Roof*, Bock and Harnick's other masterpiece playing across the street, there was something akin to an exhale throughout the community as they took a collective moment to enjoy the melodies of the past even as *Hamilton* broke new ground a few blocks away. The old collided with the new as the industry moved forward, and *She Loves Me* became the first Broadway musical to be live-streamed online, with a full pro-shot production released across the globe.

As the run of *She Loves Me* came to an end, Paul invited the entire orchestra to dinner after the show. They surrounded a table in Follia, one of Paul's favorite Italian restaurants, and had one great family-style meal together, sharing wine and memories. With time, the conversation turned to Broadway, and to where the industry was headed. A hush fell over the room as Paul spoke for thirty minutes about the deeply intimate value of music, and how difficult it is to do correctly. He told seemingly endless stories from his career, each ending on a bittersweet note. By the end of his impromptu speech, he was in tears from the passion and fervor that had overtaken him when discussing the music that had passed into memory; every other musician in the room was openly weeping from observing it.

In many ways, *She Loves Me* was exactly the type of show Paul wanted as his last. With a stunning score, exemplary cast, and stellar production, it harkened back to exactly why he had gotten into theatre in the first place. When he had signed on to tour *Cabaret*, he had expected it to be a one-time experience in his winding life as a musician, but with time it had come to overwhelm his life completely.

Proud of what he intended to be the final bow, he put down his baton and headed home to Derin.

CHAPTER TWENTY-NINE

The Under 100 Club

You have never seen someone do so many different things with a baton. A stiletto, syringe, fishing rod, hand grenade—it's all very clear.
—SUZANNE ORNSTEIN (VIOLIN, CONCERTMASTER),
THE NEW YORK TIMES

As THE SONG GOES, THERE'S A BROKEN HEART FOR EVERY LIGHT ON Broadway. Paul has had a career punctuated by immensely influential projects, but he has also had his fair share of flops—the following are ten such shows. All played fewer than one hundred performances on Broadway and have not had a significant life after their closing.

MUSIC IS

Paul was in the middle of closing *Pacific Overtures* in San Francisco when he received a phone call from Hal Prince. Instead of continuing with the tour as planned, Hal needed Paul to go to Seattle to help George Abbott with a troubled show called *Music Is*. Mr. Abbott, who had mentored Prince in his early years, was a stalwart beacon of the theatre and showed no signs of slowing down at age eighty-nine. (Mr. Abbott continued to work until he was 100, and he was still involved in the theatre when he passed at age 107.)

The same could not be said for the show. An adaptation of *Twelfth Night*, it moved in fits and starts between the songs and the dialogue in such a way that made the viewer want to just see the original Shakespeare without the interstitial songs. Paul knew there were a handful of things he could improve (namely whipping the chorus into shape), but the show's concept was dead in the water by the time he arrived.

Still, he kept his head down, soaking up as much as he could from Mr. Abbott as they worked through kinks before performances to a sold-out Seattle crowd who, to Paul's astonishment, adored the show. After every number they would leap up cheering, as Paul would stand in the pit confused as to what they had latched onto.

When the tryout transferred to Washington, D.C., the same thing happened—the show itself wilted onstage as the audience whistled. As far as Mr. Abbott was concerned, they had a solid show that was playing great to audiences, and that would continue to play well in New York. Confused, Paul began to question his own taste as they worked through the tryout period. With his focus firmly on getting the music to a place where it deserved the response it was receiving, Paul would leap on and off the stage in order to communicate with actors and musicians in rehearsal, and after several days of this behavior, Mr. Abbott gave it a try, narrowly sticking the landing. That night, his daughter Judith Abbott, who was assistant directing the show, pulled Paul aside and asked him to use the stairs from that point on—Mr. Abbott was overextending himself to try to keep up with Paul, and at double Paul's age he risked very serious injury if he fell.

During one of the final creative team note sessions in DC, Paul finally mustered the nerve to say something about the audience reactions.

"So are we believing the audience? Because the show doesn't have a rhythm yet. I don't think we should believe the audience."

Mr. Abbott, startled—"Well who should we believe?"

"We should believe ourselves. Do we think it is great, do we think it is perfect?"

Paul knew he was not alone in thinking the show was a mess—on the plane ride from Seattle to DC he had commiserated with the company manager as to how they were possibly getting such a strong reception from such a weak show. Regardless of what was happening out of town, Paul knew that they would sink or swim based on their first preview performance. They couldn't completely rehash the show in New York, and by wasting their time out of town, their end product was lessening in quality every single day.

Careful to avoid Mr. Abbott's eye, Paul explained his reasoning—everyone in the room was an artist. Directors, choreographers, designers, musicians, everyone. They were doing a disservice to their artistic integrity and taste by ignoring their own reaction to the show in favor of the reaction of the audience. They needed to trust their guts and make a show that made them proud, regardless of the feedback they were receiving from the audiences. Mr. Abbott declined, saying that the show was in great shape, and they went to New York.

When they arrived at the St. James Theatre, they were dead in the water. The reviews positively eviscerated the show, and at the matinee following opening night, less than ten audience members showed up. They performed through the end of the week and closed after eight performances.

No one has any idea why the out-of-town audiences reacted the way they did.

A Doll's Life

A Doll's Life was the first of a series of flops following *Merrily We Roll Along* that threatened to bankrupt the Prince office. Based on Ibsen's classic play *A Doll's House*, it had reunited much of the team from *On the Twentieth Century*, including Betty Comden and Adolph Green, with the addition of Larry Grossman as the composer. This combination was wildly unsuited to the material they were given—Comden and Green were true musical comedy writers, and the dark and psychological machinations of a Norwegian playwright was about as far out of their wheelhouse as was possible.

They all gave it an honest effort, but the show collapsed in on itself even as they were building it. Once again, they decided to make the Hail Mary pass of fixing everything once they got to New York, and the show landed with a thud, closing after five performances.

GRIND

Three years after the collapse of *A Doll's Life*, Prince brought back Larry Grossman to create a musical called *Grind*, with lyrics by the witty Ellen Fitzhugh. Telling the story of a mixed-race burlesque house in 1930s Chicago, it dug deep into racial issues that plagued the lives of Black performers, with a bright and bouncing score that culminated in a race riot at the end of the show.

In theory, it was a solid idea for a show, with a solid score. The Prince office poured money into the production, making it a high-gloss, low-class spectacle of the collision of vaudevillian comedy and modern burlesque. Stubby Kaye, legendary comedian, was hired to play Gus, the club's main comic, alongside Joey Faye, a familiar face from the last days of the vaudeville circuit. The Prince office had also managed to sign Ben Vereen as the leading man for his triumphant return to the stage following his Tony-winning turn as the Leading Player in *Pippin*.

This, unfortunately, proved to be their downfall. While Stubby would keep spirits light during rehearsals, inserting and improvising increasingly hilarious comedic bits with leading lady Leilani Jones, Vereen was erratic to the point of being unreliable due to his addiction to cocaine. It wasn't unusual for Vereen to become completely uncoachable as he would skitter and slide through scenes in a world seemingly separate from anyone and everything around him. No matter what Hal or any of the creative staff told him, he came out every night with the same schtick that he had been lauded for in *Pippin*, seemingly not noticing how little it fit within the context of *Grind*. Occasionally he would call out of the show from his dressing room, five minutes before curtain, claiming sudden-onset illness.

The office persevered in hopes that Vereen would pull himself together, and they put every trick they had into the production, including an actual operating elevator that would allow for entrances and exits from within the pit. Walking to get to his spot as conductor was precarious as Paul would half stumble over hundreds of wires that were covered in moving blankets, with no actual stable floor beneath him and the musicians.

When the show opened, it was to mixed reviews, with the unfocused nature of the piece overwhelming the moments of cohesive excellence they had managed to string together. Following reviews, Vereen ceased showing up to the theatre at all, and his understudy, Obba Babatundé, effectively took over the role, with a slick wit that suited the character perfectly. With Obba as Leroy, the show began to come together in the way they had been hoping for the entire development period—as the key motivating character of the piece, his focused hand controlled the experience of the audience—if Leroy was off-center and distracted, as Vereen's Leroy had been, then the audience was left with no choice but to believe the show itself was lopsided. Obba's Leroy was as smooth and smart as any film noir playboy, and he drew the audience in as he provided someone to root for throughout the show.

As word of mouth spread of Mr. Babatundé's performance, audiences began to trickle back in, but it was too little too late. *Grind* closed after seventy-one performances, marking the final collaboration between Hal Prince and Paul.

SMILE

Paul and Marvin Hamlisch had been circling each other for more than a decade when Paul received the call to come to work on *Smile*, a musical about a local beauty pageant and the girls fighting for the title. The original music director, Robert Billig, had left the show after its workshop period in order to open *Les Misérables*, and Donna Marie Elio had recommended Paul to Marvin as a replacement.

It was a troubled show full of well-intentioned people. They could never quite pin down if they wanted to glorify or lampoon the pageant world, and the material quickly became overwritten as they attempted to fix the problem with additions rather than editing.

One of the most important things a creator needs to know when making a show is what they want to say. You cannot just have an idea—"oh, a show about Miss America–type girls could be fun." You have to know what it is you are trying to say with the idea—what your overarching premise is. Without that core to your storytelling, no amount of catchy music and flashy choreography can save a show. There has to be a reason for the audience to become invested, and unless you are putting on a strip show, beautiful girls parading in bikinis does not a story make.

While trying to find a point of view for *Smile*, Paul received the phone call from Sondheim that he was needed for *Into the Woods*. He struck a deal with Marvin that he would get the company through to their opening night on Broadway before leaving for California, which Marvin accepted—Paul had come in as a replacement music director, and while he was committed to the show and Marvin, his leaving after opening was not going to change the outcome.

Smile has gone on to become a cult classic musical, with a fan base dedicated to its score, including the standout song "Disneyland," originally performed by Jodi Benson two years before she would go on to voice Ariel in *The Little Mermaid*. *Smile* closed after forty-eight performances on Broadway, with the associate conductor, Ronald Melrose, taking over the final forty-seven performances after Paul left for *Into the Woods*.

MAIL

Some shows simply can't be saved, regardless of good intentions. It is like trying to fix a stew after too much salt has been added—at a certain point, you just have to throw out the broth.

Mail ran for thirty-seven performances in 1988, and it is best remembered as the Broadway debut of Brian Stokes Mitchell (then known as Brian Mitchell).

THE ADVENTURES OF TOM SAWYER

The Adventures of Tom Sawyer was one of the greater disappointments of Paul's career. Based on the ever-enduring children's novel, with a score by iconic songwriter Don Schlitz, the show seemed golden from the moment Scott Ellis called Paul about the project. For four months Scott, Don, Paul, and dance arranger David Krane would gather in a room, bringing together the show with a sure hand that valued collaboration above all else.

Don is what many refer to as a songsmith—the music soaks deep into his bones, and he was capable of churning out a high-quality new song for a moment in the show in ten minutes should the need arise. He wrote more than fifty songs during the investigative process, each catchy and complex in its poetry, which made for an extremely tight score once everything had been parsed down—there was not a dud song in the bunch.

When they went to New Haven for the out-of-town tryout, the show found its footing. With a smaller band and a folksy atmosphere onstage, the material was matched to the visual in a way that made it all-encompassing. It had turned into a piece of musical theatre Americana, and it was well on its way to being a modest hit when they moved into the Minskoff Theatre in New York, one of the largest theatres on Broadway. What had been a clever and intimate show was suddenly dwarfed by massive sets and a full orchestra, replacing what had been a thirteen-piece band out of town. The folksy elements were scrapped in favor of spectacle, and the show was lost inside of it all, even as children responded positively to the material itself.

The choice of theatre can make or break a show on Broadway—the size of the stage and the size of the audience are two metrics that cannot be overlooked. Just as *Sawyer* had no business playing in a massive theatre, a show as large and as grand as *Evita* would not have made sense in a small house. You have to strike the right balance between the number of seats you can sell and number of seats you can properly perform to, and unfortunately *Sawyer* was put in a position where they simply couldn't fill the theatre provided by the Nederlander Organization without sacrificing something core to the show itself.

While working on *Sawyer* out of town, Paul received a call from Susan Stroman—a year had passed since Mike Ockrent's death, and she was ready to dive in on *The Producers* with Paul and Mel Brooks. Paul made the difficult decision to stay with *Sawyer* and see it through, rather than abandoning ship to run to *The Producers*. *The Producers* went on to win twelve Tony Awards that season, beating *Sawyer* in the two categories it was nominated in.

When Paul was given the opportunity to record the score of *Sawyer*, he made a point of returning to the original thirteen-piece orchestrations. Called the "Gilly's Band," they were a true folk western orchestra, and the version of the show now available for licensing is the show that should have arrived on Broadway in the first place.

The Adventures of Tom Sawyer closed after twenty-one performances.

THE FROGS

The Frogs is perhaps the least produced musical of the Sondheim canon—originally staged by the Yale Repertory Theatre in the Yale swimming pool in 1974, it was a loose adaptation by writer/director Bert Shevelove of the Classical Greek comedy by the same name. Paul had seen the original production for its novelty, and he had filed it away as a funny experiment until the early 2000s, when he received phone calls from Stephen Sondheim and Susan Stroman.

André Bishop, the artistic director of Lincoln Center, had always been intrigued by the piece, as was Nathan Lane. The musical comedy boom of the early 2000s seemed like the perfect time to resurrect the show, and an immense amount of money was poured into the project, with Nathan writing new material for himself and the rest of the company to flesh the show out into a full production.

In many ways, working as both writer and actor is more difficult onstage than on film—as Dionysus, Nathan was forced to both be in the moment and cataloging audience reactions, taking mental notes even as he delivered punch lines. He had to be everywhere at once, which was made even more difficult as the extravagant elements of the production began to loom. At various points during the production, Nathan was dragged through a trapdoor and smashed against a pipe, John Byner was trapped in a boat suspended above the stage, and the cast was sent skyward on bungee cords and ropes in an attempt to capture the visual spectacle that had dominated the original play.

That isn't to say the atmosphere backstage was fearful—the company took the chaos in stride, trying new things and holding each other up until the end. John Byner, a famous television comic and impressionist, played Charon, the ferryman of Hades. One of his impressions was of George Jessell, an old-school vaudevillian with a highly particular voice. During a matinee, Nathan told John to do the scene at the gate as George, just to spice things up—of course, no one in the entire theatre recognized who he was imitating except for Paul and Nathan, who were sent into hysterics as the audience watched, bewildered. When they exited the stage, a young member of the ensemble pulled Nathan aside to ask what had happened to John, to which Nathan replied in his trademark deadpan "He's had a stroke" before walking to his next cue, with the ensemble member equal parts confused and concerned.

When a musical works, it is somewhat of a miracle. Everyone has to be on the same page with the same artistic voice working toward the same story. Unfortunately, the audience was not on the same page as the creative team. *The Frogs* closed after ninety-two performances.

THE PEOPLE IN THE PICTURE

There are few things that worry Paul more than when a phone call with a producer begins with "Hey, pal." They are either going to call in a favor or tell you bad news. In this case it was both.

Todd Haimes, artistic director, had spearheaded the movement that had turned Roundabout Theatre Company into a nonprofit juggernaut. When he had taken over the role in 1990, the company had been primarily known for revivals of classic plays, with Chekhov, Shakespeare, and Shaw dominating their seasons. It was Haimes who took the initiative to begin producing musicals at the Roundabout with Scott Ellis, and from that point forward he had endeavored to keep the company looking forward to discover new productions. Unfortunately, sticking your neck out as much as Todd has means that you occasionally catch an axe.

The People in the Picture was one of those axes. Focused on a grandmother's stories of the Yiddish theatre and the Holocaust, the show swung between drama and comedy, tangling itself with its own through line. The score was sufficient, but a lack of experience in musical theatre from the majority of the creative team sunk the project. Writing and directing for the stage are immensely difficult, idiosyncratic artforms, and the team were unable to patch the cracks even with Paul's expertise to lean on.

Through all the false starts and limping finishes, the company had fun. Starring Donna Murphy, Alexander Gemignani, and Chip Zien, it was immediately a family atmosphere backstage as Paul relished the opportunity to work with them all on a new piece of theatre once more.

They can't all be hits, and that is okay. Sometimes, the most important part about doing a show is the art of simply doing it. The final product may not be perfect, but the process is still worthwhile. *The People in the Picture* closed after sixty performances.

110 IN THE SHADE

110 in the Shade was a continuation of Paul and Lonny Price's collaboration at Ravinia Festival the year after the *Gypsy* debacle. Intended as a star vehicle revival for Audra McDonald, the show was originally written as the follow-up to *The Fantasticks*, with a score by Tom Jones and Harvey Schmidt, and contained many similar fanciful elements while remaining grounded by the original play, *The Rainmaker*.

It can be supremely difficult to make a musical that is based on a popular play. When a text is known front to back by fans of the original material, any adjustments or cuts come under intense scrutiny. Some audience members will be up in arms at the musicalization of their favorite monologues, or at the streamlining of the piece in order to accommodate a new viewpoint. The one major benefit of adapting a popular play is that it often guarantees good, deep roles for an actor.

Before *110 in the Shade*, Audra was working immensely hard to get out from the shadow of her own voice—her vocal talent had, in many ways, enshrined her to the public in a way that made it difficult for audiences to approach her in dramatic roles that were less vocally focused. In the years leading up to *110 in the Shade*, she had appeared in *Henry IV* and *A Raisin in the Sun*, and she had won the Tony Award for Best Featured Actress in a Play for *Raisin*, but *110 in the Shade* was considered by many to be her watershed moment as a musical drama star. She was no longer a beautiful voice who occasionally did plays, or an actress who happened to have a strong voice—as the intelligent yet insecure Lizzie she blended the two into complete unison, with her voice and her acting talent supporting each other to make an even greater whole.

During the run Will Swenson, the understudy for the male lead of *Starbuck*, performed the show opposite Audra a handful of memorable times. Their immediate chemistry extended offstage, and five years after working together in *110 in the Shade*, Audra and Will were married.

110 in the Shade ended its limited run after ninety-four performances.

PAL JOEY

Of every show on this list, *Pal Joey* is perhaps the most disheartening. It was an overwhelmingly cared for labor of love by the entire creative team, with Stockard Channing taking on the role of Vera, considered one of the most complex female characters in the pre–golden age of musical theatre.

In any other year, it could have been a hit. The score was strong, the new book was clever, and the visual immediately grabbed the attention of viewers as it invited them into a world of sophistication and sleaze that was just as arresting as it had been in 1940. They had grounded the piece in a way that would not have been possible during the original production and reinvigorated many of the original intentions of Lorenz Hart and Richard Rodgers as they peeled back the veneer on the piece to create a through line that was digestible to a modern audience.

Unfortunately, a wonderful production cannot overcome poor timing. *Pal Joey* opened December 18, 2008, in the middle of the global financial crisis. All of Broadway was suffering, but many audience members fully rebuked dark and psychological theatre in favor of escapism and hope. *Pal Joey*, a show about the underbelly of society, was the antithesis of the distraction many theatregoers were looking for, and *Pal Joey* closed after eighty-five performances.

CHAPTER THIRTY

Beyond Broadway

Paul is like a second skin when you're singing. You can feel him breathing with you, and he would be right there concentrating with you, giving you the attention you needed and what the song needed and the moment needed to make it all one. You do it together instead of feeling alone. He is a part of you. Paul is your best friend when you are up there.

—Lonny Price (Director, Actor, Writer)

If there is one thing that Paul has excelled at throughout his career, it is keeping busy. Paul has participated in approximately seven hundred concerts, workshops, readings, and recordings outside of his Broadway obligations during his fifty-year career. The following are some of his personal highlights.

Beverly Sills and the New York City Opera

Paul was first introduced to legendary soprano Beverly Sills through Hal Prince in the early 1980s—Ms. Sills had become the general director of the New York City Opera (NYCO) company following her retirement from performance, and Paul had been replaced by John Mauceri when the Prince production of *Candide* had transferred to the NYCO. Three years later Hal loaned Paul to Beverly for a production of *The Student Prince*, Sigmund Romberg's sentimental operetta, and a divine partnership was born.

Beverly Sills was a wonderful woman—intelligent, she had a deep understanding of the personal politics that it took to collaborate with multiple artistic temperaments. She knew exactly what she was looking for when she set out on a project, and she could spot brilliance in the most hidden corners of a performer. What made her and Paul's six-year partnership work was their shared adoration of music. Her ability to play the game and his ability to follow through blended perfectly to create a first for the legendary company.

Paul had never had any intentions of becoming the maestro of an opera company—while he could certainly appreciate the immense amount of artistry involved (his favorite opera is *La Bohéme*), he had almost always acted as a passive audience member rather than an active creator prior to his collaboration with Sills. Part of this was due to the language barrier—while he would sit and painstakingly translate every word of an opera's libretto in order to follow along with the story, he was by far unique in this—in the opera world, the voice is king, always. The tone and warmth of a voice's musicianship is what sells a show rather than the actual inventiveness of the plotline. It is why operatic vocalists such as Sills become household names in a way that is less common in the theatre world—opera fans are often more interested in hearing a person's rendition of a favorite aria than they are in hearing an entirely new opera.

Paul has always approached his work from a "story first" perspective. The most gorgeous trills in the world have to be supported by equally enigmatic acting, which is something that can often be hidden when a foreign-language opera is performed for an audience that does not speak the language—emoting and expression without words is often the core conceit of opera in the modern era, while language and character drive the musical theatre. In a shocking move for the NYCO, Beverly and Paul came together to reach across this artistic divide.

Together, they brought the musical theatre to the classical stage—first with *Brigadoon*, and later with *Sweeney Todd*, *South Pacific*, and *Kismet*. Performed during the core company's off-season, these productions were immensely popular for how they blended the lush-voiced members of the company with the engrossing storytelling of the American musical.

Working with a repertory company model is completely different from the commercial theatre model Paul had entered into with the Prince office. With season tickets and memberships sold long before a production comes to fruition, there is a large amount of artistic freedom behind the scenes—with tickets already sold, it was up to them to make the best artistic product they could, rather than worrying over how to establish word of mouth or target audience marketing. Opera is, in many ways, a distinct artform from the musical theatre, and the blurring of the lines that Beverly and Paul were able to achieve received attention from critics on both sides of the aisle who became deeply invested in the blending that was happening onstage.

Their partnership lasted until Beverly stepped down as the general director of the NYCO, and their friendship remained firm until her passing in 2007.

THE NEW YORK CITY BALLET (NYCB)
In the years following *Jerome Robbins' Broadway*, Paul spent a portion of his time with the NYCB, as Jerome Robbins' go-to conductor for the *West Side Story* Suite. Robbins tried for many years to lure Paul over to the dance world in a more full-time capacity, but Paul always returned to the fast-paced newness of the theatre over the set repertoire of a ballet company. When Robbins passed, Paul was permanently instated as the conductor for the *West Side Story* Suite, alongside several other music-directing jobs, including a new Richard Rodgers tribute ballet called *Thou Swell* and a balletic opera called *The Seven Deadly Sins*.

The orchestra of a ballet works their fingers to the bone. An immense amount of pressure is placed on the musicians of the NYCB to maintain absolute excellence in more than a hundred different compositions that they were expected to know at a moment's notice. The work ethic and drive required to thrive in that kind of an environment is incomparable to almost any other instrumental career path. Paul safeguarded the legacy of *West Side Story* for the NYCB until he was pushed out by the music director of the NYCB main stage during employment shakeups under Peter Martins.

THE NEW YORK PHILHARMONIC

The New York Philharmonic is the best. Plain and simple. A musician does not earn a spot in their ranks without possessing a top-tier talent and work ethic. Musicians travel from across the globe to work with the Philharmonic, and the status symbol of working with them is not one to be taken lightly.

Of course, it doesn't hurt that Paul's highest profile collaboration with them is one of the most popular concerts in the Philharmonic's history.

More than a decade had passed since the closing of *Follies* when the team at Avery Fisher Hall reached out to Steve with the idea of doing a concert of the show. It was to be an all-star cast—Barbara Cook, George Hearn, Mandy Patinkin, and Lee Remick were brought on as the four leads and were supported by the likes of Carol Burnett, Elaine Stritch, Betty Comden, Adolph Green, and Phyllis Newman, among others. The score was to be presented in full—money had been so tight that the original cast recording had been forced to cut songs in order to afford the vinyl necessary, and theatre lovers had long been clamoring to hear the show that they had missed since 1971.

Director Herbert Ross took some liberties in revitalizing the show—reprises of favorite songs were added, dialogue was changed, and in the most obvious change, "The God-Why-Don't-You-Love-Me Blues" (also called "Buddy's Blues") was changed from a trio to a solo number for Mandy Patinkin.

Normally, the song is performed with one male and two female performers, in full slapstick vaudeville pastiche. Onstage at Avery Fisher, there was nowhere near enough room for that original staging. Instead of having the three performers stand in front of the audience, robbing the number of half of its comedic value, Paul and Mandy came together with one of those ideas that is just so off-kilter that it has to work.

Mandy's vocal distortion skills had been proven on *Sunday in the Park with George* only a year prior, and they decided to return to that skill set for a new inversion of the song. He grimaced and stamped his way through the number, switching voices and physicalities between the three characters in a manner that rivaled the great Fred Allen himself. It was marvelously funny, and completely unexpected by anyone outside of the rehearsal room—everyone had thought that Carol and Phyllis would step forward to voice the chorus girls, and when Mandy instead struck his first feminine pose, the audience ripped open with laughter, watching Mandy run between the three microphones that had been set up.

The focus and determination it took to make it through "Buddy's Blues" took up the overwhelming majority of Mandy's nerves going into the performance. When a concert recording is made, the show is usually performed twice, which puts an immense amount of pressure on a performer, with the knowledge that even one bung note can be memorialized for all to see. At the first performance, Mandy walked out to sing "The Right Girl," his character's first major solo number, and he went up. With the entire Philharmonic playing behind him, he froze, staring out at the audience, who stared back.

In the span of a second, Mandy made peace with being ripped off the stage with a shepherd's crook and sent to an asylum. He began counting his blessings and mentally thanking those who had believed in him before his collapse as Paul hauled the Philharmonic to a halt, with silence ringing through the concert hall. While in reality, the halt had taken only a few short seconds, it felt like a full hour to Mandy, until he ripped his eyes away from the audience and saw Paul, looking at him with a mixture of compassion and concern as he waited to see what Mandy was going to do.

Taking a deep breath, Mandy squared his shoulders and turned back to the audience.

"I'm sorry, I'm a little nervous. Let's try it again."

Before he could finish the thought, Paul's hands were aloft and the Philharmonic was immediately back at attention, starting the song from the top. From that moment on, Mandy was free to be as bold as he wanted—the worst had already happened. That sense of risk-embracing looseness carried through the rest of the performance, and it is that night's performance of "The Right Girl" and "Buddy's Blues" that made it on the live album.

The *Follies* concert brought one particular moment of pride into Paul's life that he had never expected—his percussion teacher from college, Roland Kohloff, had become the timpanist of the Philharmonic in the intervening years, and now Paul was the one conducting him. Before the first orchestra rehearsal, Kohloff had brought Paul down into the orchestra room, where he had introduced Paul to every single member of the orchestra individually, with a pride-soaked "This is Paul Gemignani. He was my student back in the day, I am so proud of him, and you better be nice to him." He trotted Paul around the entire room, introducing him and having him shake hands in the manner of a proud parent, something Paul had never really experienced before.

Follies was far from Paul's only experience with the Philharmonic. Like the NYCB, they made multiple attempts to sway him further in their direction—lush concerts and orchestral programs pepper Paul's career, and his working relationship with Leonard Bernstein connected him just as firmly to the Philharmonic as Robbins connected him to the Ballet.

The Philharmonic does not tolerate any bullshit. They have no interest in being workhorses—they know they are the best, and they don't break their backs continually trying to defend that fact. They follow union rules to the minute, to the point that a musician will put their instrument down the second the clock ticks over, even with only a few measures left in rehearsal. There is a deep amount of respect throughout the company, both for each other and the music, and no one ever impedes on another's time.

Walking onstage at the Philharmonic is a big deal for Paul, every single time. He is always immensely nervous before that initial downbeat. Paul, like almost all artists, is deeply insecure at his core. After the *Follies* concert, he had rationalized that it had gone well only because Kohloff had told the musicians to be nice to him—once Kohloff retired, he prepared himself for a rude awakening that never came.

Throughout his entire career, Paul had never felt good enough for the jobs he found himself in. Writing it off to luck, he never felt that he himself was enough to garner the work he had accomplished. No one had ever told Paul that he should follow the path he had chosen—in fact, many had told him that he was insane, and that he was making the wrong choice. That constant fight between his heart and the wishes of others created a very deep insecurity that he had to fight every single time he walked out to a podium. No matter what, it followed him, and it is often at its strongest when he walks out in front of the Philharmonic.

To conduct the Philharmonic was an irrefutable sign that he had done something right. That he could stand there, hands aloft, where his musical idol Bernstein had made his mark, was and always is an overwhelmingly positive thing. There is always the initial terror, but with the first beat, the glorious music of the Philharmonic washes away all fear.

THE MANHATTAN SCHOOL OF MUSIC

In 1991, Paul came the closest to becoming a teacher that he has in his career. The Manhattan School of Music, one of the premier training schools in the New York area, was setting up an eight-week course on musical theatre, and Paul was brought on board to head the operation, alongside Marta Casals. They assembled a core teaching staff including Paul, Joanna Merlin, Austin Pendleton, and Carolann Page.

Each student would filter through various classes taught by the four, including everything from audition preparation to a fully realized performance at the end of the eight-week period. Everyone involved was at the top of their game—Austin Pendleton was a remarkable acting teacher capable of coaxing a stellar performance out of even the least natural performer, Joanna was, as always, a miracle, and Carolann helped to establish a vocal technique that set the students up for success in the long term in the theatre.

The program was essentially a summer camp, with twenty students acting as the matriculating body. At times during the school year, Paul would work with the orchestra students within the full program, where he helped them break free of classical music habits to understand theatrical style. Rather than teaching to a set syllabus or curriculum, he would bring in mountains of scores from various shows, and he would have the musicians sight-read through them with him at the podium—if they ever hit something that a student didn't understand, or a spot that was giving everyone stylistic trouble, he would lower his baton and they would talk it through together as a group. By treating the students as collaborators, they learned how to solve problems on their own, and as the semester progressed, they had fewer questions as they learned how to navigate on the fly.

At the end of the year, Paul set up a concert in which the orchestra would play a selection over overtures from classic shows, as well as accompany two performers on musical theatre standards—Alexander Gemignani and Kate Baldwin. Longtime musical collaborators Tedd Firth and Larry Lelli were brought on alongside the orchestra students, and the night went off without a hitch. The administration of the Manhattan School of Music were so thrilled that attempts were made to schedule a similar concert once a month for the following year, but they were hesitant to pay, which put an end to the concert series after one outing (Paul paid the four outside collaborators out of pocket).

In 2003, Paul received an honorary doctorate of musical arts from the school, shortly before the summer program was made redundant. The next year, a new program consisting of a very similar model sprouted, with significantly less expensive staff running the room. In the world of academia, bureaucracy is king.

MANDY PATINKIN: *DRESS CASUAL*

In the late 1980s, Mandy Patinkin was approached to make a solo album. While it was something he had always dreamed of doing, the fear that it would fall through had always kept him from pushing to make it a reality—when the opportunity was placed before him, he immediately went to Paul.

One of Paul's greatest skills is recognizing the potential in a person before even they know it is there. On a hunch, he connected Mandy and Paul Ford, Paul's trusted pianist, and created an artistic marriage that went on to define Mandy's solo records for the next two decades.

Unfortunately, Paul ended up cutting himself out of the equation—when a performer is as wickedly smart as Mandy, performing with just a piano accompaniment can be freeing in a concert context. When there is an entire orchestra, as there was at the Philharmonic, it is a lot harder to change things on the fly—with a good pianist, you can change song orders in the middle of the show, provided you are able to properly communicate. Paul worked together with Mandy and Paul Ford to make the record *Dress Casual*, helping to make the arrangements, and conducting the full orchestra for the album, but when the time came to tour and perform the piece, he was left behind.

This was bittersweet for the three of them. They had created that first album in Mandy's home, going through hundreds of songs together to make the right selections as they refined the idea of what exactly a Mandy Patinkin solo record should sound like. The problem was that that sound worked better when left open with a bare accompaniment, versus the full and lush orchestra that Paul provided. Mandy was no frills, with a raw quality and simplicity that required only a duo.

There were no hard feelings—Paul had known in his gut that the combination of Mandy and Paul Ford was right from the start; it was why he had connected the two of them in the first place. Paul has made a large number of recordings throughout his career, but he considers *Dress Casual* to be particularly special. It turned out exactly the way it needed to.

KRISTINA

Robin Wagner, world-renowned set designer and longtime friend of Paul's, called him in 2006 to talk about a new musical written by Benny Andersson of ABBA. Called *Kristina*, it followed the story of Swedish immigrants to America and was a proven hit in Stockholm. More of a tone poem than a musical, it engaged with the sounds of Swedish folk music and traditional music to paint an auditory picture. Paul flew to Sweden to meet with Benny, and they began to work together to refine and translate the piece for an English-speaking audience.

While workshopping in New York, a decision was made to host a concert of the material in an attempt to drum up interest for a full production—Helen Sjöholm took on the title role in 2009, and the show was performed in full to sold-out crowds for two nights. The concert was then repeated in London, to similar effect, but a full production never materialized, despite the creative team's best efforts.

ENCORES! AT NEW YORK CITY CENTER

Paul was brought in as the music director for the 2005 season of *Encores! at New York City Center*—designed to revive and elevate forgotten gems of the musical theatre, Paul put together a season consisting of *Kismet*, which reunited Marin Mazzie and Brian Stokes Mitchell in the leadings roles, *70 Girls 70*, a Kander and Ebb jewel that gives voice to older female performers (in this case spearheaded by the divine Olympia Dukakis), and *Of Thee I Sing*, a Gershwin showstopper that starred Victor Garber and Jefferson Mays, one of the most incredible comedic chameleons of the current era.

One of the difficulties with a program such as *Encores!* is the amount of red tape involved each year—estates can be tricky to handle, and when that is combined with the nonprofit sector, there are often more meetings than there are actual performances, especially when a production runs for only a few short weeks, as *Encores!* productions do. After serving a year, Paul left to film Tim Burton's *Sweeney Todd*.

PBS *GREAT PERFORMANCES*

The PBS *Great Performances* series is one of the most accessible forms of musical theatre in the United States. Anyone with a television set can tune in to watch recorded productions, concerts, and one-person shows, without ever stepping foot in New York City. Paul has participated in a number of these concerts (and a number of the concerts discussed elsewhere in this book were recorded and presented publicly via PBS), but two particularly stand out—*My Favorite Broadway* and *Company*.

The *My Favorite Broadway* series was essentially a revue of Broadway's best songs on certain themes—leading ladies and love songs. Julie Andrews was the host of both events, although she declined to sing at either—her destructive vocal surgery had occurred only a few short years before, and she had effectively retired from singing altogether. After forming a rapport together on the first concert, *The Leading Ladies*, Paul began to press Julie on the issue for the second concert, *The Love Songs*.

Michael Crawford was slated to perform "I've Grown Accustomed to Her Face" and "The Rain in Spain" from *My Fair Lady* toward the end of the evening, and Paul was determined to have Julie walk out to speak-sing the final three lines of "The Rain in Spain" with him, as she had with Rex Harrison in the original production. She balked at the idea—for the majority of her life, she had been taught that her soaring soprano was her voice, and when she had lost it, she had given up singing altogether. With Paul's guiding hand, she opened up a sliver of a chest voice, only slightly altering the key to make it more comfortable for both her and Michael.

On the night of filming, the entire audience fell apart the moment Julie walked onstage at the end of the number. She didn't have time to say a word before the room imploded. Julie was, and is, a beloved titan of the theatre, and the entire community had been desperate to hear her again. Finally, after stopping the show cold for several minutes, Julie and Michael were able to finish the song together, with the audience openly in tears. It was the first time Julie publicly sang after her surgery, and vocal appearances have been few and far between since.

Throughout Paul's career, he has done almost every Stephen Sondheim musical. Through original Broadway productions, regional performances such as Ravinia, and concerts, Paul had checked them all off, except for *A Funny Thing Happened on the Way to the Forum* and *Company*. In 2011 PBS solved half of that problem.

Company was the musical that firmly planted Steve on the map as one of the most compelling creatives the musical theatre has ever seen. It was immensely "of the moment" when it premiered and had the 1970s scrawled all over it—unfortunately, that has turned the musical into somewhat of a period piece. What was cutting edge and innovative in 1970 was well worn by 2011, and they had to find a way of making the piece engaging for an audience who hadn't necessarily lived through 1970s New York like the original audience had.

Company was the first score of Steve's that Paul had ever heard— after the *Follies* debacle, when Hal Hastings had to force him to sign on, a friend had sent Paul a record of *Company*'s original cast album. While still on tour with *Zorba*, he had played the record on his portable turntable in the hotel room and been immediately grabbed by the bossa nova–infused score.

Paul and Lonny Price settled on one simple solution to engage a modern audience—a star-studded cast whose credits overflowed the page. Neil Patrick Harris was cast as the central Bobby, and he was surrounded by Stephen Colbert, Christina Hendricks, Patti LuPone, Martha Plimpton, Anika Noni Rose, Jim Walton, Jon Cryer, Katie Finneran,

Craig Bierko, Jennifer Laura Thompson, Chryssie Whitehead, Jill Paice, and Aaron Lazar. When a production is filled with that many known names, an audience cannot help but transfer some of their love for a performer outside of the show, onto the show. It was an immensely common tactic during the golden age of Broadway—film actors would come to New York and do theatre in order to build "legitimacy," and the theatre would gain popularity from their fans coming in to see and support them. It was a win-win, and it was equally successful in resuscitating *Company*.

The entire night had a buoyant feeling, with every performer on their A game. Katie Finneran was, as always, hysterical as the neurotic newlywed Amy, and Patti brought her classic charm to Joanne, making the role her own after it had been owned by Elaine Stritch for more than forty years. But of them all, it was Neil Patrick Harris who shined the brightest. While he had been marvelous in *Assassins*, *Company* was exactly the type of show to demonstrate his remarkable skills at the style most commonly associated with musical theatre. He and Paul adjusted the seminal classic "Being Alive" for the concert, and what resulted was a notably honest and open portrayal, free of the baggage that the role of Bobby had begun to carry.

It was a beautifully youthful night, and it was the perfect way to check *Company* off of Paul's to-do list.

SONDHEIM: A CELEBRATION AT CARNEGIE HALL

Paul has conducted more than one hundred concerts throughout his career, many of which have been tributes to his dear friend Stephen Sondheim. Of those concerts, he considers *Sondheim: A Celebration at Carnegie Hall* and the *80th Birthday Concert* to be the best.

Working with Susan Stroman and Scott Ellis on the Carnegie Hall concert was wonderful—the two of them had sort of grown up together, and they had a glorious understanding that made working with them smooth sailing from the outset. When the three of them are in a room, there is no artifice. They know one another and trust one another at such a level that they can be their true artistic selves together, without any masking or hiding. That kind of trust is rare, and it is something Paul has treasured his entire career.

The Carnegie Hall concert is renowned for the quality of its performances—be it Dorothy Loudon delivering a heart- and gut-busting madness medley of "Losing My Mind" and "You Could Drive a Person Crazy," thirteen-year-old Daisy Eagan performing the elderly etude "Broadway Baby," or Madeline Kahn presenting a neurotically funny "Not Getting Married," every performer hit it out of the park. It set the standard for what a Sondheim tribute could be, and every concert since has had to rise to the standards it set.

SONDHEIM 80TH BIRTHDAY CONCERT

The *80th Birthday Concert* has become somewhat of a legend—it served as the introductory production for a new generation of theatre fans and cemented Sondheim in their minds as the pinnacle of achievement.

Much of the mythic quality of the concert can be attributed to the work of its director, Lonny Price. It was Lonny who picked the performers, Lonny and Paul who selected the material, and Lonny who came up with the "Red Dress" concept for the second half of the night, a concept that has been endlessly copied ever since. As a devoted Sondheim fan who had eagerly anticipated each new show since he was a child, Lonny knew the canon inside and out and was able to pick exciting and interesting material for every performer, with many performing songs they had never before sung in public. He blended comedy and pathos, from the dueling Sweeneys (George Hearn and Michael Cerveris, who had both played the titular role thirty years apart, split "A Little Priest" against Patti LuPone's Mrs. Lovett, who had previously played opposite them both) to full vocal re-creation (Bernadette Peters and Mandy Patinkin had reunited to perform "Move On").

Paul served as joking foil throughout the concert, with false starts of the *Sweeney Todd* overture puncturing particularly saccharine moments. The New York Philharmonic has something called the "Lenny Camera"—named for Leonard Bernstein, they had carved a hole into the wall to fit a camera in order to capture Bernstein conducting. Bernstein was the first maestro to capture the public's attention in such a way that they cared to see his face as he worked, and Lonny made the decision to film Paul, cutting to him throughout the evening in order to give the general public a glimpse into the jolly nature rarely witnessed outside of the isolation of the pit.

In Paul's first Sondheim concert, *Sondheim: A Musical Tribute*, the ladies of Sondheim had done a series of numbers back-to-back in order to close out the concert—Lonny took that idea to the moon. With every woman dressed by Diane Von Furstenberg in a vivid shade of red, an energy of electric proportions spread through the room—first, Patti LuPone's "The Ladies Who Lunch," then Marin Mazzie's "Losing My Mind," and in quick succession, Audra McDonald's "The Glamorous Life," Donna Murphy's "Could I Leave You," Bernadette Peters' "Not A Day Goes By," and finally, Elaine Stritch's "I'm Still Here."

By the time Elaine had gotten up to sing, the theatre was a live wire of emotion. Elaine, at age eighty-five, was nearly deaf and refused to wear a hearing aid.

The first night of the recording, Elaine fell apart. She had been tip-toeing around memory problems for years, and the emotions coursing through the room combined with her difficulty hearing Paul and the Philharmonic created an unfortunate cocktail. Lyrics would flow in and out of her head as Paul would slow the instrumentation down, looping vamps over and over as he tried to will the words from his head into hers. He held her hand in every way but physical and was able to guide her to a steady landing, where the orchestra finished beside her, even after the calamity.

The second day, she remembered her words but was so staunchly focused on not losing them that she paid little attention to the tempo and rhythms as previously rehearsed. Sensing the potential coming storm, Paul verbally urged her to begin and deconstructed the music as they played, following her every step to make it seem that they had reimagined the piece prior. What resulted was an underscored monologue that ripped the roof off of the theatre. Every word from her mouth was honest—she stood in her red satin heels and jaunty cap, alive and irrefutably *here*. As the audience began to laugh, she came alive, brash, heartbreaking and bold as she had been when "The Ladies Who Lunch" had been written for her forty years prior. When she hopped in her heels, desperately affirming that she was still here, after all these years, the audience leapt to their feet, with tears shed across the auditorium.

If you watch the PBS recording of the concert, you will find moments of unbridled humanity in every transition—keep your eyes on Marin Mazzie after she finishes "Losing My Mind." First, she grabs the hand of neighboring Donna Murphy, one of her closest friends since the pair had worked together on *Passion*. Then, as the lights dim, and Audra rises, Marin reaches back and pulls on the tails of Paul's tuxedo, looking all the world like a young girl playing with the edge of her father's coat. It is a sweet moment of support and gratitude, and hundreds of these little moments can be found throughout the evening.

What made the *80th Birthday Concert* so remarkable was that it managed to capture the sense of community that has sprung up around Sondheim's work. It was far more than performers walking onstage, singing a song, and walking off. It was an outpouring of love and respect for Steve, and for how much incredible art and friendship he had given every person onstage. The concert ends with nearly a thousand performers swarming the auditorium in a heart-stopping arrangement of "Sunday" from *Sunday in the Park with George*. Weeping, Steve clung to Paul when he reached the stage as the room erupted with a raucous rendition of "Happy Birthday."

It is unlikely that that birthday celebration will ever be beat.

CHAPTER THIRTY-ONE

Film Projects

There is a reason that so exacting a master as Stephen Sondheim has insisted on working with the inimitable Paul Gemignani over so many years and collaborations—Paul has the impeccable precision and ear of the finest conductors—and an infallible drummer's pulse—but his main thing is his heart. It's the first thing you meet in the morning rehearsal, that beam of positivity that somehow he sustains throughout the day—that gives artists room to breathe, create, fail, and ultimately surf the high of a great session. Everyone looked forward to the music rehearsals, and it was largely because of the embrace of his enveloping optimism. He was a taskmaster and slid over nothing, but it was in the spirit of sharing confidence; the confidence he had in you to meet this great music where it dovetailed with your own voice and unique experience. I watched him do this over and over with every actor, and the gift of lifting from an artist the best they have, well, no wonder Steve keeps him close. He is a treasure. And try as I might to figure out how he does what he does, I can't say I am able to effectively parse it out from my memory of our sessions. I just know I went home after a day's work less tired than when I went in in the morning—elevated by the music, his shared delivery of it with us, and his unflagging spirit. This is a man that loves what he does, and that energy is irresistible.

*—*MERYL STREEP (ACTOR, SINGER)

While Paul is rightfully considered a master of live theatrical performance, he has occasionally dabbled in the world of captured performance. This is a representation of his cinematic footprint.

Kramer vs. Kramer

Kramer vs. Kramer was Paul's first true film experience outside of the adaptation of *A Little Night Music*. His long-term first trumpet player, Wilmer Wise, had suggested him as conductor for the sonata. Paul and Wilmer had had a long-standing relationship since Wilmer had first subbed in on *A Little Night Music* on Broadway—through Wilmer, he met a number of musicians that he continued to work with decades after Wilmer stepped away from Broadway, including a young Wynton Marsalis, who Wilmer would personally call in as his sub on *Sweeney Todd*.

Reds

In 1981, Paul tackled his most significant film soundtrack recording— *Reds*. An epic historical drama produced, directed, cowritten by, and starring Warren Beatty, it followed an American journalist in Russia during the Bolshevik Revolution. Filming took place across five different countries, and Paul was tasked with maintaining the score, composed by Stephen Sondheim, throughout filming.

Paul and Warren had a wonderful working relationship—Warren was very free-form, and the pair were able to collaborate on the soundscape of the film, with Warren trusting Paul to produce the right tone for the film. Paul made a point of watching the dailies after every shoot day in order to understand the exact tone needed by the music underscoring the scene—since he was unable to perform in tandem with the actors, as he would in a live production, he spent an immense amount of time analyzing the raw footage itself in order to capture the emotion after the fact.

While examining the dailies of a protest scene, Paul noticed a problem with the audio and visual synchronization. They had recorded a chorus singing "The Internationale," the initial anthem of the USSR, and actors had sung over it to make it seem that the twenty extras were actually two hundred strong. While the chorus sounded great, there were moments in the footage where the actors' lips would not match—entire phrases would match exactly, and then the entire group of actors would appear to forget the words at the exact same time, and then sync up together at the same time.

Baffled, Paul called Warren. Somehow, no one on set had realized that the actors were singing the Russian lyrics to "The Internationale" over a Ukrainian recording—while moments of the song synced up, due to the similarity of the two languages, there were entire sequences where everything fell apart visually. With no time to refilm the sequence, Paul had to find a Russian chorus in the United States to rerecord the song with the exact same tempo as the original recording, so as to match the preshot film. Paul, Warren, and several assistants ended up in Philadelphia of all places to record with the Mendelssohn Club, and the sequence was salvaged as a montage that could be cleverly edited.

SOUTH PACIFIC

The 2005 performance of *South Pacific* at Carnegie Hall was one of the most significant highlights of Paul's career. A beloved favorite from a young age, *South Pacific* had always been a musical that had drawn him in, and when PBS called with the idea of doing a *Great Performances* broadcast starring Brian Stokes Mitchell and Reba McEntire, he was immediately intrigued.

Stokes is one of Paul's favorite male performers—he knows just enough about music to be dangerous. They had previously created his solo Carnegie Hall show together, as well as its associated album, and they had developed a shorthand while working that was incredibly effective. Together, they created a new arrangement for "This Nearly Was Mine," one of the seminal songs in Act 2. While they had the original 1949 orchestrations on the music stands of the Orchestra of St. Luke's, Paul and Stokes reinvented moments throughout the song by carefully selecting who would play when and Paul would silence certain instruments, regardless of written orchestration. Changing an arrangement as swiftly as they did is an immensely difficult task, and the fact that the orchestra was able to accommodate them in the moment was a testament to how incredibly disciplined they were in their work, and in their focus on Paul. This unique arrangement of "This Nearly Was Mine" has gone on to be one of the highlights of the 2005 recording, as one of the moments that made the production feel fresh, unlike many musical readings.

Reba was the best Nellie Paul could have ever hoped to have worked with. She had a sunshiney Southern optimism that made her perfect for the cockeyed optimist, and her chemistry with Stokes made the show feel brand new—in the decades that had followed the original success of *South Pacific*, a performance tradition had been formed that aligned closely with the original interpretations of Mary Martin and Ezio Pinza—Paul, Stokes, and Reba made the collective decision to throw out those half-a-century-old line readings, and they worked on the piece as if it was a completely new musical, breathing fresh life into it that positively sparkled.

It was an immensely quick process—they had two weeks to rehearse before the show was presented, book in hand, before paying audiences at Carnegie Hall. Audiences went wild. At the end of "This Nearly Was Mine," the orchestra tapped on their stands, applauding Paul and Stokes in a gesture of respect and admiration that is extremely rare in the world of musical theatre—while it is tradition at some classical venues such as the Metropolitan Opera to applaud the first run of a production from the stand, this type of celebration is rare in the middle of a show in between numbers. If you watch the official film release of the concert from PBS, you can see the violin section tapping swiftly as the audience roars.

After filming, Mary Rodgers approached Paul with tears in her eyes. The eldest daughter of Richard Rodgers, she embraced Paul and affirmed how deeply Richard would have appreciated the production, nearly bowling Paul over. For his efforts he received the Primetime Emmy Award for Outstanding Music Direction in 2006, the highest competitive award for music direction.

Fledgling plans for the future were made with the idea of a full-scale revival starring Stokes and Reba, alongside Jason Danieley, who had played Lieutenant Cable, but funding unfortunately fell through.

SWEENEY TODD

Twenty-five years after working on the original *Sweeney Todd*, Paul was called to Sondheim's house to talk to film director Tim Burton about a movie adaptation. It was to be Burton's first live-action musical (excluding his reimagining of *Charlie and the Chocolate Factory*), and it was important to him that the show was translated correctly. With Paul on board to music-direct and supervise, and with Sondheim's blessing, the film took off like a shot, starring Johnny Depp, Helena Bonham Carter, Alan Rickman, Sacha Baron Cohen, and Jaime Campbell Bower. Burton was committed to doing the film as much like a Broadway production as possible, and the majority of the cast rehearsed in London, after which Paul would fly to New York to rehearse Alan Rickman, and to Los Angeles to rehearse Johnny Depp and Sacha Baron Cohen before the beginning of production. These weekly trips were nearly overwhelming, and Paul racked up more frequent flyer miles working on the film than he had in the thirty-six years of his career prior. At the end of the rehearsal period, rather than having a sitzprobe as a standard musical production would have, Paul recorded with the orchestra sans performers, and the cast then recorded their vocals over those tracks. This approach is not uncommon in recording movie musicals, as it gives the director the most control in selecting takes—by having each performer record separately, difficult moments can be pinpointed and perfected without having to worry about the best take for one person containing a mistake from another. Unfortunately, this method can make true unity between performers difficult.

In a film musical, the role of a musical director is quite different than in a theatrical musical. A film has a principal recording supervisor, who handles the day-to-day work and the postproduction—in *Sweeney Todd*, and later *Into the Woods* and *Mary Poppins Returns*, Paul's partner was Mike Higham, a brilliant musician in his own right. Once Paul's work is complete in rehearsal, Mike takes over putting the pieces together. Paul's final responsibility on *Sweeney* following the tricoastal rehearsals was conducting the orchestra over which the voices of the cast were layered.

No expenses were spared in capturing the epic sonic scale of *Sweeney Todd* for the film. A seventy-eight-piece orchestra was hired, as opposed to the original twenty-seven, and Jonathan Tunick reorchestrated the entire score for the film. The multiday process was exhaustive, with multiple takes of almost every song recorded so as to have options available. The workload was immense, as was the timeline. Paul, ever the professional, was able to guide the orchestra through the swells of the score and adeptly used the sheer force of the increased number, who followed him eagerly. At the close of recording, Paul, Jonathan, and Steve received a raucous six-minute standing ovation from the orchestra.

While every song in the stage show was recorded, the majority of the ballads ended up on the cutting room floor—the pacing of the film had to be swifter than the three-hour stage show, and the dramatic function of songs such as the opening "Ballad of Sweeney Todd" (and Paul's whistle) made less sense than cutting straight to the cinematic action. All was not lost, however, as the orchestral recordings Paul had made of the ballads were used as underscoring for the scenes of dialogue, keeping the music flowing consistently throughout the entire film. What had started around Sondheim's piano had turned into a cultural touchstone of a musical, and the film went on to make more than $150 million worldwide.

This was not the only full-circle moment *Sweeney Todd* brought into Paul's life in the early 2000s. In 2005, Alexander took on the role of the Beadle in John Doyle's inventive revival of the show, with the performers playing their own instruments onstage rather than having an orchestra in the pit. The infant who had been born in the midst of the original production had grown to take on the role that had given the team such trouble in the original casting.

INTO THE WOODS

Into the Woods was a glorious time. There are many different ways of producing a movie musical, and Rob Marshall's method is exactly how Paul prefers to work—he rehearses his productions as though they were going to be a live show, and the music is given a true weight. They make three separate vocal recordings so as to have options in the editing booth—they record the song once, live as if it were a cast recording, twice, with the performers singing over a perfect orchestral track created by Paul, and thrice, with the performers singing on set over the tracks as they perform the scene itself.

By having these options, it makes it significantly easier to make the right choice—there is no such thing as a perfect take with a bung note. The songs are rehearsed and recorded so many times that come filming, the performers know exactly where the bull's-eye is, and any of the recordings can be dubbed over should the need arise, which makes it much easier to combine the best vocal take and the best acting take. Many of the clinical problems of prerecording are also removed in this process—when everyone records the songs together, after rehearsing them together, there is significantly less disconnect than when a vocalist records their half of a duet independent from their vocal partner.

The cast of *Into the Woods* was a delightful group—in particular, Emily Blunt, Meryl Streep, and Christine Baranski kept smiles and laughter flowing throughout the process. After having worked with Rob as a performer on *The Rink*, it was a wonderful full-circle moment to come together on *Into the Woods*, and he quickly climbed Paul's personal list of favorite collaborators after their experience creating *Into the Woods* together.

MARY POPPINS RETURNS
Mary Poppins Returns was one of those projects where the colleagues make the experience. David Krane, a longtime collaborator of Paul's, arranged the dance music and underscoring. A lovely man, he worked closely with Paul to polish the piece's music as brightly as possible, like they had on productions of *Big*, *She Loves Me*, *The Adventures of Tom Sawyer*, and *110 in the Shade*. Reuniting with Emily Blunt and Meryl Streep was a blessing, and working with Lin-Manuel Miranda and Ben Whishaw was a joy—in particular, Ben brought a fresh approach to his first musical that was infectious, and it reminded Paul of how much fun a project can be when seen through the eyes of a first timer.

Unfortunately, Paul was unable to reunite with Angela Lansbury when she was brought in to portray the Balloon Lady after Julie Andrews turned down the end-of-the-film cameo. Due to Angela's schedule, he created a track for her to record separately from him, and he was unable to sneak onto the set to see her forty-five years after they had first worked together on *Sondheim: A Musical Tribute*.

CHAPTER THIRTY-TWO

Kiss Me, Kate 2019

The job of a music director is so big that it's almost impossible to be equally good at every facet of it. Conducting, yes, but also shaping and forming the piece, speaking the language of musicians, choreographers, directors, producers, and actors—requiring you to be part teacher, colleague, taskmaster, consensus builder, and psychiatrist, and of course all of the administrative duties. It is the only job that has these different roles: department head, member of the creative team, and on top of that, performer. Paul is good at all of it. He amazes me. People can be quick to judge music directors only on the part of the job they see, that is, the head bobbing in the pit, but the fact is it's a huge job. I am amazed at the way Paul goes about it, and I learn a lot when I work with him.

—ERIC STERN (MUSIC DIRECTOR, ARRANGER)

PAUL RETURNED TO BROADWAY ONE FINAL TIME. THE ROUNDABOUT Theatre Company had done a gala presentation of *Kiss Me, Kate* in 2016 with a star-studded cast, and its reception had been strong enough that they had decided to make it a full production. The gala's music director had other obligations, and at Scott Ellis's request Paul was brought on to music-direct *Kiss Me, Kate* for the second time, with a cast already compiled and ready to go.

It was mostly a straightforward second revival—the version of the show that was available to be licensed was the version with the adjustments Paul, John Guare, and Michael Blakemore had made in 1999, and Paul was able to maintain those prior decisions, and fight for more wide-sweeping changes. What had been borderline acceptable in 1999 was blatant in 2019, and Amanda Green (daughter of Adolph Green) was recruited to heal the most troubling aspects of the book, with lyrics and scenes adjusted to be more appropriate. One song in particular proved troublesome—"Always True to You in My Fashion" had played amazing in the original production and had gone over as a coyly sexy number in 1999, but by 2019 it dragged and fell inward under the weight of its own contrivance. The team worked closely with the piece to shorten and rework it into a moment of performative humor, and the wonderful Warren Carlyle filled the number with eye-catching choreography to distract from poorly aged lyrics.

Lois, the character who sings "Always True," can be difficult to cast. A sex kitten gone mainstream, her chemistry with her gambling-addict boyfriend Bill has to be passionately turbulent without ever taking away from the core love story of Lilli and Fred. Both Bill and Lois are the more adult edges of the earnestly romantic piece, and they have become the harder characters to cast as time has gone on. Corbin Bleu and Stephanie Styles were brought on to reinterpret the pair, with a more teasing energy applied to scenes that had previously teetered on the line of being toxic.

Kelli O'Hara headed the 2019 revival of *Kiss Me, Kate* as Lilli, carrying the torch from Marin marvelously, as Will Chase took over for Brian Stokes Mitchell. Both supremely talented, they swiftly stepped into their roles as the show came together around them. A role like Lilli had several potential vocal pitfalls for a performer, but O'Hara navigated them without so much as a worry on Paul's end. Unfortunately, that could not be said of the entire company.

Paul knows when a person is lip-syncing. The musculature of the throat gives it away to a trained eye almost immediately, even when an untrained audience member would have no idea. During the run of the revival, one of the supporting players in the show began lip-syncing the opening and closing numbers, with little physical and facial gags thrown to the audience in an attempt to garner a laugh instead of singing the vocal line they were supposed to be on. Paul went backstage to talk it out with the player, assuming they were having vocal fatigue after having had vocal stamina problems earlier in the run. The performer denied lip-syncing, and Paul was left to question his hearing as he watched the following two performances, where the performer continued to mouth along to the opening and closing. This was no small matter. Music had guided Paul's life since before he could properly form memory, and the idea that he might be losing his hearing was a deep, foundation-shattering fear. Finally, Paul had the sound designer single out the performer's microphone in his headphones so he could listen to them in isolation—they were producing no sound.

With this irrefutable evidence, Paul again went to the performer, explaining the problem in their dressing room in private. Paul is more than willing to work with performers when there are vocal issues—there are a number of potential fixes, including changing the line they sing to a more comfortable place, such as moving a soprano down to the alto line, or if that was too strenuous, Paul could have given them outright permission to lip-sync along. He had done it before—in *On the Twentieth Century*, strategic mouthing had been what had gotten the company through the stratospheric score unscathed. No matter what Paul did, the performer refused to admit that they weren't singing, even when confronted with the evidence.

Paul, and other music directors, cannot help someone if they refuse to admit there is a problem. He is more than willing to accommodate a performer's needs, but to blatantly lie to his face was the quickest way the performer could ensure that Paul would never hire them again. Theatre is collaborative, and a lone wolf "I'll tough it out" strategy hurts everyone involved.

Outside of that thorn, Paul had a wonderful time revisiting *Kiss Me, Kate*. It was, and is, the kind of show that exemplifies why he got into the business—gorgeous music, fantastic performers, and a great working environment. At the same time, Alexander began work on the 2019 revival of *West Side Story*, as a music director. After a decades-long career as an actor (garnering a Tony nomination for his work in *Carousel*), he had returned to the pit, picking up the baton as his father prepared to set it aside. As Paul had begun to say no to upcoming projects, Alexander had said yes, and Alex became the go-to music director for the Sondheim canon.

As Paul settled into one more Broadway run, he tried to focus on the moments of joy—the bustle backstage at half hour, the knowing glances from onstage friends, and the pristine silence of the theatre in the hour he spent sitting in the orchestra section, long before anyone else had arrived. After fifty years, the theatre still held the magic of possibility for him. It was also bittersweet.

Marin Mazzie, immense talent, compassionate collaborator, and dear friend, passed away from ovarian cancer on September 13, 2018, shortly before the revival of *Kiss Me, Kate* went into rehearsals. Paul had loved her, as had anyone who had ever known her—she radiated kindness and curiosity and had been the epitome of strength in the community, performing until only a few short weeks before her death. She had lived up to her middle name until the end—Joy.

The creative team had created what is called a star's entrance for *Kiss Me, Kate* in 1999—Lilli walks onstage, and the motion around her stops, allowing time for the audience to applaud as the actress takes the stage with grace. In the 2019 revival, a clothing rack filled with Marin's costumes was whisked in front of a door before revealing Kelli O'Hara as Lilli, wearing the same hat Marin had worn for her star entrance twenty years prior. Every night, Paul played the show's opening, "Another Op'nin Another Show," and looked out at these pieces of Marin, tethering his past to his future. He had outlived yet another collaborator, the final vicar tending the fire long after the cathedral had begun to crumble.

Exactly one month after the closing of *Kiss Me, Kate* came the shattering news that Hal Prince had passed away. After a short illness, he had passed in Keflavik, Iceland, with little fanfare or warning—Paul had learned of his death when he had read his obituary in *The New York Times* the following morning. There had been no calls or condolences, only the stark finality of the newsprint.

For all of their disagreements and disillusions, Paul had loved Hal. He had been more than just a colleague, and far more than just a boss. What they had built, alongside Stephen Sondheim and Jonathan Tunick, had been utterly remarkable. They had influenced the sound of the American musical in ways unheard of since the work of Oscar Hammerstein II, and it was the theatre created by Prince that had attracted Paul to the musical theatre in the first place, when he had first seen *Cabaret* all those years ago. Even after the door had been shut following the *Roza* debacle, he had continued sending Christmas cards and congratulations notes to Hal every year and for every production, knowing that Hal would send a short thank-you note regardless of their professional detachment. While they had only actually spoken in person a handful of times after 1987, Paul had never given up hope that a resolution might one day be achieved—unfortunately, they simply ran out of time.

In some ways, Hal's death was the perfect conclusion to his life—he had been able to truly live up to the end, traveling around the world checking on productions and making grand plans for potential revivals and new shows. Hal was the kind of person who simply needed his work—he needed something new and exciting to dig into, and he had never willingly stepped back, even as he had passed age ninety. His final production, *Prince of Broadway*, had been a retrospective revue, much in the fashion established by *Jerome Robbins' Broadway*. Everyone had expected him to continue on like his mentor, George Abbott, who had opened his final show at the age of one hundred.

When Hal passed at age ninety-one, it was his last surprise.

Chapter Thirty-Three

On Fathers and Sons

BY ALEXANDER GEMIGNANI

I CAN DISTINCTLY REMEMBER A LUNCH TABLE FULL OF ELEMENTARY school kids laughing at me when I was asked to explain what my dad did for a living. I was in the second grade and when I said "music director" and was met with a sea of perplexed faces, I defiantly stood up and imitated what conducting looked like. And they all laughed, because it looked silly.

And it is! It is silly. Stand up with a little white stick in your hand and wave your arms around, sway from side to side and . . . dance in place. For a living. That's silly. Or perhaps deeply vulnerable.

As I lifted my baton as music director and conductor of the 2019 revival of *West Side Story*, I remembered that lunchroom. The orchestra was vamping the "Promenade" as the Sharks and Jets ominously circled the stage; Gladhand blew the whistle, and in that split second of silence before the drums kicked in for "Mambo," I realized: *Yes! Silliness is the key!* It has to have flow, freedom, and, above all, vulnerability. It has to be expressive, intense, and jovial or you simply aren't doing it correctly.

As I sat down to write this, I was trying to distill the experience of what it's like watching my dad conduct and lead a show from the pit. And "vulnerability" is the word that kept coming to mind. I'm not sure how teachable it is with words, but if you watch Dad do it, it's like nothing else. And that's true artistry, isn't it? Not having anything in the way between you and the art; a free flow of point of view and expression.

That is why people (including me) continue to hunger to work with my father. The child-like joy he brings to being that vessel of musical communication. The vulnerability, effervescence, and unedited flow of musical expression that allows a show to sparkle and groove.

I realized in that "Mambo" moment that the most important thing my father taught me about music direction, more than the business advice and more than the love of musicians and actors, is that you cannot be afraid to bring your full self to the music. If you work fearlessly and vulnerably from that childlike place, you will get the very best out of your collaborators and the process can be magical.

Dad is fond of saying, while flapping his right hand up and down: "this little stick doesn't make any noise." Well, I respectfully disagree; I have always been able to hear the music coming from him.

BY AUGUST DANNEHL

Whenever I'm asked about Paul, and I eagerly launch into the story of how he became my stepfather at age twelve, I am reminded of a simple yet powerful lesson his presence in my life has taught me. It's a value that has guided me both in and out of the entertainment business, but can be best summed up by a principle that will likely resonate with anyone reading this book: The show must go on.

Paul taught me not only about the importance of having goals, but having the tenacity and dedication it takes to achieve them. Just as a show's company exhibits preparedness and adaptability to ensure the curtain goes up on every performance, Paul has inspired me (and countless others) to work hard, stay focused, and, above all else, believe in myself and my aspirations.

When the Twin Towers fell in 2001 and our community reeled in the wake of death and destruction, Paul and the rest of Broadway fought to keep the doors open and the lights on. They made sacrifices and banded together to stay true to that inherent principle; the show must go on. As a young high school student with aspirations to attend New York University film school, I was inspired by their response to the tragic events of 9/11 and considered ways to join the cause. After a motivational discussion with Paul and some insight into his own military experience, I decided to put college on hold and join the Navy—a decision that would change the rest of my life.

I am incredibly lucky to have had Paul as a father figure. His unique combination of empathy, work ethic, and imperviousness to bullshit pulls out the best in all of us. And like the countless performers and musicians Paul has mentored over the years, I can attest to just how crucial his support and direction has been in my life.

Since Paul became my stepdad at such a pivotal time in my childhood, I often think about what his life was like at that age. He was not born into this business (as I was) nor did his parents nurture his inherent talents or passion for music. Even though he was choosing a career field already rife with disappointment, struggle, and emotional tumult, Paul didn't let his parents' passivity deter him from following his dreams. It is, again, an example of the most important lesson I've learned from Paul Gemignani—no matter who doubts you, no matter what obstacles you face, no matter how hard or seemingly impossible the journey becomes, the show must go on.

CHAPTER THIRTY-FOUR
The Importance of Collaboration

THERE IS NO CREATION WITHOUT COLLABORATION. IT TAKES FULL COMmitment from every member of a team to create a worthwhile product. This is not only true for the arts—think back to grade school, and the dreaded group projects. Which turned out the best—the ones where everyone did their part and talked through the presentation beforehand, or the ones where half of the team flaked and a few members were left to carry the project on their backs?

That same concept carries through to every single industry—business meetings, surgical consults, even social media networks all rely on collaboration. When a person isolates themselves, the system breaks down. Human beings are inherently social creatures, and whatever work we may produce alone is almost universally outweighed by the work we can do together.

This collaborative empathy is the core of what it takes to make a musical. A distinct understanding of the moving parts around you can completely change how you approach a project, for the better. Below is an outline of the hands a musical will pass through before being presented to the public—while it is not an exhaustive list (and there are alternative routes to theatrical success, especially in the age of the internet), take the time to familiarize yourself with every stage involved in this traditional collaborative process for Broadway.

*Either a **book writer**, a **lyricist**, or a **composer** will get an idea— sometimes these positions are held by the same person (Stephen*

Sondheim is both a composer and a lyricist) but often times, they are three distinct roles (consider Betty Comden, Adolph Green, and Cy Coleman). That idea can come from almost anywhere—in the twenty-first century, movies have become popular fodder for inspiration, but anything from a good book to an overheard conversation on the train can be the spark of creation.

These three can labor over the initial creative stages for years. Somewhere within that time frame, a **producer** (or producers) will become involved. A producer is the person in charge of raising the money needed to put on the show. They are the business part of show business, and it is their job to make sure the show is able to exist outside of the original three's minds, by bringing **backers** on board. Backers are essentially investors—they put money into a show in hopes that it is a success, and that they make a profit.

Once enough money has been raised to get a project on its feet, a larger creative team will get involved. A **director** is essentially the boss of how a show looks—they decide who goes where on the stage and are often the deciding factor on important decisions down the road. Some directors are also producers (such as Hal Prince), but that combination is becoming increasingly rare as musicals become more and more expensive to put on. A **choreographer** is in charge of the dance throughout the show (if there is any) and both directors and choreographers will have a number of **associates or assistants** throughout the entire process.

An **orchestrator** will be hired in order to flesh out the composer's work, and a **dance arranger** will communicate with the orchestrator, the composer, and the choreographer to underscore dance sequences. A **music copyist** (such as Katharine Edmonds) works hand in hand with the orchestrator and the composer to write out a rehearsal score prior to the fully orchestrated copy. A **music director** will work with every person previously mentioned to make sure everyone is collaborating in such a way to make the music sound as good as possible. It has become increasingly common for a show to bring on a **dramaturg**, who handles the history and research for the production, and a **dialect** *coach* may be brought on if specific accents are utilized throughout the production.

A **music contractor** *(who is occasionally the same person as the music director) will hire* **musicians** *to play for the production—this can range from a pianist and a violinist to a full symphonic orchestra, depending on the show's needs and budget. These musicians then have a* **house contractor** *(such as Roger Shell on* She Loves Me*), who serves as the liaison between the company and the musicians' union. There are union representatives throughout the company for the* **fourteen different unions** *involved in putting on a musical (the Broadway League negotiates agreements between these unions).*

A **casting director** *is brought on to cast the* **actors** *and any other associated performers—if there are children in a show, you will need* **child wranglers***, animals need their own* **specialty handlers***, and if there is a special acrobatic track in your show, you need to cast a* **stunt performer***.*

Of course, no actors or musicians are hired until you know what you are rehearsing for, meaning you need a **theatre owner***, a* **general manager***, a* **company manager***, a* **production stage manager***, and a* **stage manager***. If you have any special technical moments in your show, you will need a dedicated* **technical supervisor***, and perhaps a* **fly rig operator***. If there is any movement that is not dance, that is put together by a* **fight director** *(such as Rick Sordelet).*

While the performers are rehearsing and getting the show on its feet, the design team works diligently to create the production around the performances. A **set designer***, a* **lighting designer***, a* **costume designer***, and a* **sound designer** *are the bare minimum. Those four will almost always have a number of assistants, and a costume designer likely has an entire costume team, ranging from* **pattern makers** *to* **sewers** *to* **dressers***, who are all intimately involved in getting garments on performers. A design team will have a number of* **electricians***,* **carpenters***,* **technicians***,* **painters***, and* **engineers** *involved. Broadway productions also have a* **hair and wig designer** *and a* **makeup designer***. (Fun little piece of trivia—you are almost* *never seeing a performer's actual hair onstage if it is long. Even if it looks like their real hair, chances are that it is a custom-built wig to maintain consistency. Productions can have more than a hundred wigs, depending on the grandeur of the show and the number of costume changes.)*

*Once a show exits rehearsals and moves into a theatre, a whole new crop of people come into play. You have the **box office staff** handling tickets, the **front of house staff** handling audience members, the **merchandise workers** hawking any souvenirs, **bartenders** selling refreshments, and **ushers** seating patrons. Backstage you have **stagehands, props masters, wardrobe supervisors**, and the **doorman**, who serves as the barrier between the show and the outside world.*

*A show requires publicity, meaning there will be a **photographer**, a **videographer**, a **publicist**, and numerous **creative directors** involved. Performers often have **agents**, **managers**, and **publicists** of their own who are involved closely in the publicity process, and promotional events may be arranged outside of the show, which require additional work from everyone involved.*

That is sixty-five separate jobs before a production even reaches opening night. It is, frankly, a miracle that a musical ever comes to fruition. The jobs bolded here are far from the only jobs involved—almost all of these positions have assistants, associates, or partners. It takes 130 people to put on a single performance of *The Phantom of the Opera* on Broadway.

Don't let this knowledge weigh on you—while it can seem insurmountable when you're in the early stages, with only one or two collaborators, this is actually very good news. Why?

No matter who you are in the chain of command, you are never alone. No one makes a decision without someone by their side. In Paul's music department, he is constantly collaborating with his musicians, the assistant conductor, the orchestrator, the music copyist, the dance arranger, and the sound department before he then works with the director, the choreographer, or any other member of the creative team. There is no such thing as an isolated incident—everyone is interwoven to create an artistic tapestry that has seemingly no end and no beginning—it is why it is so difficult to pin down exactly who came up with things when questioned years after the fact.

For example, take the 2004 revival of *Assassins*. At the end of the "Ballad of Guiteau," Joe Mantello instructed Denis O'Hare to climb the stairs to the gallows in order to end the song. Denis, listening to the new bouncy arrangement Michael Starobin had written, decided to dance his way up the stairs. Joe liked that moment, and the choice stayed in. The number of stairs in the staircase designed by set designer Robert Brill determined exactly how Denis could dance up the set, and their shallow and rickety design made the moment appear even more dangerous. The lighting designer put a spotlight on Denis to emphasize his movement to the audience, and Paul closely watched Denis's every move to make sure the music matched exactly with what he was doing—when he stomped his feet, he was supported by the musicians on either side of the boxes in Studio 54. When he ascended the staircase to "heaven" and is finally hanged out of view of the audience, a fake body outfitted by the costume department and put together by the props department was dropped from the rafters by stagehands, following the music cue and the call from the stage manager, who had been timing everything onstage exactly in order to make the moment go off without a hitch.

That is one moment in one song in one musical—winding collaborative stories like that one exist for almost every second of your favorite show. In order to operate in the theatrical industry (or in any industry), you need to understand and have a respect for every single person working around you. The doorman is just as important as the producer when it comes to creating a full-circle, healthy working experience, and no person's opinion is inherently better or worse than someone else's. Listen to everyone, and share your own ideas with everyone, because it is in that mix that real excellence is brewed.

CHAPTER THIRTY-FIVE

Advice to Artists

ADVICE IS ALWAYS SUBJECTIVE AND SELECTIVE—WHAT WORKS FOR ONE person may not work for another, and oftentimes circumstances dictate what can actually be applied from one person's life experience to another. The following are ten core truths that have guided Paul throughout his career—take whatever resonates with you.

1. Always believe in yourself.
   You have value. Do not lose sight of that core fact. You are, inherently, enough, and you deserve to be in whatever room you work your way into. Your ideas have merit, and your experiences give you a breadth of knowledge different from anyone else.

2. Trust what you feel.
   You need to trust yourself. If any inventor stuck strictly to the rules, we would have no innovation—it is the same in the arts. There are no rules when it comes to creation.

3. Take all the advice seriously, and discard whatever doesn't help you.
   You will come up against many, many experts who may or may not be giving you the correct advice for you. When you're young and inexperienced, the tendency is to take everything people tell you as gospel. Take in all of the advice that you possibly can, process it all, but when push comes to shove you need to take the part that speaks to you and throw out the rest.

4. Don't just learn your job. Learn what everyone is doing around you. Be observant about what happens around you. Be ready to do the job of whoever is above you or next to you. Understand what the lighting team does, or the sound team, or anyone else—understand the machine as a whole. When you know the how and why of everything else, the role of the music becomes crystal clear. Don't isolate yourself, you are a conduit.

5. Never forget the reason you're doing what you're doing.
When you get frustrated, when you're spending more time working your survival job than doing anything with your art, when you go to endless auditions and never get in, remember why you're doing this. You have no choice when the love pours out of your marrow. There's a reason you slog through the bullshit. Your soul and your heart know where you should be and what your voice is, and you need to trust it. When everyone tries to take that away from you, remember you're the boss of your own attitude.

6. Don't stop working until you are satisfied with yourself and the results. You can always go back, but if you give up you will never know what's ahead of you. If you have an ambition to do something, don't quit halfway up the ladder because "I can deal with this being my peak." Don't give up halfway, keep climbing until you either can't anymore or your intuition tells you that you have found the right stopping place.

7. Listen to all criticism or suggestions as if it were not about your work before brushing it off.
One of the things that is difficult about the arts is that everyone has an opinion, and there aren't many empirical facts. People tend to listen to their own opinions, but there is nothing wrong with listening to others and agreeing with their opinion. We argue to defend ourselves, but there is no forward motion without trying other ideas. No one is an island. You gain so much more knowledge toward solving a problem by letting everyone share their sides, and

finding a way to combine the ideas at play. Don't talk over each other to feel valuable and smart.

8. See all sides of a conflict.
One of the best things you can do is learn to listen. We all think we listen, but we don't, especially if we are eager and impetuous and have lots of opinions. You have to learn to listen and not just hear.
Every job is not your dream job. Plain and simple. Your hands will end up tied, and one of the hardest parts of being an artist is when you have to give your all to a process that isn't quite clicking. You have to muster the same energy and creative spirit as you would for your favorite project in the world, and the key to navigating these difficulties is actively listening to those around you. You're all in the same hole—it is up to you if you'll climb out bloody or brave.

9. Never stop working to be better than you are. The best is relative. Don't ever stop working for yourself. Be the best in your own eyes. Your satisfaction is the mark of success, not any other metric.

10. No matter what else you do, *always* follow your heart. It speaks your truth and you should always listen to it.
Your intuition is your foundation—it is what makes you, you. It can go by many names—intuition, instinct, the still small voice, a sixth sense. That inner voice pushes you where you need to go—trust it. Don't trust others' claims that you will be a failure, trust the voice inside of you.

Security has many different definitions. Security can be physical safety and trust. Security can also be financial stability and comfort. Above all, when you consider security as a personal endeavor, consider this definition: Security is happiness. Contentment. A cat sitting in a window purring is security—it is where it wants to be doing what it wants to do.

If Paul had lived by his parents' definition of security, he would have lived out his life as a high school music teacher in California. By trusting his heart, he found his own security in the theatre.

Only you can define what makes up your personal security. Only you can assign value to your own experiences. It is your life to lead, and your responsibility to decide on your own definition.

CHAPTER THIRTY-SIX

The Interpretive Artist

IN OUR MODERN WORLD, AN INCREDIBLE PREMIUM HAS BEEN PUT ON creative arts—ingenuity, invention, and ideas are the name of the proverbial game, with an artist judged based on how unexpected or unique their creation is. To create something wholly new is often the aim—the idea of the mythic artistic genius, who creates masterworks free of outside inspiration is a narrative that many cling to, valuing this individualistic idea as the pinnacle of artistic achievement.

This framework leaves out the incredibly critical work done by interpretive artists such as Paul. In the musical theatre, there are only a small handful of true creative artists—the composer, the lyricist, and the book writer. Every other person on the project, from the design team to the director, is an interpretive artist. They take what has been created by the creators and evolve it into a living and breathing piece of art. An orchestrator takes the original score and fleshes it out to fill the space with music; the choreographer takes that music and devises movement to it; the music director takes that orchestration and that choreography and creates a cohesive whole in order to support the performers; the performers elevate the work done by everyone who came before them in the chain to actualize the story into a physical piece of storytelling.

Every single link in this chain is important. From the assistant who copyedits dialogue to the designer who makes massive visual decisions based on the core material from the creators, it takes clear communication and drive from every member to create a piece of good theatre. A transcendent production is one that understands and embraces this collaboration. So why is it that the American theatrical industry so consistently buys into the lone-genius theory of an artist?

In short, it is because it is a compelling story. Human beings love the idea of individualism—stories of heroes and villains populate the oldest stories on record, and the idea that one person could have a profound impact is one that many people subscribe to in an attempt to define human worth. This is particularly true of American society. This individual-first attitude, rather than a community outlook, can be found in everything from children's bedtime stories to political discourse, with every aspect of American society affected by where they fall on the spectrum of individualism. America is a country obsessed with legacy, and the American theatre is no different.

When Paul received his Lifetime Achievement Award from the Antoinette Perry Awards in 2001, he was the first music director to be awarded a Tony Award since Shepard Coleman had received the final Tony Award for Best Conductor and Musical Director in 1964, for *Hello Dolly!* The category was then discontinued due to a lack of interest from the general public and a belief that it was impossible to single out the work of a music director in order to evaluate it.

Paul received his award only due to an immense amount of pressure being put on the awarding committee by Luther Henderson, a fellow music director. In 1996, Paul and a team of musicians had successfully lobbied the committee to instate the Tony Award for Best Orchestrations, by making the argument that an orchestrator's work could be judged based on the reading of the score, since the nominators refused to consider orchestrations a living art form—that credit they gave to the composer via the Best Score award. Of course, for every Tony Award that Stephen Sondheim ever won for Best Score, he made a point of celebrating his collaborators for bringing the score to life. Even as he openly acknowledged this inherent truth, that it takes more than one person to breathe life into a piece of music, orchestrators and music directors had been shut out from being awarded—should a production win Best Musical, Best Revival of a Musical, or Best Original Score, they are not one of the members of the creative team who are awarded.

Paul's fight on behalf of orchestrators sent a ripple through the industry—musicians had, across the board, been trained to keep their head down in regards to the respect that comes with recognition. As the most powerful music director in the business, Paul was perhaps the only person with the cache to make the stand that he did. He had built up decades of personal and professional respect across the entire industry and had used that power to uplift the theatrical community as a whole by championing the role of the orchestrator.

It was on these grounds that Luther Henderson fought for Paul's Lifetime Achievement Award. Paul had revolutionized the role of the music director and had been left unrecognized for his contributions to twenty Tony Award–winning musicals. Luther's passionate plea worked just enough to get Paul his statue, but during the ceremony, Paul's speech was cut from public broadcast, as it was deemed unimportant to the proceedings.

His speech, printed here for the first time, went as follows.

Thank you, I'm breathing. I love the theatre. I love actors. I love performers. It is why I went into it. This is a great honor. I have to thank some people really quickly, or Elliot will start to play.

Elliot Lawrence, who had brought Paul back from the brink of being a school bus driver, was conducting the orchestra at the ceremony.

The two guys that gave me—or gave a bebop drummer from California—a good job in this town when we first started. One of them has gone to that great orchestra pit in the sky, and his name was Hal Hastings. And the other one is back there—you can't see him yet but you will, the musicians are on the stage for a change, is Elliot Lawrence.

I'd also like to thank the musicians that have worked for me over the years, that are usually in a hole—actually, where you people are.

Paul points directly at the camera crews pushed up against the lip of the stage.

Usually in a hole that nobody ever sees. They are great artists, they are very committed to the theatre, and you know? This little white stick makes no noise without them. So, if you wouldn't mind thanking them for me, I would appreciate it.

Uproarious applause.

Now there are two other gentlemen in my life, that without them I wouldn't be standing here. One of them has helped more young artists than I know of, I don't know anybody else who has helped as many young artists as this man has, he still is helping them, he is still doing new musicals by people you've never heard of, he is still helping chore- ographers who you've never heard of, he is still helping young musical directors who you've never heard of, and his name is Hal Prince.

The other person, who has fed my musical soul since I met him in 1971, and has kept me honest, taught me so much, and made me care about music more than I thought I could, is Steve Sondheim.

Paul begins to cry as the audience applauds once more. After settling himself, he throws a winking aside to the front row of the audience, many of whom were performers he had worked with.

I just want to say I'm glad I'm usually down there because this is really hard.

I just want to say thank you to all of you, for all of the people that I've worked with. You're all great and I love you all. And without my family—Augie, Alexander, and beloved Derin, none of this would matter. Thanks very much.

Paul's tears were not for himself, or for his own legacy. He had not gotten into the industry with any expectations of awards or commenda- tions—this was no long-awaited day or finally achieved dream. His tears were for every member of the theatrical community who never had the chance to stand on that stage. Every musician, every conductor, every stagehand, every technician, and every single backstage worker deserves to be recognized for their work toward creating a piece of theatre. While Paul's award may bear his name, in reality it should be etched with the names of every interpretive artist whose work has been looked over in search of flashier creatives.

Today, as you finish this book and finish learning Paul's story, I ask one simple thing of you.

Thank the interpretive artists in your life. Show appreciation for the people who give their all without recognition. Thank your teachers, your coworkers, anyone who uplifts and supports you as you work toward a common goal.

There is no such thing as a lone success story. Every person's life is a collaboration.

Thank you for acknowledging and experiencing Paul's.

"Dear Paul - Here we are, as always: you as Jesus Christ and me as Mephistopheles. Love, Steve."

PHOTO BY RIVKA KATVAN

CODA

Here's to Us! Who's Like Us? Damn Few!

ON NOVEMBER 26, 2021, IN THE EARLY HOURS OF A GENTLE DAY AT HIS Roxbury, Connecticut, home, Stephen Joshua Sondheim passed away at the age of 91. News of his death rocketed through the entertainment world as remembrances and recollections were shared worldwide. Within twenty-four hours, a portrait began to emerge of a generous, thoughtful, and deeply inquisitive man, one who had fostered connection and collaboration with almost everyone he came across.

Steve was one of the last members of the "old guard"—that is, those creatives who had been working in American musical theatre before the AIDS crisis ravaged the generation that was to follow them. While many had made incredible art after Sondheim's golden period in the 1970s and 1980s, he had lingered in the minds of devotees across the globe, with the promise of a new show seemingly always on the horizon.

To those who knew him personally, the loss was shattering. Many gathered together to grieve, bonded forever through their experiences working on his art. Members of the Broadway community at large, past and present, paid tribute to the man who had, in many cases, changed their views on music and theatre forever.

When the news reached Paul, he was at home in South Carolina, far from the public mourning that had begun throughout New York City and the rest of the world. To lose Steve was to lose not only a treasured colleague, but a brother or, as Paul had regularly described Steve, his own artistic soul, outside of his body yet tethered all the same. Through Steve's music, Paul had found himself.

In 1973, over their shared drink before Paul had taken over *A Little Night Music* following the death of Harold Hastings, Steve had imparted one simple, seemingly innocuous piece of advice: "Just do what you do." The tender trust of that remark had echoed throughout their entire collaboration and friendship. Steve had never wanted Paul to be anyone but himself, a far cry from the harsh home life he had left behind in California, and in Steve, Paul found a mirror of his musical mind, which markedly proved that he was not, in fact, alone in the world. For fifty years, the pair had moved forward through life, leaving their mark in the annals of musical theatre history. Steve wrote the music; Paul helped to bring it to life.

When asked to describe their bond, Stephen Sondheim struggled. The undisputed master of the lyric and the American stage could not find the words to describe the relationship between himself and Paul: "It can't be expressed. It's like trying to explain why you're in love with somebody. There's no explanation; it just is."

Paul Gemignani, According to His Colleagues

Performers

"It is rare in this business that you meet someone who is incredibly powerful, incredibly talented, incredibly loyal, AND who has the best damn sense of humor! Roll all of those up into one, and you have Paul Gemignani. What a lucky woman I am to have met this man when I was 19 and to still have his friendship at 58. I have so much love and respect for him and can die a happy woman because Paul is in my life."—Donna Marie Asbury

"There is nobody better than Paul. If I ever do another one man show, I want Paul with me. He is the best there is, and I love him to death."—Mario Cantone

"Before I wanted to be an actor, I wanted to be Paul. He was who I wanted to be, and when I'm with him, I am in awe."—Will Chase

"Paul Gemignani has had an enormous influence in my life, since we first met doing 'Sweeney Todd.' He inspires confidence whenever he waves a baton or gives an insightful note about the interpretation of some of the most beautiful and complicated music I have been privileged to originate. 'Assassins' at Playwrights Horizons is most memorable for his looks from the pit as we performed to often bewildered audiences. He was our rock and supplied unconditional support. I treasure my time with him and wish he could be knighted. I love him."—Victor Garber

"Paul is the Rolls Royce of music directors."—Nathan Lane

"Working with Paul on 'Sweeney Todd' was a most memorable highlight in my musical career."—Angela Lansbury

"I met Paul Gemignani in 1990 when I was cast as Sara Jane More in the original production of 'Assassins' Off-Broadway at Playwrights Horizons. This was my first time working with Stephen Sondheim, Jerry Zaks, and Paul. I was scared because I heard that Jerry always fired one person from each of his shows. So, the first time the entire cast met with Paul to learn 'Everybody's Got the Right,' I was convinced I was going to be fired because I don't read music, and this is SONDHEIM! So, Paul teaches the song and then asks if anyone wants to tape it. I shakily raise up my tape recorder, thinking this is it, and then see that the whole cast had also raised up their tape recorders as well. Paul taught me not only how to sing but to interpret the songs. He was the best coach, supporter, and audience, and he did it all with a twinkling eye. Without him, I don't know if I would have gone on to sing in so many musicals. He taught me to sing, and I made him laugh, and we have been friends all of these years. Thank you, Paul. I miss you and love you dearly!"—Debra Monk

"Paul is the most unflappable person. He sits there, taking in life, watching the rest of us release our power through constantly flapping our wings, until everyone else catches up with the answer he knew all along."—Kelli O'Hara

"I love this man. Had he not come into my life I do not think I would have had the gift of the musical career that he was highly responsible in giving birth to. By marrying me to Paul Ford and supporting that relationship, and conducting my solo albums and encouraging me to do them, he launched me on a 30-plus-year journey that defined my life in terms of music. Without him it never would have happened."—Mandy Patinkin

"My strongest memories of Paul go back to 'Merrily We Roll Along,' 1981, when he guided the young cast with a sure and gentle hand. There was understandably a lot of tension running through the cast during our short run. We were so lucky to have his expertise and sense of humor."—Jim Walton

CREATIVE TEAM

"Paul gave me my first Broadway job. As a recent grad (Manhattan School of Music, Class of 1975), having credits in summer stock and one Off-Broadway show, Paul let me audition for him and—on the spot—hired me as rehearsal and pit pianist for 'Pacific Overtures.' We had plenty of good times at the rehearsals at the Jerome Robbins Studio and during the tryouts in Boston and Washington. Though I worked with Paul on two other shows the following year, it was 40 years later that we did 'She Loves Me' and then 'Kiss Me, Kate.' The difference was that, for these recent shows, I served as orchestrator rather than pianist. My favorite moment was during the first orchestra reading of 'She Loves Me.' I had had snuck in a new counterpoint into the final chorus, quoting 'Tonight at Eight' from Act I against the 'She Loves Me' melody. Though it wouldn't have been noticed by many, Paul shot me a glance of appreciation and disbelief. I'm very fond of our reconnection, perhaps 'parallel lines who meet.'"—Larry Hochman

"Paul is simply the 'master maestro.' He's not only brilliant musically, but there is not a finer collaborator alive. Paul has it all—a sharp and clever wit, a compassionate soul, a deep connection to all artists, and a supreme gut instinct that never fails to excite and inspire.

He is truly the coolest of rock stars—who also just happens to be a national treasure."—Rob Marshall and John DeLuca

"Working with Paul is a joy. I always hold up everybody else to his standard. He is the standard, and no one has gone higher than that, ever. Working with Paul is rapture."—Tony Meola

"When I first worked with Paul, he was already widely regarded as the master of his craft while I was on the very lowest rung of the professional ladder. Despite our different levels, he always shared a friendly hello with me and a kind word, making me feel like an equal member of the team. I'll always be grateful to him for setting the example that one can be at the top of their game and yet still be a wonderful human being. He's such a legend."—Caroline Roberts

"I have been lucky enough to be a stage manager on five Broadway shows with Paul. The first two were as an assistant to my mentor, Beverley Randolph, who had a long history of shows with PG, dating from the early 1980s. Paul was the first 'Bway MD' with whom I really worked, and he set a high standard that has been rarely met by others. Being in the rehearsal room with Paul is magical—whether it's witnessing him guide a cast to give their best version of a song or watching him actually grow numbers in a new work out of a few notes from a composer. Paul is simply the best at all of it. I treasure his friendship deeply. The times we have spent together at restaurants and bars during out-of-town tryouts or hanging out in the front row of the House or SM office before a show have been among the highlights of my career. His quick wit and humor, matched by his drive for excellence and his love of art, is unparalleled. He makes me and everyone around him better."—Scott Rollison

"I was fortunate to work with Paul on a production of 'Showboat' for Carnegie Hall. He is one of the greats of American musical theater, not only a consummate musician but a theatrical force. When you look at the great musicals of the 1970s, 1980s and 1990s, you see him everywhere. I have often wondered what it was like to be in the room during the creation of the shows that are keystones in our American musical theater legacy; having a chance to work with Paul gave me some inkling."—Francesca Zambello

"Paul was one of the first Broadway professionals I was lucky enough to meet and work with when I first arrived in New York City. I was, and always will be, grateful to bear witness to his awesome talent and enormous respect for musicals. I miss Paul when he's not around. He's just the best."—Michael Zimmer

CHOREOGRAPHERS
"Paul recognizes the connection between the physicalization of the human body and music more than any other music director I have ever worked with. When Paul conducts, he dances."—Jason Sparks

MUSICIANS

"One of the greatest pleasures of my Broadway career was to perform as drummer/percussionist under the baton of Paul Gemignani during the Broadway performances of 'Follies,' 'Candide,' and 'On the Twentieth Century.' What stands out most for me was not only Paul's ability to control the different factions involved within any performance, but his unique sense of doing so with a firm hand flavored with a subtle sense of humor. As a result, not only did the actors and musicians deliver their strong support of him, but we always did so feeling good. Paul is, and always will be, my mentor. He is the shining light of the art of musical performance. And as a result, he will never be forgotten!"
—Nick Cerrato

"Paul is the best conductor I have ever seen at managing to take care of the singers and musicians at the same time. Everybody is taken care of. The singers and the actors feel like he is looking out for them, and the musicians in the orchestra feel like he is looking out for them. It all goes on at the same time, and I have never seen another conductor do that as well as Paul."—Theodore Firth

"Paul Gemignani is the person who steps back in the room and sees how everything needs to be put together. He sees how the music needs to help the story, and how the actors need to tell the story through the song. He is the mastermind. Paul knows what every part needs to do, and he knows how to assemble them. He is a genius."—Larry Lelli

"Paul is a great conductor/music director. He shows the orchestra what he needs and trusts his musicians to do their job. And it's always about the music first. I love working with him."—Kathleen Nester

"I've played for a lot of great conductors over the years ranging from classical, pop, and Broadway. Paul is by far my favorite conductor. He stands on a podium all his own. There is no one that can touch him."—Roger Shell

"Paul carries such authority and is so gifted that you don't want to mess up or cross him. It is kind of like Father Knows Best. He created something where he could make you joyously anticipate what tomorrow was going to bring. Each day proved to be very telling and full of discoveries and magical moments, and he was able to instill that in every one of us who had the pleasure of being in his midst."—Timothy Shew

"Paul is a musician, musical director, visionary, leader, teacher, arbitrator, and fierce defender of his orchestras. He is a master at restructuring a song or orchestration (on the fly, no less!) and of shaping a phrase while allowing the artists (on stage and in the pit) to express themselves freely. It is his relentless pursuit of the highest caliber performance, every night, his quick sense of humor (that keeps everyone from taking themselves too seriously) and ability to assemble an orchestra with positive energy that enable Paul to bring out the best in the musicians lucky enough to work with him. Paul is a rare gift to musical theater, to the music business as a whole, and to those lucky enough to call him a friend."—Eric Weidman

COMPOSERS
"Paul Gemignani is a genius maestro dude and there lives a great dancer in his body!"—Benny Andersson

"Paul and I became friends and collaborators longer ago than many of you have been alive! He is now considered—correctly, I believe—the symbol and authoritative voice for an entire generation of musical theater creators."—John Kander

SOUND DEPARTMENT
"Immediately, upon being introduced to Paul, a veteran of so many classic Broadway cast albums, I was struck by his kindness and willing to accept me—not having previously produced recordings in this genre—as an equal participant in figuring out how to plan the album. It became very apparent to me why he had achieved his one-of-a-kind status in the industry. No nonsense, a good, dry sense of humor, and a true professional with wonderfully creative ideas."—Steve Epstein

"Paul is one of my best friends in show business. When I came on 'Grind,' I had vinyl after vinyl after vinyl that had his name on it. To be in the room with him was an amazing experience, and I was in awe of everyone around me. Out of everyone, Paul was genuinely interested in how I was doing and how he could help. He really cared."—David Gotwald

ORCHESTRATORS

"I had been engaged for my second Sondheim musical, 'Follies,' and arrived at Jerome Robbins's rehearsal studio for the first day of rehearsal, where I was introduced by Hal Hastings, Hal Prince's long-time conductor, to his assistant and rehearsal drummer, a jovial, red-headed bear of a man named Paul Gemignani. Due to our similar backgrounds in jazz as well as shared attitudes toward life, along with a zany sense of the ridiculous, we immediately formed a personal and professional camaraderie that persists to this day."—Jonathan Tunick

MUSIC DIRECTORS

"Paul Gemignani has held the status of music director 'legend' for years and years. He was the first 'famous' music director I took note of when I was discovering Broadway, and I knew him to be 'Sondheim's guy.' I have always held him in the highest of regard and I have always loved watching him conduct, especially with his signature beat-pattern on jazzy songs where he looks like he's playing a ride cymbal, drummer that he is. I got lucky enough to work with him on a Broadway show called 'The People in the Picture,' and I kept pinching myself every time he would pass along a word of encouragement or share a story from all the shows he's done in his career. I will admit that I was intimidated to work with him because his presence can seem towering (that deep voice! the dark lenses!), but I was relieved to learn what a sweet and gentle human he is. I always smile when I get a message from Paul because I'm giddy to be on his radar, and I'm grateful that I've been able to commune with someone who I've respected for so long. To Paul!" —Alex Lacamoire

Acknowledgments

When I was first approached to write this book, I never could have imagined how it would change my life. I was a twenty-two-year-old college student living in a studio apartment in New York, pacing a hole in the floor as the COVID-19 pandemic turned the theatre district I held so dear into a barren void of silence. On May 5, 2020, within that silence, the phone rang.

On the other end of the line was Jennifer Ashley Tepper, a woman I have long admired, and who I am immensely grateful to now call a friend. She connected me to Paul, and changed my life with that single act of kindness. It is no surprise to me that Hal Prince loved her. I like to say that in that moment of trust and support, she "Merrily'd me"—that is, finding a passionate young adult and opening the doors between them and their destiny. I am eternally grateful.

This book would not exist without the hundreds of hours of interviews and statements readily given by so many of Paul's ingenious collaborators. I am forever touched by their honesty and passion and count every moment in their presence to be a blessing. Thank you to Jason Alexander, Benny Andersson, Donna Marie Asbury, Christine Baranski, John Beal, Laura Benanti, Jane Brockman, Mario Cantone, Len Cariou, Nick Cerrato, Michael Cerveris, David Chase, Paula Leggett Chase, Will Chase, Jim Coleman, Graciela Daniele, Sylvia D'Avanzo, Annbritt duChateau, Joanna Merlin, Scott Ellis, Steve Epstein, Tedd Firth, Victor Garber, Jonathan Goldblith, David Gotwald, Debbie Gravitte, Harriet Rawlins Hill, Larry Hochman, Jennifer Hoult, Joanna Hunter, Alvin Ing, Glen Kelly, David Krane, Robert La Fosse, Mary Ann Lamb, Nathan Lane, Angela Lansbury, James Lapine, Larry Lelli, Patti LuPone, Richard Maltby Jr., Joe Mantello, Kathleen Marshall, Rob Marshall, Alan

Menken, Tony Meola, Mark Mitchell, Debra Monk, Donna Murphy, Kathleen Nester, Kelli O'Hara, Mandy Patinkin, Bernadette Peters, Seymour "Red" Press, Lonny Price, Chita Rivera, Scott Taylor Rollison, Dan Moses Schreier, Roger Shell, Timothy Shew, Stephen Sondheim, Jason Sparks, Michael Starobin, Eric Stern, Susan Stroman, Jonathan Tunick, Jim Walton, Eric Weidman, Francesca Zambello, Michael Zimmer, and Steve Zweigbaum.

Thank you to John, Barbara, Carol, Shana, Jess, Laurel, Meaghan, and everyone at Applause Books, for lifting this book from my laptop to the printing press.

Thank you to Derin Altay, August Dannehl, and Alexander Gemignani, who opened their lives to me with immediate trust. Your faith in handing me your stories is an honor.

Thank you to the friends who accepted every 4:00 a.m. text with grace, and whose support and good humor kept my feet on the ground throughout the tornado—Casey Berner, Cossette Woo, Allison Kann, Angelika Airam, Ashlea Gilliam, Marc Bonanni, Ali Sousa, Alyssa Jennette, Justine Velasquez, Alison Regan, Taylor Buhrts, and Veronika Lindroth.

Krupa Malawade is one of the best friends a person can have. Her patience, kindness, and readiness to help made writing this book feel not only possible, but plausible. Her persistent support means the world, and I could not ask for a better partner in crime.

Zachary Agatstein is one of the most remarkable people I have ever met. His empathy, intelligence, genuine interest, and overwhelming dedication inspire me daily. I couldn't have dreamed of a better pre-editor, and I am a better person because you are in my life. Where I go, you go.

At the start of this process, I was forced to leave New York until the end of the pandemic. My beloved brother, Patrick, drove a U-Haul from Ohio to Manhattan to make sure I was safe, and as I sat crying in the passenger seat, his presence comforted me without words. It is a rare thing to have such unshakable love and devotion from a sibling, and I count myself lucky to call him my best bud.

My mother, Cynthia, is the ultimate cheerleader. She has openly encouraged my various passions since before I could form words, and when I began work on this book, she immediately switched into supportive copyeditor mode. I'd promise not to use so many obscure words in the next one, but we both know you raised me to be loquacious.

Much like Paul, I was lucky to have incredible teachers who pointed me in the right direction before I could even read the map. Thank you to David Monseur, Laurence Maslon, Kent Gash, Aleksei Grinenko, Rick Church, Barbara Tirrell, Lynn Reese, Stephen Stern, Melissa Hasebrook, Mark Wilkinson, Scott Yant, and Jen Waldman.

To M, A, and R—there is not a day in which I am not grateful for your presence in my life. Your guidance is my north star, and I will never stop working to be worthy of you.

Paul. Working with you on this book has been one of the greatest honors of my life. Your faith in me has been overwhelming, and it is by your support and kindness that these pages have been bound. Your commitment to compassion is remarkable, and we would all do well to follow your luminous example. That you have trusted me with your life story is the most precious gift, and I deeply hope that my words were sufficient in capturing even an ounce of your personal magic.

If you are a burgeoning music director and would like to contact Paul, he may be reached at StreetOfDreams2022@gmail.com.

Last, I thank you, dear reader. Your presence is invaluable, and I am overjoyed that you have taken the time to so fully engage with this book as to read to the end of the acknowledgments (seriously, kudos).

Ní neart go cur le chéile.

Career Time Line

Broadway

All credits are as music director unless otherwise specified.

- *Zorba* (November 16, 1968–August 9, 1969) *(as percussionist)*
- *Follies* (April 4, 1971–July 1, 1972) *(as percussionist and replacement music director)*
- *A Little Night Music* (June 5, 1973–August 3, 1974)
- *The Visit* (November 25, 1973–February 16, 1974) *(as music consultant)*
- *Holiday* (December 26, 1973–February 16, 1974) *(as music consultant)*
- *Candide* (May 13, 1974–January 4, 1976)
- *Love for Love* (November 11, 1974–November 30, 1974) *(as composer of incidental music)*
- *Pacific Overtures* (January 11, 1976–June 27, 1976)
- *Music Is* (December 20, 1976–December 26, 1976)
- *Side by Side by Sondheim* (April 18, 1977–March 19, 1978) *(as music supervisor)*
- *On the Twentieth Century* (February 19, 1978–March 18, 1979)
- *Sweeney Todd* (March 1, 1979–June 29, 1980)
- *Evita* (September 25, 1979–June 26, 1983) *(as music supervisor and replacement music director)*
- *West Side Story* (February 14, 1980–November 30, 1980) *(as music contractor)*

- *Merrily We Roll Along* (November 16, 1981–November 28, 1981)
- *A Doll's Life* (September 23, 1982–September 26, 1982)
- *Dreamgirls* (February 7, 1983–December 11, 1983) *(as conductor following pre-Broadway work as music supervisor)*
- *Zorba* (October 16, 1983–September 2, 1984) *(as music supervisor)*
- *The Rink* (February 9, 1984–August 4, 1984)
- *Sunday in the Park with George* (May 2, 1984–October 13, 1985)
- *Grind* (April 16, 1985–June 22, 1985)
- *Smile* (November 24, 1986–January 3, 1987)
- *Into the Woods* (November 5, 1987–September 3, 1989)
- *Mail* (April 14, 1988–May 15, 1988) *(as music supervisor and contractor)*
- *Jerome Robbins' Broadway* (February 26, 1989–September 1, 1990)
- *Crazy for You* (February 19, 1992–January 7, 1996)
- *Passion* (May 9, 1994–January 7, 1995)
- *Big* (April 28, 1996–October 13, 1996)
- *1776* (August 14, 1997–June 14, 1998)
- *High Society* (April 27, 1998–August 30, 1998)
- *Kiss Me, Kate* (November 18, 1999–December 30, 2001)
- *The Adventures of Tom Sawyer* (April 26, 2001–May 13, 2001)
- *Into the Woods* (April 30, 2002–December 29, 2002)
- *Assassins* (April 22, 2004–July 18, 2004)
- *The Frogs* (July 22, 2004–October 10, 2004)
- *Pacific Overtures* (December 2, 2004–January 30, 2005)
- *110 in the Shade* (May 9, 2007–July 29, 2007)
- *Pal Joey* (December 18, 2008–March 1, 2009)
- *The People in the Picture* (April 28, 2011–June 19, 2011)
- *The Mystery of Edwin Drood* (November 13, 2012–March 10, 2013)

- *She Loves Me* (March 17, 2016–July 10, 2016)
- *Kiss Me, Kate* (March 14, 2019–June 30, 2019)

National Tours (as music director/conductor)
- *Cabaret* (November 20, 1966–September 6, 1969) *(as percussionist and assistant conductor)*
- *Zorba* (December 26, 1969–August 30, 1970)
- *Follies* (July 3, 1972–October 1, 1972)
- *Pacific Overtures* (August 31, 1976–December 18, 1976)
- *Jerome Robbins' Broadway* (October 2, 1990–September 8, 1991)
- *Crazy for You* (May 11, 1993–August 6, 1995)
- *Kiss Me, Kate* (June 19, 2001–June 16, 2002)

National Tours (as music supervisor)
- *On the Twentieth Century* (June 9, 1979–November 25, 1979)
- *Evita* (September 25, 1980–March 27, 1983)
- *Sweeney Todd* (October 23, 1980–September 20, 1981)
- *Sweeney Todd* (February 22, 1982–July 17, 1982)
- *Evita* (February 23, 1982–July 8, 1984)
- *Zorba* (January 25, 1983–June 30, 1985)
- *Zorba* (December 31, 1985–August 3, 1986)

Films and Filmed Productions
- *Pacific Overtures* (1976)
- *A Little Night Music* (1978)
- *Kramer vs. Kramer* (1979)
- *Reds* (1981)
- *Broadway Goes to Washington* (1982)
- *Sweeney Todd* (1981) *(as music supervisor)*

- *Follies in Concert* (1985)
- *Sunday in the Park with George* (1985)
- *Into the Woods* (1987)
- *Side by Side by Sondheim* (1987)
- *Into the Woods* (1989)
- *New York City Opera: A Little Night Music* (1990)
- *Sondheim: A Celebration at Carnegie Hall* (1992)
- *Passion* (1995)
- *My Favorite Broadway: The Leading Ladies* (1998)
- *My Favorite Broadway: The Love Songs* (2000)
- *Kiss Me, Kate* (2003)
- South Pacific *in Concert from Carnegie Hall* (2005)
- *Sweeney Todd* (2007)
- *Camelot* (2008)
- *Sondheim! The Birthday Concert* (2010)
- *Company* (2011)
- *Into the Woods* (2014)
- *She Loves Me* (2016)
- *Mary Poppins Returns* (2018)

CONCERTS AND ONE-NIGHT-ONLY EVENTS

- *Sondheim: A Musical Tribute*—March 11, 1973
- *Follies in Concert*—September 6–7, 1985
- *Sondheim: A Celebration at Carnegie Hall*—June 10, 1992
- *Sunday in the Park with George*—May 15, 1994
- *Into the Woods*—November 9, 1997
- *Passion*—October 20, 2004
- *South Pacific*—June 9, 2005

- *Camelot*—May 7–10, 2008
- *She Loves Me*—December 5, 2011
- *Assassins*—December 3, 2012

RECORDINGS (CAST ALBUMS ARE BOLDFACED)
- *Sondheim: A Musical Tribute*—1973
- *A Little Night Music*—1976
- **Pacific Overtures—1976**
- **On the Twentieth Century—1978**
- **Sweeney Todd: The Demon Barber of Fleet Street—1979**
- **Merrily We Roll Along—1981**
- **A Doll's Life—1982**
- *A Stephen Sondheim Evening*—1983
- **Zorba—1983**
- **The Rink—1984**
- **Sunday in the Park with George—1984**
- *Follies in Concert*—1985
- **Grind—1985**
- *Sondheim*—1985
- *Lost in the Stars: The Music of Kurt Weill*—1985
- *Broadway Extravaganza, Vol. 1: Symphonic Recollections*—1987
- *Carousel*—1987
- *Digital Trip Down Broadway*—1987
- **Into the Woods—1987**
- *Broadway!*—1988
- *Symphonic Pictures: Phantom of the Opera/Jesus Christ Superstar*—1988
- **Jerome Robbins' Broadway—1989**
- *Mandy Patinkin*—1989

- *Dress Casual with Mandy Patinkin*—1989
- *Man of La Mancha*—1990
- **Assassins—1991**
- *Kismet*—1991
- *Broadway's Best: Overtures and Dances*—1992
- **Crazy for You—1992**
- *Sondheim: A Celebration at Carnegie Hall*—1992
- *Standing Room Only with Jerry Hadley*—1992
- *Golden Days: Songs of Romberg, Friml and Herbert with Jerry Hadley*—1993
- *In the Real World with Jerry Hadley*—1993
- **Merrily We Roll Along—1993**
- *The Men in My Life with Marilyn Horne*—1994
- **Passion—1994**
- *Anyone Can Whistle*—1995
- *Broadway Legend*—1995
- **A Christmas Carol—1995**
- **Big—1996**
- *An Evening at Carnegie Hall with Betty Buckley*—1996
- *Leading Man with Thomas Hampson*—1996
- **1776—1997**
- **High Society—1998**
- *My Favorite Broadway: The Leading Ladies*—1998
- *Do Re Mi*—1999
- **Kiss Me, Kate—1999**
- *The Frogs*—2000
- *My Favorite Broadway: The Love Songs*—2000
- *Evening Primrose*—2001

- *Into the Woods*—**2002**
- *A Tale of Two Cities*—2002
- *Renee and Bryn: Under the Stars*—2003
- *Assassins*—**2004**
- *The Frogs*—**2004**
- *Pacific Overtures*—**2005**
- *South Pacific in Concert at Carnegie Hall*—2005
- *Wall to Wall Stephen Sondheim*—2005
- *110 in the Shade*—**2007**
- *Sweeney Todd: The Demon Barber of Fleet Street*—2007
- *Kristina at Carnegie Hall*—2009
- *The People in the Picture*—**2011**
- *The Mystery of Edwin Drood*—**2012**
- *Into the Woods*—2014
- *She Loves Me*—**2016**
- *Mary Poppins Returns*—2018
- *Kiss Me, Kate*—**2019 Broadway Cast**

Show Reference

Pacific Overtures

The Westernization of Japan, told in Kabuki style.

December 31, 1975–January 11, 1976–June 27, 1976
Winter Garden Theatre
193 Performances
13 Previews

Musical Numbers

Act 1

Prologue
The Advantages of Floating in
the Middle of the Sea
There Is No Other Way
Four Black Dragons
Chrysanthemum Tea
Poems
Welcome to Kanagawa
March to the Treaty House
Someone in a Tree
Lion Dance

Act 2

Please Hello
A Bowler Hat
Pretty Lady
Next

Creative Team

Music and Lyrics by Stephen Sondheim
Book by John Weidman
Additional Material by Hugh Wheeler
Directed by Harold Prince
Choreographed by Patricia Birch
Kabuki consultant—Haruki Fujimoto
Martial Arts Sequence by Soon-Tek Oh

Music Directed by Paul Gemignani
Conducted by Paul Gemignani
Orchestrated by Jonathan Tunick
Dance music by Danny Troob

Scenic Design by Boris Aronson
Costume Design by Florence Klotz
Lighting Design by Tharon Musser
Sound Design by Jack Mann
Makeup Design by Richard Allen
Wig Design by Richard Allen and Paul Huntley
Masks and Dolls by E. J. Taylor
Assistant to Miss Klotz—Domingo Rodriguez
Assistant to Miss Musser—Marilyn Rennagel

Production Stage Manager: George Martin
Stage Manager—John Grigas
Assistant Stage Manager—Carlos Gorbea
Technical Supervisor—John J. Moore

General Manager—Howard Haines
Company Manager—Leo K. Cohen
Casting—Joanna Merlin

Cast

Mako—Reciter, Shogun, Jonathan Goble, Emperor Meiji
Soon-Tek Oh—Tamate, Samurai, Storyteller, Swordsman
Isao Sato—Kayama
Yuki Shimoda—Lord Abe
Sab Shimono—Manjiro
Ernest Abuba—Samurai, Adams, Noble
James Dybas—Councillor, Old Man, French Admiral
Timm Fujii—Son, Priest, Kanagawa Girl, Noble, British Sailor
Haruki Fujimoto—Servant, Commodore Matthew Calbraith Perry
Larry Hama—Williams, Lord of the South, Gangster

Ernest Harada—Physician, Madam, British Admiral
Alvin Ing—Shogun's Mother, Observer, Merchant, American
Admiral
Patrick Kinser-Lau—Shogun's Companion, Kanagawa Girl, Dutch
Admiral, British Sailor
Jae Woo Lee—Fisherman, Sumo Wrestler, Lord of the South
Freddy Mao—Councillor, Samurai's Daughter
Tom Matsusaka—Imperial Priest
Freda Foh Shen—Shogun's Wife
Mark Hsu Syers—Samurai, Thief, Soothsayer, Warrior, Russian
Admiral, British Sailor
Ricardo Tobia—Observer
Gedde Watanabe—Priest, Kanagawa Girl, the Boy
Conrad Yama—Grandmother, Sumo Wrestler, Japanese Merchant
Fusako Yoshida—Shamisen accompaniment
Genji Ito—Percussion

Proscenium Servants, Sailors, and Townspeople
Kenneth S. Eiland, Timm Fujili, Joey Ginza, Susan Kikuchi, Patrick
Kinser-Lau, Diane Lam, Tony Marinyo, Kevin Maung, Kim Miyori,
Dingo Secretario, Mark Hsu Seyers, Freda Foh Shen, Ricardo Tobia,
Gedde Watanabe, Leslie Watanabe

Understudies
Ernest Abuba (Swordsman, Abe, First Councillor), Patrick Kins-
er-Lau (Manjiro), Jae Woo Lee (Reciter), Freddy Mao (Samurai,
Storyteller), Tony Marinyo (Third Councillor), Tom Matsusaka
(Kayama), Ricardo Tobia (Second Councillor), and Gedde Watanabe
(Tamate)

AWARDS
30th Tony Awards
Wins
Best Costume Design
Best Scenic Design

Nominations
Best Musical
Best Book of a Musical
Best Original Score
Best Actor in a Musical—Mako
Best Featured Actor in a Musical—Isao Sato
Best Choreography
Best Direction of a Musical
Best Lighting Design

21st Drama Desk Awards
Wins
Outstanding Costume Design
Outstanding Set Design

Nominations
Outstanding Musical Book
Outstanding Music and Lyrics
Outstanding Featured Actor in a Musical—Haruki Fujimoto
Outstanding Choreography
Outstanding Director of a Musical

A Little Night Music (Film)

A tangled web of affairs centered on actress Desirée Armfeldt and the men who love her.

Released September 5, 1977
Filmed September 7, 1976–October 29, 1976
Filmed in Vienna, Austria

Cast

Elizabeth Taylor—Desiree Armfeldt
Diana Rigg—Charlotte Mittelheim
Len Cariou—Frederick Egerman
Lesley-Anne Down—Anne Egerman
Hermione Gingold—Mme. Armfeldt
Laurence Guittard—Carl-Magnus Mittelheim
Christopher Guard—Erich Egerman
Lesley Dunlop—Petra
Chloe Franks—Fredericka Armfeldt
Heinz Marecek—Frid
Jonathan Tunick—Conductor
Hubert Tscheppe—Franz
Rudolph Schrympf—Band Conductor
Franz Schussler—the Mayor
Johanna Schussler—the Mayoress
Jean Sincere—Box Office Lady in Theatre
Dagmar Koller—First Lady
Ruth Brinkman—Second Lady
Anna Veigl—Concierge
Stephan Paryla—Uniformed Sergeant
Eva Dvorska—First Whore

Lisa De Cohen—Second Whore
Kurt Martynow—Major Domo
Gerty Barek—Cook
James De Groat—Footman
Mason Cardiff—Desiree's child
Elaine Tomkinson—Fredericka Armfeldt (singing voice)

Side by Side Sondheim

A revue.

April 13, 1977–April 18, 1977–March 19, 1978
Music Box Theatre and Morosco Theatre
384 Performances
6 Previews

Musical Numbers

Act 1

Comedy Tonight
Love Is in the Air
If Momma Was Married
(*music by Jule Styne*)
You Must Meet My Wife
The Little Things You Do
    Together
Getting Married Today
I Remember
Can That Boy Foxtrot
Company
Another Hundred People
Barcelona
Marry Me a Little
I Never Do Anything Twice
Bring on the Girls
Ah, Paree!
Buddy's Blues
Broadway Baby
You Could Drive a Person Crazy

Act 2

Everybody Says Don't
Anyone Can Whistle
Send in the Clowns
We're Gonna Be Alright
(*music by Richard Rodgers*)
A Boy Like That/I Have a
    Love
(*music by Leonard Bernstein*)
The Boy from . . .
(*music by Mary Rodgers*)
Pretty Lady
You Gotta Have a Gimmick
(*music by Jule Styne*)
Losing My Mind
Could I Leave You?
I'm Still Here
Conversation Piece
Side by Side by Side

CREATIVE TEAM
Music and Lyrics by Stephen Sondheim
Directed by Ned Sherrin
Musical staging by Bob Howe

Music Directed by Ray Cook
Music Supervisor—Paul Gemignani
Pianists—Daniel Troob and Albin Konopka

Scenic Design by Peter Docherty
Costume Design by Florence Klotz
Lighting Design by Ken Billington
Sound Design by Jack Mann
Hair Design by Vidal Sassoon Salons
Assistant to Mr. Billington—Jeremy Johnson

Stage Manager—John Grigas
Assistant Stage Manager—Artie Masella

General Manager—Howard Haines
Casting—Joanna Merlin

CAST
David Kernan
Millicent Martin
Fernanda Maschwitz
Julie N. McKenzie
Ned Sherrin

Standbys
Jack Blackton, Fernanda Maschwitz, Bonnie Schon, and Carol
Swarbrick

NOTABLE REPLACEMENTS
Georgia Brown
Nancy Dussault

Hermione Gingold
Larry Kert
Burr Tillstrom

AWARDS
31st Tony Awards
Nominations
    Best Musical
    Best Featured Actor in a Musical—David Kernan
    Best Featured Actor in a Musical—Ned Sherrin
    Best Featured Actress in a Musical—Millicent Martin
    Best Featured Actress in a Musical—Julie N. McKenzie

22nd Drama Desk Awards
Nominations
    Unique Theatrical Experience
    Outstanding Actress in a Musical—Julie N. McKenzie

ON THE TWENTIETH CENTURY

A classic comedy aboard a Twentieth Century Limited train from Chicago to New York.

February 9, 1978–February 19, 1978–March 18, 1979
St. James Theatre
449 Performances
11 Previews

MUSICAL NUMBERS

Act 1

Stranded Again
On the 20th Century
I Rise Again
Indian Maiden's Lament
Veronique
I Have Written a Play
Together
Never
Our Private World
Repent
Mine
I've Got It All
On the Twentieth Century
(Reprise)

Act 2

Entr'acte
Five Zeros
Sextet
She's a Nut
Max Jacobs
Babbette
The Legacy

CREATIVE TEAM

Book and Lyrics by Betty Comden and Adolph Green
Music by Cy Coleman

Based on the play by Ben Hecht, Charles MacArthur, and Bruce
   Millholland
Directed by Harold Prince
Musical Staging by Larry Fuller
Assistant Choreographer—Gerald Teijelo

Musical Director—Paul Gemignani
Orchestrated by Hershy Kay
Music Contractor—Mel Rodnon
Assistant Conductor—Nick Cerrato

Scenic Design by Robin Wagner
Costume Design by Florence Klotz
Lighting Design by Ken Billington
Sound Design by Robin Wagner
Hair Design by Richard Allen

Production Stage Manager—George Martin
Stage Manager—E. Bronson Platt
Assistant Stage Managers—Gerald Teijelo and Andrew Cadiff

General Managers—Joseph Harris and Ira Bernstein
Business Manager—Frank Scardino
Casting—Joanna Merlin

CAST

Imogene Coca—Letitia Primrose
John Cullum—Oscar Jaffee
Madeline Kahn—Lily Garland
George Lee Andrews—Max Jacobs
Tom Batten—Conductor Flanagan
Willi Burke—Imelda, Dr. Johnson
Kevin Kline—Bruce Granit

Ensemble

Susan Cella, Maris Clement, George Coe, Peggy Cooper, Keith Davis, Dean Dittman, Quitman Fludd III, Karen Gibson, Ray Gill, Ken Hilliard, David Horwitz, Mel Johnson Jr., Judy Kaye, Craig Lucas, Carol Lugenbeal, Carol Lurie, Sal Mistretta, Hal Norman, Charles Rule, Stanley Simmonds, Rufus Smith, Ray Stephens, Melanie Vaughan, David Vogel, and Joseph Wise

Understudies

Christine Ebersole (Lily Garland), Mel Johnson Jr. (Porter), and Ted Williams (Porter)

NOTABLE REPLACEMENTS

Betty Comden—Letitia Primrose
Judy Kaye—Lily Garland
Richard Cooper Bayne—Maxwell Finch
Christine Ebersole—Agnes
Lee Goodman—Owen O'Malley
Jeff Keller—Max Jacobs
Melanie Vaughan—Agnes
Ted Williams—Redcap
Nicholas Wyman—Bruce Granit

AWARDS

32nd Tony Awards

Wins

Best Book of a Musical
Best Original Score
Best Actor in a Musical—John Cullum
Best Featured Actor in a Musical—Kevin Kline
Best Scenic Design—Robin Wagner

Nominations

Best Musical
Best Actress in a Musical—Madeline Kahn

Best Featured Actress in a Musical—Imogene Coca
Best Direction of a Musical—Hal Prince

23rd Drama Desk Awards
Wins
Outstanding Featured Actor in a Musical—Kevin Kline
Outstanding Music
Outstanding Costume Design
Outstanding Set Design

Nomination
Outstanding Actress in a Musical—Judy Kaye

1978 Theatre World Awards
Judy Kaye

SWEENEY TODD—THE DEMON BARBER OF FLEET STREET

A wronged barber returns to Victorian London to exact revenge.

February 6, 1979–March 1, 1979–June 29, 1980
Uris Theatre
557 Performances
19 Previews

MUSICAL NUMBERS

Act 1

The Ballad of Sweeney Todd
No Place Like London
The Barber and His Wife
The Worst Pies in London
Poor Thing
My Friends
Green Finch and Linnet Bird
Ah, Miss
Johanna
Pirelli's Miracle Elixir
The Contest
Wait
Kiss Me
Ladies in Their Sensitivities
Quartet
Pretty Women
Epiphany
A Little Priest

Act 2

God, That's Good!
Johanna (Reprise)
By the Sea
Not While I'm Around
Parlour Songs
City on Fire
Final Scene
The Ballad of Sweeney Todd
(Reprise)

CREATIVE TEAM

Music and Lyrics by Stephen Sondheim
Book by Hugh Wheeler
Directed by Harold Prince
Dance and Movement by Larry Fuller
Based on a version of "Sweeney Todd" by Christopher Bond

Music Directed by Paul Gemignani
Conducted by Paul Gemignani
Orchestrated by Jonathan Tunick
Assistant Music Directed by Les Scott

Scenic Design by Eugene Lee
Costume Design by Franne Lee
Lighting Design by Ken Billingston
Sound Design by Jack Mann
Hair and Wig Design by Lyn Quiyou
Makeup Design by Barbara Kelly

Production Stage Manager: Alan Hall
Stage Manager: Ruth E. Rinklin
Assistant Stage Manager: Arthur Masella
Technical Director: Arthur Siccardi

General Manager: Gatchell & Neufeld, Ltd.
Company Manager: Drew Murphy
Management Associate: Douglas C. Baker
Casting: Joanna Merlin

CAST

Len Cariou—Sweeney Todd
Angela Lansbury—Mrs. Lovett
Victor Garber—Anthony Hope
Ken Jennings—Tobias Ragg
Merle Louise—Beggar Woman
Edmund Lyndeck—Judge Turpin

Sarah Rice—Johanna
Joaquin Romaguera—Pirelli
Jack Eric Williams—the Beadle

Members of the Company
Duane Bodin, Walter Charles, Carole Doscher, Nancy Eaton, Jonas Fogg, Mary-Pat Green, Skip Harris, Marthe Ihde, Betsy Joslyn, Nancy Killmer, Frank Kopyc, Spain Logue, Craig Lucas, Pamela McLernon, Duane Morris, Robert Ousley, Richard Warren Pugh, and Maggie Task

Understudies
Walter Charles (Sweeney Todd), Cris Groenendaal (Anthony Hope), Skip Harris (Tobias Ragg), Betsy Joslyn (Johanna), Frank Kopyc (Pirelli), Pamela McLernon (Beggar Woman), Robert Ousley (Judge Turpin), Richard Warren Pugh (the Beadle), and Maggie Task (Mrs. Lovett)

NOTABLE REPLACEMENTS
George Hearn—Sweeney Todd
Dorothy Loudon—Mrs. Lovett
Cris Groenendaal—Anthony Hope
Betsy Joslyn—Johanna

Nancy Callman
Robert Henderson *(understudy Anthony Hope)*
Michael Kalinyen *(understudy the Beadle)*
Kevin Marcum
Carolyn Marlow
Candace Rogers *(understudy Johanna)*

AWARDS
33rd Tony Awards
Wins
Best Musical
Best Book of a Musical

Best Original Score
Best Actor in a Musical—Len Cariou
Best Actress in a Musical—Angela Lansbury
Best Direction of a Musical
Best Costume Design
Best Scenic Design

Nomination
Best Lighting Design

24th Drama Desk Awards
Wins
Outstanding Musical
Outstanding Book
Outstanding Actor in a Musical—Len Cariou
Outstanding Actress in a Musical—Angela Lansbury
Outstanding Featured Actor in a Musical—Ken Jennings
Outstanding Featured Actress in a Musical—Merle Louise
Outstanding Director of a Musical
Outstanding Lyrics
Outstanding Music

Nominations
Outstanding Choreography
Outstanding Costume Design
Outstanding Lighting Design
Outstanding Set Design

1979 Theatre World Awards
Sarah Rice
Ken Jennings

EVITA

The life and death of Argentine first lady Eva Peron.

September 10, 1979–September 25, 1979–June 26, 1983
Uris Theatre
1,567 Performances
17 Previews

MUSICAL NUMBERS

Act 1

A Cinema in Buenos Aires;
July 26, 1952
Requiem for Evita
Oh What a Circus
On This Night of a Thousand
Stars
Eva Beware of the City
Buenos Aires
Goodnight and Thank You
The Art of the Possible
Charity Concert
I'd Be Surprisingly Good
for You
Another Suitcase in Another
Hall
Perón's Latest Flame
A New Argentina

Act 2

On the Balcony of the Casa
Rosada
Don't Cry for Me Argentina
High Flying Adored
Rainbow High
Rainbow Tour
The Actress Hasn't Learned
(the Lines You'd Like to
Hear)
And the Money Kept Rolling
In (and Out)
Santa Evita
Waltz for Eva and Che
She Is a Diamond
Dice Are Rolling
Eva's Final Broadcast
Montage
Lament

CREATIVE TEAM

Music by Andrew Lloyd Webber
Lyrics by Tim Rice
Book by Tim Rice
Directed by Harold Prince
Choreographed by Larry Fuller
Assistance to Mr. Fuller by Linda Papworth

Musical Directed by Rene Wiegert
Music orchestrated by Andrew Lloyd Webber and Hershy Kay
Assistant Musical Directed by Edward Strauss
Music Contractor by Paul Gemignani
Music Preparation by Chelsea Music Services, Inc., Mathilde
   Pincus, and Al Miller

Scenic Design by Timothy O'Brien and Tazeena Firth
Costume Design by Timothy O'Brien and Tazeena Firth
Projection Design by Timothy O'Brien and Tazeena Firth
Lighting Design by David Hersey
Sound Design by Abe Jacob
Makeup Design by Richard Allen
Assistant to Mr. Jacob: Larry Spurgeon
Hair Design by Richard Allen
Assistant to Mr. Allen: Esther Teller
Assistant to Mr. O'Brien and Ms. Firth: Donna Thomas
Production Stage Manager: George Martin
Stage Manager: John Grigas
Assistant Stage Managers: Carlos Gorbea and Andy Cadiff

General Manager: Howard Haines
Company Manager: John Caruso
Assistant to Mr. Haines: Nina Skriloff
Casting: Joanna Merlin

CAST
Bob Gunton—Perón
Patti LuPone—Eva Perón
Mandy Patinkin—Che
Jane Ohringer—Perón's Mistress
Mark Syers—Magaldi
Terri Klausner—Alternate Eva Perón

People of Argentina
Seda Azarian, Dennis Birchall, Peppi Borza, Tom Carder, Robin Cleaver, Anny De Gange, Mark East, Megan Forste, Bridget Francis, Nicole Francis, Teri Gill, Carlos Gorbea, Pat Gorman, Re, David Hays, Michael Lichtefeld, Carol Lugenbeal, Paula Lynn, Morgan MacKay, Peter Marinos, Sal Mistretta, Jack Neubeck, Marcia O'Brien, Nancy Opel, Michael Pastryk, Davia Sacks, James Sbano, David Staller, Michelle Stubbs, Robert Tanna, Clarence Teeters, Susan Terry, Phillip Tracy, David Vosburgh, Mark Waldrop, Sandra Wheeler, Brad Witsger, John Leslie Wolfe, Nancy Wood, Christopher Wooten, and John Yost

Understudies
Tom Carder (Che), Rex David Hays (Perón), Sal Mistretta (Magaldi), Nancy Opel (Eva Perón), and Nancy Wood (Perón's Mistress)

NOTABLE REPLACEMENTS
Derin Altay—Eva Perón
Loni Ackerman—Eva Perón
Florence Lacey—Eva Perón
Pamela Blake—Alternate Eva Perón
Patricia Hemenway—Alternate Eva Perón
Nancy Opel—Alternate Eva Perón

Anthony Crivello—Che
Scott Holmes—Che

James Sbano—Che
James Stein—Che
David Cryer—Perón
Jack Neubeck—Perón
Cynthia Hunt—Perón's Mistress
Peter Marinos—Magaldi
James Whitson—Magaldi

AWARDS
34th Tony Awards
Wins

Best Musical
Best Book of a Musical
Best Original Score
Best Actress in a Musical—Patti LuPone
Best Featured Actor in a Musical—Mandy Patinkin
Best Direction of a Musical
Best Lighting Design

Nominations

Best Featured Actor in a Musical—Bob Gunton
Best Scenic Design
Best Costume Design
Best Choreography

25th Drama Desk Awards
Wins

Outstanding Musical
Outstanding Actress in a Musical—Patti LuPone
Outstanding Featured Actor in a Musical—Bob Gunton
Outstanding Director of a Musical
Outstanding Lyrics
Outstanding Music

Nominations

 Outstanding Actor in a Musical—Mandy Patinkin
 Outstanding Choreography
 Outstanding Costume Design
 Outstanding Lighting Design

MERRILY WE ROLL ALONG

The story of three friends, beginning in 1980 and moving backward toward 1955.

October 8, 1981–November 17, 1981–November 28, 1981
Alvin Theatre
16 Performances
44 Previews

MUSICAL NUMBERS

Act 1
The Hills of Tomorrow
Merrily We Roll Along
Rich and Happy
Merrily We Roll Along
Old Friends
Like It Was
Franklin Shepard, Inc.
Merrily We Roll Along
Old Friends (Reprise)
Merrily We Roll Along
(Reprise)
Not a Day Goes By
Now You Know

Act 2
It's a Hit!
Merrily We Roll Along
Good Thing Going
Merrily We Roll Along
Bobby and Jackie and Jack
Not a Day Goes By
Opening Doors
Our Time
The Hills of Tomorrow

CREATIVE TEAM
Book by George Furth
Music by Stephen Sondheim
Lyrics by Stephen Sondheim
From the play by George S. Kaufman and Moss Hart

Directed by Harold Prince
Choreographed by Larry Fuller
Assistant Choreographer: Janie Gleason
Originally Choreographed by Ron Field

Music orchestrated by Jonathan Tunick
Musical Director: Paul Gemignani
Assistant Conductor: Tom Fay and Les Scott

Scenic Design by Eugene Lee
Costume Design by Judith Dolan
Lighting Design by David Hersey
Sound Design by Jack Mann
Makeup Design by Richard Allen
Hair Design by Richard Allen
Projection Consultant: Westerfield/Quitt Productions, Ltd.

General Manager: Howard Haines
Assistant Manager: David Musselman
Production Stage Manager: Beverley Randolph
Stage Manager: Richard Evans
Assistant Stage Manager: Steve Knox

Casting: Joanna Merlin

CAST

Ann Morrison—Mary Flynn
Lonny Price—Charley Kringas
James Weissenbach (replaced in previews)—Franklin Shepard
Jim Walton—Franklin Shepard
Jason Alexander—Joe
Terry Finn—Gussie
Sally Klein—Beth

Members of the Company
Marianna Allen, James Bonkovsky, David Cady, Liz Callaway, Donna Marie Elio, Geoffrey Horne, Paul Hyams, Steven Jacob, Mary Johansen, David Loud, Marc Moritz, Tonya Pinkins, Abby Pogrebin, Daisy Prince, Forest D. Ray, Clark Sayre, Tom Shea, David Shine, Gary Stevens, and Maryrose Wood

Understudies
Marianna Allen (Gussie), James Bonkovsky (Joe), David Cady (Franklin Shepard), Liz Callaway (Mary Flynn), David Loud (Charley Kringas), and Daisy Prince (Beth)

AWARDS
36th Tony Awards
Nomination
Best Original Score

27th Drama Desk Awards
Win
Outstanding Lyrics

Nomination
Outstanding Music

1982 Theatre World Awards
Ann Morrison

Dreamgirls

Greed, hate, and romance intertwine with three young women in the music industry.

December 9, 1981–December 20, 1981–August 11, 1985
Imperial Theatre
1,521 Performances
10 Previews

Musical Numbers

Act 1

I'm Lookin' for Something
Goin' Downtown
Takin' the Long Way Home
Move (You're Steppin' on My Heart)
Fake Your Way to the Top
Cadillac Car
Cadillac Car (on the Road)
Cadillac Car (in the Recording Studio)
Cadillac Car (Reprise)
Steppin' to the Bad Side
Party, Party
I Want You Baby
Family
Dreamgirls
Press Conference
Only the Beginning
Heavy/Stop Bringing Us Down
Drivin' Down the Strip
It's All Over
And I Am Telling You I'm Not Going
Love Love You Baby

Act 2

Act II Opening
I Am Changing
One More Picture
   Please
When I First Saw You
Got to Be Good Times
Ain't No Party
I Meant You No Harm
Quintette
The Rap
Firing of Jimmy
I Miss You Old Friend
One Night Only
One Night Only (Disco)
I'm Somebody
Chicago/Faith in Myself
Hard to Say Goodbye,
   My Love
Dreamgirls (Reprise)

CREATIVE TEAM

Music by Henry Krieger
Book and Lyrics by Tom Eyen
Directed by Michael Bennett
Choreographed by Michael Bennett and Michael Peters

Music orchestrated by Harold Wheeler
Musical Director: Yolanda Segovia
Vocal arrangements by Cleavant Derricks

Scenic Design by Robin Wagner
Assistant to Mr. Wagner: Linda Hacker
Costume Design by Theoni V. Aldredge
Associate Costume Designer: Frank Krenz
Lighting Design by Tharon Musser
Assistant to Ms. Musser: Gregg Marriner
Sound Design by Otts Munderloh
Hair Design by Ted Azar
Assistant to Mr. Munderloh: Cynthia J. Hawkins
Special Assistants to Ms. Aldredge: Suzy Benzinger and
   Woody Lane

Production Stage Manager: Jeff Hamlin
Stage Managers: Zane Weiner and Frank di Filia
Technical Coordinator: Arthur Siccardi
Assistant Stage Manager: Jacqueline Yancey

General Managers: Marvin A. Krauss Associates, Inc., Eric M.
   Angelson, Gary Gunas, and Steven C. Callahan
Casting: OLAIYA

CAST

Obba Babatundé—C. C. White
Cleavant Derricks—James Thunder Early
Loretta Devine—Lorrell Robinson

Ben Harney—Curtis Taylor Jr.
Jennifer Holliday—Effie Melody White
Sheryl Lee Ralph—Deena Jones
Deborah Burrell—Michelle Morris
Vondie Curtis-Hall—Marty
Tony Franklin—Wayne
David Thomé—Frank

Ensemble
Cheryl Alexander, Phylicia Ayers, Charles Bernard, Paul Binotto, Candy Darling, Ronald Dunham, Stephanie Eley, Sheila Ellis, Thomas Scott Gordon, Tenita Jordan, Linda Lloyd, Carol Logen, Joe Lynn, Frank Mastrocola, Jamie Patterson, Wellington Perkins, Scott Plank, Brenda Pressley, Charles Randolph-Wright, Larry Stewart, David Thomé, and Weyman Thompson

Understudies
Cheryl Alexander (Lorrell Robinson), Phylicia Ayers-Allen (Deena Jones), Vondie Curtis-Hall (Curtis Taylor Jr.), Sheila Ellis (Effie Melody White), Tony Franklin (C. C. White), Linda Lloyd (Michelle Morris), Milton Craig Nealy (Marty, Jerry), Scott Plank (Frank), Larry Stewart (James Thunder Early), and Weyman Thompson (Wayne)

NOTABLE REPLACEMENTS
Hinton Battle—James Thunder Early
David Alan Grier—James Thunder Early
Linda Leilani Brown—Deena Jones
Deborah Burrell—Deena Jones
Terry Burrell—Lorrell Robinson
Cheryl Alexander—Lorrell Robinson
Lawrence Clayton—C. C. White
Tony Franklin—C. C. White
Wellington Perkins—C. C. White
Roz Ryan—Effie Melody White

Julia McGirt—Effie Melody White
Vanessa Townsell—Effie Melody White
Terry Burrell—Michelle Morris
Brenda Pressley—Michelle Morris

AWARDS
36th Tony Awards
Wins

Best Book of a Musical
Best Actor in a Musical—Ben Harney
Best Actress in a Musical—Jennifer Holliday
Best Featured Actor in a Musical—Cleavant Derricks
Best Choreography
Best Lighting Design

Nominations

Best Musical
Best Direction of a Musical
Best Original Score
Best Featured Actress in a Musical—Sheryl Lee Ralph
Best Featured Actor in a Musical—Obba Babatundé
Best Scenic Design
Best Costume Design

27th Drama Desk Awards
Wins

Outstanding Actress in a Musical—Jennifer Holliday
Outstanding Featured Actor in a Musical—Cleavant Derricks
Outstanding Music
Outstanding Lighting Design
Outstanding Set Design

Nominations

Outstanding Musical
Outstanding Actress in a Musical—Sheryl Lee Ralph

Outstanding Featured Actor in a Musical—Ben Harney
Outstanding Director of a Musical
Outstanding Lyrics
Outstanding Costume Design

1982 Theatre World Awards
Jennifer Holliday

THE RINK

A mother and daughter reconcile in the midst of the sale of the family's dilapidated roller rink.

January 12, 1984–February 9, 1984–August 4, 1984
Martin Beck Theatre
204 Performances
29 Previews

MUSICAL NUMBERS

Act 1

Colored Lights
Chief Cook and Bottle Washer
Don't Ah Ma Me
Blue Crystal
Under the Roller Coaster
Not Enough Magic
We Can Make It
After All These Years
Angel's Rink and Social
    Center
What Happened to the Old
    Days?
Colored Lights (Reprise)

Act 2

The Apple Doesn't Fall
Marry Me
We Can Make It (Reprise)
Mrs. A
The Rink
Wallflower
All the Children in a Row

CREATIVE TEAM

Book by Terrence McNally
Music by John Kander; Lyrics by Fred Ebb
Directed by A. J. Antoon

Choreographed by Graciela Daniele
Assistant Choreographer: Tina Paul

Musical Director: Paul Gemignani
Dance arrangements by Tom Fay
Music orchestrated by Michael Gibson

Scenic Design by Peter Larkin
Costume Design by Theoni V. Aldredge
Lighting Design by Marc B. Weiss
Sound Design by Otts Munderloh
Hair Design by J. Roy Helland
Assistant to Mr. Larkin: William Barclay
Assistant to Mr. Weiss: Susan A. White
Associate Costume Design: Frank Krenz
Assistant to Mr. Munderloh: Kurt Fischer
Personal Assistant to Ms. Aldredge: Caroline Newcomb

Production Stage Manager: Ed Aldridge
Stage Manager: Craig Jacobs
Assistant Stage Manager: Tom Capps

Special Effects by Justin Zizes
Magic Consultant: William Schmeelk
Dance Captain: Rob Marshall
Skating Instructor: April Allen

Casting: Johnson-Liff Associates
Casting Associate: Andrew M. Zerman

CAST

Liza Minnelli—Angel
Chita Rivera—Anna
Jason Alexander—Leno, Lenny, Punk, Uncle Fausto

Ronn Carroll—Ben, Dino's Father, Mrs. Silverman, Sister
   Philomena
Kim Hauser—Little Girl
Scott Ellis—Lucky, Sugar, Punk, Arnie, Suitor, Bobby Perillo,
   Danny
Scott Holmes—Guy, Dino, Father Rocco, Debbie Duberman
Mel Johnson Jr.—Buddy, Hiram, Mrs. Jackson, Charlie, Suitor,
   Junior Miller
Frank Mastrocola—Tony, Tom, Punk, Suitor, Peter Reilly

Standbys
   Patti Karr (Anna) and Lenora Nemetz (Angel)

Understudies
   Rob Marshall (Lino, Lucky, Tony), Frank Mastrocola (Guy), Kimi
   Parks (Little Girl), and Jim Tushar (Ben, Buddy)

NOTABLE REPLACEMENTS
   Stockard Channing—Angel
   Scott Ellis—Mrs. Antonelli
   Frank Mastrocola—Danny
   Kimi Parks—Little Girl
   Standby: Mary Testa (Angel)
   Understudy: Barclay DeVeau (Little Girl)

AWARDS
38th Tony Awards
Win
   Best Actress in a Musical—Chita Rivera

Nominations
   Best Original Score
   Best Actress in a Musical—Liza Minnelli
   Best Scenic Design
   Best Choreography

29th Drama Desk Awards
Win

Outstanding Actress in a Musical—Chita Rivera

Nominations

Outstanding Musical
Outstanding Actress in a Musical—Liza Minnelli
Outstanding Director of a Musical
Outstanding Lighting Design
Outstanding Set Design

Sunday in the Park with George

Two lovers struggle to connect through the painting A Sunday Afternoon on the Island of La Grande Jatte.

April 2, 1984–May 2, 1984–October 13, 1985
Booth Theatre
604 Performances
35 Previews

Musical Numbers

Act 1

Sunday in the Park with George
No Life
Color and Light
Gossip
The Day Off
Everybody Loves Louis
Finishing the Hat
We Do Not Belong Together
Beautiful
Sunday

Act 2

It's Hot Up Here
Chromolume #7
Putting It Together
Children and Art
Lesson #8
Move On
Sunday

Creative Team

Music and Lyrics by Stephen Sondheim
Book by James Lapine
Directed by James Lapine

Musical Director: Paul Gemignani
Music orchestrated by Michael Starobin

Scenic Design by Tony Straiges
Costume Design by Patricia Zipprodt and Ann Hould-Ward
Lighting Design by Richard Nelson
Sound Design by Tom Morse
Hair and Wig Design by Charles LoPresto
Hair Design by Richard Allen
Makeup Design by Richard Allen
Mr. Patinkin's hair designed by J. Roy Helland
Mr. Patinkin's makeup designed by J. Roy Helland

General Manager: Robert Kamlot
Company Manager: Richard Berg
Production Stage Manager: Charles Blackwell
Stage Managers: Fredric H. Orner and Loretta Robertson
Technical Supervisor: Theatrical Services, Inc.

Special Effects by Bran Ferren
Casting: John S. Lyons

Suggested by the painting *A Sunday Afternoon on the Island of La Grand Jatte* and the life of painter Georges Seurat
Set and costume design adapted from the Seurat painting from the Art Institute of Chicago

CAST

Mandy Patinkin—George
Bernadette Peters—Dot, Marie
Barbara Bryne—Old Lady, Blair Daniels
Dana Ivey—Yvonne, Naomi Eisen
Charles Kimbrough—Jules, Bob Greenberg
Mary D'Arcy—Celeste #2, Elaine
Danielle Ferland—Boy bathing in the River, Louise
Sue Anne Gershenson—Woman with baby carriage, Photographer
Cris Groenendaal—Man lying on the bank, Louis, Billy Webster
John Jellison—Man with bicycle, Museum Assistant

Kurt Knudson—Mr. Lee Randolph
Judith Moore—Nurse, Mrs. Harriet Pawling
Nancy Opel—Young Man sitting on the bank, Frieda, Betty
William Parry—Boatman, Charles Redmond
Michele Rigan—Little Girl
Brent Spiner—Franz, Dennis
Melanie Vaughan—Celeste #1, Waitress
Robert Westenberg—Soldier, Alex

Understudies

Sue Anne Gershenson (Young Man sitting on the bank, Frieda, Betty, Celeste #1, Nurse, Celeste #2, Elaine), Ray Gill (Franz, Dennis, Man with bicycle, Man lying on the bank, Louis, Billy Webster, Soldier, Alex, Mr. Lee Randolph), Joanna Glushak (Dot, Marie, Celeste #1, Nurse, Celeste #2, Elaine), Cris Groenendaal (Franz, Dennis, Soldier, Alex), John Jellison (Man lying on the bank, Louis, Billy Webster, Jules, Bob Greenberg, Boatman, Charles Redmond), Michele Rigan (Boy bathing in the River, Louise), Robert Westenberg (George (Act I), George (Act II)), and Sara Woods (Old Lady, Blair Daniels, Nurse, Mrs. Harriet Pawling, Yvonne, Naomi Eisen)

NOTABLE REPLACEMENTS

Joanna Glushak—Dot, Marie
Betsy Joslyn—Dot, Marie
Maryann Plunkett—Dot, Marie
Robert Westenberg—George
Cris Groenendaal—George
Harry Groener—George

AWARDS
36th Tony Awards
Wins

Best Scenic Design
Best Lighting Design

Nominations

    Best Musical
    Best Book of a Musical
    Best Original Score
    Best Direction of a Musical
    Best Actress in a Musical—Bernadette Peters
    Best Actor in a Musical—Mandy Patinkin
    Best Featured Actress in a Musical—Dana Ivey
    Best Costume Design

27th Drama Desk Awards

Wins

    Outstanding Musical
    Outstanding Book
    Outstanding Director of a Musical
    Outstanding Orchestration
    Outstanding Lyrics
    Outstanding Lighting Design
    Outstanding Set Design
    Outstanding Special Effects

Nominations

    Outstanding Actor in a Musical—Mandy Patinkin
    Outstanding Actress in a Musical—Bernadette Peters
    Outstanding Featured Actor in a Musical—Charles Kimbrough
    Outstanding Music
    Outstanding Costume Design

1985 Pulitzer Prize for Drama

INTO THE WOODS

Characters from the Grimm and Perrault fairy tales collide, with unfortunate results.

September 29, 1987–November 5, 1987–September 3, 1989
Martin Beck Theatre
765 Performances
43 Previews

MUSICAL NUMBERS

Act 1

Prologue: Into the Woods
Hello, Little Girl
I Guess This Is Goodbye
Maybe They're Magic
I Know Things Now
A Very Nice Prince
Giants in the Sky
Agony
It Takes Two
Stay with Me
On the Steps of the Palace
Ever After

Act 2

Prologue: So Happy
Agony (Reprise)
Lament
Any Moment
Moments in the Woods
Your Fault
Last Midnight
No More
No One Is Alone
Children Will Listen

CREATIVE TEAM

Music and Lyrics by Stephen Sondheim
Book by James Lapine
Directed by James Lapine

Music orchestrated by Jonathan Tunick
Musical Director: Paul Gemignani
Musical Staging by Lar Lubovitch

Scenic Design by Tony Straiges
Lighting Design by Richard Nelson
Costume Design by Ann Hould-Ward
Sound Design by Alan Stieb and James Brousseau
Hair Design by Phyllis Della Illien
Costumes based on original concepts by Patricia Zipprodt

Production Stage Manager: Frank Hartenstein
Stage Manager: Johnna Murray
Assistant Stage Managers: Marianne Cane and James Dawson
Production Supervisor: Peter Feller Sr.

General Manager: David, Strong, Warner, Inc.
Company Manager: Sandra Carlson
Casting: Joanna Merlin

CAST

Tom Aldredge—Narrator, Mysterious Man
Joanna Gleason—Baker's Wife
Bernadette Peters—Witch
Robert Westenberg—Wolf, Cinderella's Prince
Chip Zien—Baker
Barbara Bryne—Jack's Mother
Kim Crosby—Cinderella
Danielle Ferland—Little Red Riding Hood
Merle Louise—Cinderella's Mother, Grandmother, Giant
Ben Wright—Jack
Maureen Davis—Sleeping Beauty
Joy Franz—Cinderella's Stepmother
Philip Hoffman—Steward
Jean Kelly—Snow White

Edmund Lyndeck—Cinderella's Father
Kay McClelland—Florinda
Lauren Mitchell—Lucinda
Chuck Wagner—Rapunzel's Prince
Pamela Winslow—Rapunzel

Understudies
Jeff Blumenkrantz (Jack, Rapunzel's Prince, Steward), Maureen Davis (Rapunzel, Little Red Riding Hood, Snow White), Suzanne Douglas (Cinderella, Witch, Sleeping Beauty), Joy Franz (Witch), Philip Hoffman (Baker, Cinderella's Father), Jean Kelly (Rapunzel, Little Red Riding Hood), Carolyn Marlow (Cinderella's Step-mother, Jack's Mother, Cinderella's Mother, Grandmother, Giant), Kay McClelland (Baker's Wife), Lauren Mitchell (Baker's Wife), Michael Piontek (Jack, Rapunzel's Prince, Cinderella's Prince, Wolf), Chuck Wagner (Cinderella's Prince, Wolf), and Pamela Winslow (Cinderella, Lucinda, Florinda)

NOTABLE REPLACEMENTS
Ellen Foley—Witch
Betsy Joslyn—Witch
Phylicia Rashad—Witch
Nancy Dussault—Witch
Joy Franz—Witch
Kay McClelland—Baker's Wife
Mary Gordon Murray—Baker's Wife
Lauren Mitchell—Baker's Wife
Cynthia Sikes—Baker's Wife, Witch
Philip Hoffman—Baker
Dean Butler—Rapunzel's Prince
Don Goodspeed—Rapunzel's Prince
Patricia Ben Peterson—Cinderella
LuAnne Ponce—Little Red Riding Hood
Dick Cavett—Narrator
Edmund Lyndeck—Mysterious Man
Marin Mazzie—Rapunzel

Awards
42nd Tony Awards
Wins

Best Book of a Musical
Best Original Score
Best Actress in a Musical—Joanna Gleason

Nominations

Best Musical
Best Direction of a Musical
Best Featured Actor in a Musical—Robert Westenberg
Best Scenic Design
Best Costume Design
Best Lighting Design
Best Choreography

33rd Drama Desk Awards
Wins

Outstanding Musical
Outstanding Book of a Musical
Outstanding Featured Actor in a Musical—Robert Westenberg
Outstanding Featured Actress in a Musical—Joanna Gleason
Outstanding Lyrics

Nominations

Outstanding Actress in a Musical—Bernadette Peters
Outstanding Featured Actress in a Musical—Danielle Ferland
Outstanding Director of a Musical
Outstanding Orchestration
Outstanding Music
Outstanding Costume Design
Outstanding Lighting Design
Outstanding Set Design

1988 Theatre World Awards

Danielle Ferland

JEROME ROBBINS' BROADWAY

A revue of legendary director choreographer Jerome Robbins' theatrical career.

January 9, 1989–February 26, 1989–September 1, 1990
Imperial Theatre
663 Performances
55 Previews

MUSICAL NUMBERS

Act 1

Gotta Dance
Papa, Won't You Dance with Me?
Shall We Dance?
New York, New York
Sailors on the Town
Ya Got Me
Charleston
Comedy Tonight
I Still Get Jealous
West Side Story Suite

Act 2

The Small House of Uncle Thomas
You Gotta Have a Gimmick
I'm Flying
On a Sunday by the Sea
Mr. Monotony
Tradition
Tevye's Dream
Sunrise, Sunset
Wedding Dance
Some Other Time
New York, New York (Reprise)
Finale from On the Town

CREATIVE TEAM

Featuring Music by Irving Berlin, Leonard Bernstein, Jerry Bock, Moose Charlap, Morton Gould, Hugh Martin, Richard Rodgers, Stephen Sondheim, and Jule Styne

Featuring Lyrics by Sammy Cahn, Irving Berlin, Betty Comden, Adolph Green, Oscar Hammerstein II, Sheldon Harnick, Carolyn Leigh, Hugh Martin, and Stephen Sondheim
Narrative continuity by Jason Alexander

Entire Production Choreographed and Directed by Jerome Robbins
Co-Director: Grover Dale
West Side Story Co-Choreographer: Peter Gennaro
Assistants to Mr. Robbins: Cynthia Onrubia, Victor Castelli, and Jerry Mitchell

Music orchestrated by Sid Ramin and William D. Brohn
Music continuity by Scott Frankel
Musical Director: Paul Gemignani

Production Scenic Designer: Robin Wagner
Supervising Costume Designer: Joseph G. Aulisi
Scenic Design by Boris Aronson ("Fiddler on the Roof"), Jo Mielziner ("The King and I," "Gypsy"), Oliver Smith ("On the Town," "Billion Dollar Baby," "High Button Shoes," "West Side Story"), Robin Wagner ("Peter Pan," "Broadway at Night") and Tony Walton ("A Funny Thing Happened on the Way to the Forum")
Assistant Scenic Design: Atkin Pace, Thomas Peter Sarr, and Charles E. McCarry
Assistant to Oliver Smith: Campbell Baird
Costume Design by Joseph G. Aulisi ("Peter Pan," "Miss Liberty," and "Call Me Madam" ("Mr. Monotony")), Alvin Colt ("On the Town"), Raoul Pène Du Bois ("Gypsy"), Irene Sharaff ("Billion Dollar Baby," "West Side Story," "The King and I"), Tony Walton ("A Funny Thing Happened on the Way to the Forum"), Miles White ("High Button Shoes"), and Patricia Zipprodt ("Fiddler on the Roof")
Assistant Costume Design: Mary L. Hayes, Marsha L. Eck, and Richard Schurkamp

Lighting Design by Jennifer Tipton
Assistant to Mr. Aulisi: Douglas C. Petitjean
Assistant Lighting Design: David Finn and David Neville
Sound Design by Otts Munderloh
Assistant to Mr. Munderloh: Serge Ossorguine
Hair Design by J. Roy Helland
Makeup Design by J. Roy Helland

General Manager: Leonard Soloway; Company Manager: Brian
  Dunbar
Assistant General Manager: Abby Evans
Production Supervisor: Charles Blackwell
Production Stage Manager: Beverley Randolph
Stage Manager: Jim Woolley

Casting: Jay Binder
Flying by Foy

CAST

Jason Alexander	Jeffrey Lee Broadhurst
Charlotte d'Amboise	Christophe Caballero
Robert La Fosse	Mindy Cartwright
Susann Fletcher	Irene Cho
Nancy Hess	Jamie Cohen
Susan Kikuchi	Camille de Ganon
Michael Kubala	Donna Di Meo
Jane Lanier	Donna Marie Elio
Joey McKneely	Mark Esposito
Luis Perez	Scott Fowler
Faith Prince	Angelo H. Fraboni
Debbie Shapiro	Ramon Galindo
Scott Wise	Nicholas Garr
Richard Amaro	Gregory Garrison
Dorothy Benham	Carolyn Goor

Michael Scott Gregory
Andrew Grose
Alexia Hess
Louise Hickey
Eric A. Hoisington
Barbara Hoon
JoAnn M. Hunter
Scott Jovovich
Pamela Khoury
Mary Ann Lamb
David Lowenstein
Michael Lynch
Greta Martin
Joey McKneely
Julio Monge
Troy Myers
Maria Neenan

Jack Noseworthy
Steve Ochoa
Kelly Patterson
James Rivera
Tom Robbins
George Russell
Greg Schanuel
Renée Stork
Mary Ellen Stuart
Linda Talcott
Leslie Traye
Ellen Troy
Andi Tyler
Elaine Wright
Barbara Yeager
Alice Yearsley

NOTABLE REPLACEMENTS

Alan Ariano, Cleve Asbury, Harrison Beal, Bill Brassea, Bill Burns, Christophe Caballero, Tony Caligagan, Mindy Cartwright, Christopher Childers, Christine DeVito, Colleen Durham, Denise Faye, Colleen Fitzpatrick, Angelo H. Fraboni, Jeff Gardner, Lyd-Lyd Gaston, Sean Grant, Ned Hannah, Alexia Hess, Kipling Houston, JoAnn M. Hunter, K. Craig Innes, Cherylyn Jones, Lisa Leguillou, John MacInnis, Terrence Mann, Karen Mason, Maureen Moore, Troy Myers, Maria Neenan, Steve Ochoa, Jacquie Porter, James Rivera, Erin Robbins, Tony Roberts, Mary Rotella, Greg Schanuel, Scott Spahr, Dorothy Stanley, Linda Talcott, Nancy Ticotin, Leslie Trayer, Ellen Troy, Sergio Trujillo, Andi Tyler, Marc Villa, Deanna D. Wells, and Lori Werner

AWARDS
43rd Tony Awards
Wins
Best Musical
Best Direction of a Music
Best Actor in a Musical—Jason Alexander
Best Featured Actor in a Musical—Scott Wise
Best Featured Actress in a Musical—Debbie Shapiro
Best Lighting Design

Nominations
Best Actor in a Musical—Robert La Fosse
Best Actress in a Musical—Charlotte d'Amboise
Best Featured Actress in a Musical—Jane Lanier, Faith Prince

34th Drama Desk Awards
Wins
Outstanding Musical
Outstanding Actor in a Musical—Jason Alexander
Outstanding Lighting Design

Nominations
Outstanding Actor in a Musical—Scott Wise
Outstanding Actress in a Musical—Faith Prince, Debbie Shapiro

CRAZY FOR YOU

A would-be song and dance man does whatever it takes to win the heart of the woman he loves.

January 31, 1992–February 19, 1992–January 7, 1996
Shubert Theatre
1,622 Performances
21 Previews

MUSICAL NUMBERS

Act 1

K-ra-azy for You
I Can't Be Bothered Now
Bidin' My Time
Things Are Looking Up
Could You Use Me
Shall We Dance?
Someone to Watch Over Me
Slap That Bass
Embraceable You
Tonight's the Night
I Got Rhythm

Act 2

The Real American Folk Song
Is a Rag
What Causes That?
Naughty Baby
Stiff Upper Lip
They Can't Take That Away
from Me
But Not for Me
Nice Work If You Can Get It
Finale

CREATIVE TEAM

Music by George Gershwin
Lyrics by Ira Gershwin
Additional lyrics by Gus Kahn and Desmond Carter
Book by Ken Ludwig
Directed by Mike Ockrent
Choreographed by Susan Stroman
Associate Director: Steven Zweigbaum

Assistant Choreographer: Chris Peterson
Conceived by Ken Ludwig and Mike Ockrent
Inspired by material by Guy Bolton and John McGowan

Dance arrangements by Peter Howard
Incidental music arranged by Peter Howard
Music orchestrated by William D. Brohn
Musical Director: Paul Gemignani
Additional orchestrations by Sid Ramin

Scenic Design by Robin Wagner
Costume Design by William Ivey Long
Lighting Design by Paul Gallo
Sound Design by Otts Munderloh
Hair Design by Angela Gari
Makeup Consultant: Randy Mercer
Additional Hair Styles and Principal Wigs by Paul Huntley
Assistant Scenic Design: Dave Peterson, Atkin Pace, and Maureen
    Going
Associate Costume Design: Scott Traugott
Assistant Costume Design: Nancy Palmatier
Associate Lighting Design: Michael Lincoln
Assistant Lighting Design: Robert Jared and Vivien Leone
Assistant to Mr. Gallo: David Weiner
Assistant Sound Design: Scott Sanders
General Manager: Gatchell & Neufeld, Ltd.
Company Manager: Abbie M. Strassler
Production Manager: Peter Fulbright
Stage Managers: John Bonanni and Mindy Farbrother
Production Stage Manager: Steven Zweigbaum

CAST

Jodi Benson—Polly Baker
Harry Groener—Bobby Child
Bruce Adler—Bela Zangler
John Hillner—Lank Hawkins

Michele Pawk—Irene Roth
Ronn Carroll—Everett Baker
Jane Connell—Mother
Tripp Hanson, Brian M. Nalepka, Hal Shane—The Manhattan
Rhythm Kings
Beth Leavel—Tess
Stephen Temperley—Eugene
Amelia White—Patricia

Ensemble

Fred Anderson, Jeffrey Lee Broadhurst, Gerry Burkhardt, Pamela
Everett, Joel Goodness, Tripp Hanson, Ida Henry, Michael Kubala,
Paula Leggett, Stacey Logan, Penny Ayn Maas, Jean Marie, Salomé
Mazard, Casey Nicholaw, Judine Hawkins Richárd, Ray Roderick,
and Louise Ruck

Understudies

Gerry Burkhardt (Everett Baker), Michael Kubala (Bobby Child,
Lank Hawkins, Bela Zangler), Beth Leavel (Polly Baker), Paula Leg-
gett (Tess), Penny Ayn Maas (Patsy), Jessica Molaskey (Irene Roth,
Patricia), Casey Nicholaw (Eugene), and Amelia White (Mother)

NOTABLE REPLACEMENTS

Karen Ziemba—Polly Baker
James Brennan—Bobby Child
Melinda Buckley—Tess
Carleton Carpenter—Everett Baker, Bela Zangler
Al Checco—Bela Zangler, Everett Baker
Roger Horchow—Everett Baker, Bela Zangler
John Jellison—Bela Zangler, Everett Baker
Daren Kelly—Lank Hawkins
Kay McClelland—Irene Roth
Pia Zadora—Irene Roth
Colleen Smith Wallnau—Patricia

AWARDS
46th Tony Awards
Wins

Best Musical
Best Choreography
Best Costume Design

Nominations

Best Book of a Musical
Best Direction of a Musical
Best Actor in a Musical—Harry Groener
Best Actress in a Musical—Jodi Benson
Best Featured Actor in a Musical—Bruce Adler
Best Lighting Design

37th Drama Desk Awards
Wins

Outstanding Musical
Outstanding Choreography

Nominations

Outstanding Featured Actor in a Musical—Bruce Adler
Outstanding Featured Actress in a Musical—Michelle Pawk
Outstanding Orchestration/Musical Adaptation
Outstanding Costumes
Outstanding Set Design
Outstanding Direction of a Musical

PASSION

A tale of love, loss, and desperation in a remote Italian military outpost.

March 24, 1994–May 9, 1994–January 7, 1995
Plymouth Theatre
280 Performances
52 Previews

MUSICAL NUMBERS
One Act
Happiness
First Letter
Second Letter
Third Letter
Fourth Letter
I Read
Transition
Garden Sequence
Trio
Soldiers' Gossip
I Wish I Could Forget You
Flashback
Sunrise Letter
Is This What You Call Love?
Forty Days
Loving You
Letter from Clara
Christmas Carol (in Italian)
Farewell Letter
No One Has Ever Loved Me
Finale

CREATIVE TEAM

Music and Lyrics by Stephen Sondheim
Book by James Lapine
Based on the film *Passione d'Amore* directed by Ettore Scola
Directed by James Lapine
Associate Director: Jane Comfort

Music orchestrated by Jonathan Tunick
Musical Director: Paul Gemignani

Scenic Design by Adrianne Lobel
Costume Design by Jane Greenwood
Lighting Design by Beverly Emmons
Sound Design by Otts Munderloh
Hair Design by Phyllis Della
Dialect Coach: Deborah Hecht

General Manager: Marvin A. Krauss Associates, Inc.
Company Manager: Nina Skriloff
Associate Company Manager: Elizabeth M. Blitzer
Production Stage Manager: Beverley Randolph
Technical Supervisor: Fred J. Gallo Jr.

CAST

Donna Murphy—Fosca
Jere Shea—Giorgio
Tom Aldredge—Doctor Tambourri
William Duff-Griffin (replaced in previews)—*Doctor Tambourri*
Linda Balgord—Fosca's Mother
George Dvorsky—Private Augenti
Gregg Edelman—Colonel Ricci
Cris Groenendaal—Major Rizzolli
Juliet Lambert—Mistress
Marin Mazzie—Clara
Marcus Olson—Sergeant Lombardi

William Parry—Lieutenant Barri
Matthew Porretta—Ludovic
Francis Ruivivar—Lieutenant Torasso
John Leslie Wolfe—Fosca's Father

Understudies

Linda Balgord (Fosca), Gibby Brand (Doctor Tambourri, Fosca's Father, Private Augenti, Sergeant Lombardi), George Dvorsky (Giorgio, Ludovic), Colleen Fitzpatrick (Fosca, Clara, Fosca's Mother, Mistress), Juliet Lambert (Clara), Frank Lombardi (Private Augenti), William Parry (Colonel Ricci), Matthew Porretta (Giorgio), and John Leslie Wolfe (Lieutenant Torasso, Major Rizzolli, Lieutenant Barri, Sergeant Lombardi)

NOTABLE REPLACEMENTS
John Antony—Private Augenti
Colleen Fitzpatrick—Ludovic
T. J. Meyers—Major Rizzolli
Christopher Peccaro—Ludovic
Peter Reardon—Soldier
Andy Umberger—Fosca's Father

AWARDS
48th Tony Awards
Wins

Best Musical
Best Book of a Musical
Best Original Score
Best Actress in a Musical—Donna Murphy

Nominations

Best Actor in a Musical—Jere Shea
Best Featured Actor in a Musical—Tom Aldredge
Best Featured Actress in a Musical—Marin Mazzie
Best Direction of a Musical

Best Costume Design
Best Lighting Design

39th Drama Desk Awards
Wins

Outstanding Musical
Outstanding Book
Outstanding Actress in a Musical—Donna Murphy
Outstanding Orchestrations
Outstanding Lyrics
Outstanding Music

Nominations

Outstanding Actor in a Musical—Jere Shea
Outstanding Director of a Musical
Outstanding Costume Design
Outstanding Lighting Design
Outstanding Set Design

1994 Theatre World Awards
Jere Shea

A CHRISTMAS CAROL

Music by Alan Menken
Lyrics by Lynn Ahrens
Book by Mike Ockrent and
Lynn Ahrens
Based on Charles Dickens' 1843
novella of the same name

Directed by Mike Ockrent
Choreographed by Susan Strohman
Music Orchestrated by
Michael Starobin

BIG

Music by David Shire
Lyrics by Richard Maltby Jr.
Book by John Weidman
Based on the 1988 film of the
same name

Directed by Mike Ockrent
Choreographed by Susan
Strohman

Musical Director:
  Paul Gemignani

Scenic Design by Tony Walton
Costume Design by William
  Ivey Long
Lighting Design by Jules Fisher
  and Peggy Eisenhauer
Sound Design by Tony Meola
Projections by Wendall K.
  Harrington

Music Orchestrated by Douglas
  Besterman
Electronic music designed by
  Brian Besterman
Musical Director: Paul
  Gemignani

Scenic Design by Robin Wagner
Costume Design by William Ivey
  Long
Lighting Design by Paul Gallo
Sound Design by Steve Canyon
  Kennedy
Moving Lights Programmer:
  Paul J. Sonnleitner

Produced in association with
  F.A.O. Schwarz

1776

The events leading up to the signing and ratification of the Declaration of Independence.

July 16, 1997–August 14, 1997–June 14, 1998
Gershwin Theatre
333 Performances
34 Previews

MUSICAL NUMBERS

Act 1

Sit Down, John
Piddle, Twiddle and Resolve
Till Then
The Lees of Old Virginia
But Mr. Adams
Yours, Yours, Yours
He Plays the Violin
Cool, Cool, Considerate Men
Momma Look Sharp

Act 2

The Egg
Molasses to Rum
Compliments
Is Anybody There?

CREATIVE TEAM

Music by Sherman Edwards
Lyrics by Sherman Edwards
Book by Peter Stone
From a concept by Sherman Edwards

Directed by Scott Ellis
Choreographed by Kathleen Marshall
Assistant Director: Chris Kahler
Assistant Choreographer: Danny Wright

Music orchestrated by Brian Besterman
Dance arrangements by Peter Howard
Musical Director: Paul Gemignani
Assistant Musical Director: Mark Mitchell

Scenic Design by Tony Walton
Costume Design by William Ivey Long
Lighting Design by Brian Nason
Sound Design by Brian Ronan
Hair and Wig Design by David Brian Brown
Associate Scenic Design: Klara Zieglerova
Assistant Lighting Design: Tiffany Yelton

Production Supervisor: Michael Curry
Production Manager: Glenn Merwede
Production Stage Manager: Lori M. Doyle
Stage Manager: David Sugarman

CAST

Tom Aldredge—Stephen Hopkins
Joseph Cassidy—Leather Apron
Michael Cumpsty—John Dickinson
MacIntyre Dixon—Andrew McNair
Dashiell Eaves—Courier
Gregg Edelman—Edward Rutledge
Linda Emond—Abigail Adams
Tom Riis Farrell—Lewis Morris
Merwin Foard—Richard Henry Lee
John Herrera—Roger Sherman
Pat Hingle—Benjamin Franklin
Jerry Lanning—Rev. John Witherspoon
Kevin Ligon—George Read
David Lowenstein—Joseph Hewes
Daniel Marcus—Robert Livingston
Michael X. Martin—Dr. Josiah Bartlett

Michael McCormick—Caesar Rodney
Bill Nolte—Col. Thomas McKean
Guy Paul—Charles Thomson
Richard Poe—John Hancock
Ben Sheaffer—Painter
Brent Spiner—John Adams
Ric Stoneback—Samuel Chase
Paul Michael Valley—Thomas Jefferson
Lauren Ward—Martha Jefferson
Robert Westenberg—Dr. Lyman Hall
Michael Winther—James Wilson

Understudies

Joseph Cassidy (Roger Sherman, Richard Henry Lee, Edward Rutledge), Rob Donohoe (Dr. Josiah Bartlett, Stephen Hopkins, Caesar Rodney, Andrew McNair), Rebecca Eichenberger (Abigail Adams, Martha Jefferson), Tim Fauvell (Lewis Morris, Robert Livingston, Samuel Chase, Joseph Hewes), John Herrera (John Adams), James Hindman (Rev. John Witherspoon, Col. Thomas McKean, Dr. Lyman Hall, Charles Thomson), David Lowenstein (James Wilson), Michael X. Martin (John Dickinson), Michael McCormick (John Hancock), Bill Nolte (Benjamin Franklin), Tom Roland (Benjamin Franklin), and Ben Sheaffer (George Read, Thomas Jefferson, Leather Apron, Courier)

Notable Replacements

Carolee Carmello—Abigail Adams
Michael McCormick—John Adams

Awards

51st Tony Awards

Nominations

Best Revival of a Musical
Best Direction of a Musical
Best Featured Actor in a Musical—Gregg Edelman

43rd Drama Desk Awards
Win

Outstanding Featured Actor in a Musical—Gregg Edelman

Nominations

Outstanding Revival of a Musical
Outstanding Actor in a Musical—Brent Spiner
Outstanding Direction of a Musical

HIGH SOCIETY

A socialite's wedding brings together high and low classes in a tangled web of love and honor.

March 31, 1998–April 27, 1998–August 30, 1998
St. James Theatre
144 Performances
27 Previews

MUSICAL NUMBERS

Act 1

High Society
Ridin' High
Throwing a Ball Tonight
Little One
Who Wants to Be a
　Millionaire?
I Love Paris
She's Got That Thing
Once Upon a Time
True Love

Act 2

High Society (Reprise)
Let's Misbehave
I'm Getting Myself Ready
　for You
Once Upon a Time (Reprise)
Just One of Those Things
Well, Did You Evah?
You're Sensational
Say It with Gin
Ridin' High (Reprise)
It's All Right with Me
He's a Right Guy
Samantha
True Love (Reprise)

CREATIVE TEAM

Music and Lyrics by Cole Porter
Additional lyrics by Susan Birkenhead
Book by Arthur Kopit

Based on the play *The Philadelphia Story* by Philip Barry
Also based on the movie *High Society*, owned by Turner
    Entertainment Co.
Directed by Christopher Renshaw
Replacement Director: Des McAnuff
Musical Staging by Lar Lubovitch
Replacement Choreographer: Wayne Cilento
Associate Choreographer: Marcia Milgrom Dodge
Assistant Director: Anders Cato

Dance arrangements by Glen Kelly
Music orchestrated by William David Brohn
Musical Director: Paul Gemignani

Scenic Design by Loy Arcenas
Associate Scenic Design: Myung Hee Cho
Assistant Scenic Design: Emily Beck, Ann Keehbauch, Russell
    Parkman, Michael V. Sims, and Mikiko Uesugi
Assistants to the Scenic Designer: Anthony Bishop, Andrew Sachs,
    and Matthew Anderson
Costume Design by Jane Greenwood
Assistant Costume Design: MaryAnn D. Smith and Jan Finnell
Lighting Design by Howell Binkley
Associate Lighting Design: Chad McArver
Assistant Lighting Design: Les Dickert
Sound Design by Tony Meola
Associate Sound Design: Kai Harada
Hair and Wig Design by Paul Huntley

General Manager: Stuart Thompson
Associate General Manager: Florie Seery
Company Manager: Kimberly Kelley
Assistant Company Manager: Thia Calloway
Production Supervisor: Steven Zweigbaum
Technical Supervisor: Gene O'Donovan

Stage Manager: Rolt Smith
Assistant Stage Manager: Tamlyn Freund
Technical Supervision: Aurora Productions

CAST

Stephen Bogardus—Mike Connor
Melissa Errico—Tracy Samantha Lord
Daniel McDonald—C. K. Dexter Haven
John McMartin—Uncle Willie
Randy Graff—Liz Imbrie
Lisa Banes—Margaret Lord
Barry Finkel—Chester
Daniel Gerroll—Seth Lord
Kisha Howard—Sunny
Betsy Joslyn—Patsy
Anna Kendrick—Dinah Lord
Marc Kudisch—George Kittredge
William Ryall—Edmund
Jeff Skowron—Stanley
Jennifer Smith—Polly
Dorothy Stanley—Peg
Glenn Turner—Arthur

Understudies

Barry Finkel (Seth Lord, Uncle Willie), William Ryall (Seth Lord, Uncle Willie), Holiday Segal (Dinah Lord), Sarah Solie Shannon (Tracy Samantha Lord), Jeff Skowron (Mike Connor), Jennifer Smith (Liz Imbrie, Margaret Lord), and Dorothy Stanley (Liz Imbrie, Margaret Lord)

AWARDS

52nd Tony Awards

Nominations

Best Featured Actor in a Musical—John McMartin
Best Featured Actress in a Musical—Anna Kendrick

44th Drama Desk Awards
Nominations

    Outstanding New Musical
    Outstanding Actress in a Musical—Melissa Errico
    Outstanding Featured Actor in a Musical—John McMartin
    Outstanding Featured Actress in a Musical—Anna Kendrick

1998 Theatre World Awards
    Anna Kendrick

Kiss Me, Kate 1999

A divorced couple reunite to perform in a musical adaptation of The Taming of the Shrew.

October 25, 1999–November 18, 1999–December 30, 2001
Martin Beck Theatre
881 Performances
28 Previews

Musical Numbers

Act 1

Another Op'nin' Another Show
Why Can't You Behave
Wunderbar
So in Love
We Open in Venice
Tom, Dick or Harry
I've Come to Wive It Wealthily in Padua
I Hate Men
Were Thine That Special Face
Cantiamo D'Amore
Kiss Me, Kate

Act 2

Too Darn Hot
Where Is the Life That Late I Led?
Always True to You (In My Fashion)
From This Moment On
Bianca
So in Love (Reprise)
Brush Up Your Shakespeare
Pavane
I Am Ashamed That Women Are So Simple
Kiss Me, Kate (Reprise)

Creative Team

Music and Lyrics by Cole Porter
Book by Sam Spewack and Bella Spewack
From *The Taming of the Shrew*, by William Shakespeare
Uncredited contributions by John Guare

Directed by Michael Blakemore
Choreographed by Kathleen Marshall
Associate Choreographer: Rob Ashford

Music orchestrated by Don Sebesky
Dance arrangements by David Chase
Musical Director: Paul Gemignani

Scenic Design by Robin Wagner
Associate Scenic Design: David Peterson
Costume Design by Martin Pakledinaz
Associate Costume Design: Marion Williams
Assistant Costume Design: Eden Miller and Kristian Kraai
Assistant to Mr. Pakledinaz: Juliet Ouyoung
Lighting Design by Peter Kaczorowski
Assistant Lighting Design: Traci Klainer and Michael P. Jones
Moving Light Programmer: Josh Weitzman and Kai Harada
Sound Design by Tony Meola
Wig Design by Paul Huntley

General Manager: 101 Productions, Ltd.
Company Manager: Ron Gubin
Associate Company Manager: Elie Landau
Production Supervisor: Steven Zweigbaum
Production Manager: Arthur Siccardi
Stage Manager: Àra Marx
Assistant Stage Manager: Elaine Bayless

CAST

Marin Mazzie—Lilli Vanessi/Katharine
Brian Stokes Mitchell—Fred Graham/Petruchio
Michael Berresse—Bill Calhoun/Lucentio
Ron Holgate—Harrison Howell
John Horton—Harry Trevor/Baptista
Adriane Lenox—Hattie

Stanley Wayne Mathis—Paul
Michael Mulheren—Second Man
Amy Spanger—Lois Lane/Bianca
Lee Wilkof—First Man

Ensemble
Eric Michael Gillett, Patty Goble, Blake Hammond, JoAnn M. Hunter, Darren Lee, Nancy Lemenager, Michael X. Martin, Kevin Neil McCready, Carol Lee Meadows, Elizabeth Mills, Linda Mugleston, Robert Ousley, Vince Pesce, Cynthia Sophiea, and Jerome Vivona

Understudies
Patty Goble (Lilli Vanessi/Katharine), Blake Hammond (First Man, Second Man), JoAnn M. Hunter (Lois Lane/Bianca), Nancy Lemenager (Lois Lane/Bianca), Michael X. Martin (Fred Graham/Petruchio, Second Man, Harrison Howell), Kevin Neil McCready (Bill Calhoun/Lucentio), Robert Ousley (Harry Trevor/Baptista), Vince Pesce (Hortensio (Second Suitor), T. Oliver Reid (Paul, Hortensio (Second Suitor), Gremio (First Suitor), Cynthia Sophiea (Hattie), and Jerome Vivona (Gremio (First Suitor)

NOTABLE REPLACEMENTS
Carolee Carmello—Lilli Vanessi/Katharine
Burke Moses—Fred Graham/Petruchio
David Elder—Bill Calhoun/Lucentio
Kevin Neil McCready—Bill Calhoun/Lucentio
JoAnn M. Hunter—Lois Lane/Bianca
Janine LaManna—Lois Lane/Bianca
Walter Charles—Harrison Howell
Mamie Duncan-Gibbs—Hattie
Herb Foster—Harry Trevor/Baptista

AWARDS
54th Tony Awards
Wins

> Best Revival of a Musical
> Best Actor in a Musical—Brian Stokes Mitchell
> Best Direction of a Musical
> Best Costume Design
> Best Orchestrations

Nominations

> Best Actress in a Musical—Marin Mazzie
> Best Featured Actor in a Musical—Michael Berresse
> Best Featured Actor in a Musical—Michael Mulheren
> Best Featured Actor in a Musical—Lee Wilkof
> Best Choreography
> Best Scenic Design
> Best Lighting Design

45th Drama Desk Awards
Wins

> Outstanding Revival of a Musical
> Outstanding Actor in a Musical—Brian Stokes Mitchell
> Outstanding Director of a Musical
> Outstanding Orchestrations
> Outstanding Set Design of a Musical
> Outstanding Costume Design

Nominations

> Outstanding Actress in a Musical—Marin Mazzie
> Outstanding Featured Actor in a Musical—Lee Wilkof
> Outstanding Featured Actor in a Musical—Michael Mulheren
> Outstanding Choreography

ASSASSINS

Nine people attempt to justify their assassination attempts against the US president.

Off Broadway
> December 18, 1990–February 16, 1991
> Playwrights Horizons Wilder Theater
> 73 Performances

Broadway
> March 31, 2004–April 22, 2004–July 18th 2004
> Studio 54
> 101 Performances
> 26 Previews

MUSICAL NUMBERS
(2004 Broadway iteration)
> Everybody's Got the Right
> The Ballad of Booth
> How I Saved Roosevelt
> Gun Song
> The Ballad of Czolgosz
> Unworthy of Your Love
> The Ballad of Guiteau
> Another National Anthem
> Something Just Broke
> Everybody's Got the Right (Reprise)

CREATIVE TEAM

Off Broadway

Music and Lyrics by
    Stephen Sondheim
Book by John
    Weidman
Directed by Jerry
    Zaks
Choreographer by
    D. J. Giagni
Based on an idea by
    Charles Gilbert Jr.

Musical Director:
    Paul Gemignani
Music orchestrated
    by Michael Starobin

Scenic Design by
    Loren Sherman
Costume Design by
    William Ivey Long
Lighting Design by
    Paul Gallo
Sound Design by
    Scott Lehrer

Production Stage
    Manager—Clifford
    Schwartz

Broadway

Music and Lyrics by Stephen Sondheim
Book by John Weidman
Directed by Joe Mantello
Musical Staging by Jonathan Butterell
Based on an idea by Charles Gilbert Jr.

Musical Director: Paul Gemignani
Music orchestrated by Michael Starobin

Scenic Design by Robert Brill
Costume Design by Susan Hilferty
Lighting Design by Jules Fisher and
    Peggy Eisenhauer
Sound Design by Dan Moses Schreier
Hair and Wig Design by Tom Watson
Projection Design by Elaine J. McCarthy
Lead Assistant Set Designer: Tobin Ost
Assistant Costume Design: Maiko
    Matsushima
Assistant Lighting Design: Scott Davis
Associate Sound Design: David Bullard
Assistant Projection Design: Jacob
Daniel Pinholster

Roundabout General Manager: Sydney
    Davolos
Company Manager: Nichole Larson
Production Stage Manager: William
Joseph Barnes
Stage Manager: Jon Krause

Roundabout Technical Supervisor:
Steve Beers Special Effects Equipment
by Jauchem & Meeh, Inc.

1990 Playwrights Horizons Cast

Proprietor—William Parry Leon
Leon Czolgosz—Terrence Mann
John Hinckley—Greg Germann
Charles Guiteau—Jonathan
Hadary
Giuseppe Zangara—Eddie
Korbich
Samuel Byck—Lee Wilkof
Lynette Fromme—Annie
Golden
Sara Jane Moore—Debra Monk
John Wilkes Booth—Victor
Garber
Balladeer—Patrick Cassidy
David Herold—Marcus Olson
Bartender—John Jellison
Emma Goldman—Lyn Greene
James Garfield—William Parry
James Blaine—John Jellison
Hangman—Marcus Olson
Warden—John Jellison
Billy—Michael Shulman
Gerald Ford—William Parry
Lee Harvey Oswald—Jace
Alexander

2004 Broadway Cast

Proprietor—Marc Kudisch
Leon Czolgosz—James Barbour
John Hinckley—Alexander Gem-
ignani
Charles Guiteau—Denis O'Hare
Giuseppe Zangara—Jeffrey Kuhn
Samuel Byck—Mario Cantone
Lynette Fromme—Mary
Catherine Garrison
Sara Jane Moore—Becky Ann
Baker
John Wilkes Booth—Michael
Cerveris
Balladeer—Neil Patrick Harris
David Herold—Brandon Wardell
A Housewife—Kendra
Kassebaum
Emma Goldman—Anne L.
Nathan
James Garfield—Merwin Foard
James Blaine—James Clow
Billy—Eamon Foley
David Herold—Brandon Wardell
Lee Harvey Oswald—Neil
Patrick Harris

AWARDS

58th Tony Awards

Wins

Best Revival of a Musical
Best Featured Actor in a Musical—Michael Cerveris
Best Direction of a Musical
Best Lighting Design
Best Orchestrations

Nominations

Best Featured Actor in a Musical—Denis O'Hare
Best Scenic Design

49th Drama Desk Awards
Wins

Outstanding Revival of a Musical
Outstanding Orchestrations
Outstanding Lighting Design
Outstanding Sound Design

Nominations

Outstanding Featured Actor in a Musical—Marc Kudisch
Outstanding Director of a Musical
Outstanding Set Design of a Musical

2004 Theatre World Awards

Alexander Gemignani

THE MYSTERY OF EDWIN DROOD

An unfinished Charles Dickens murder mystery reaches an unpredictable conclusion.

October 19, 2012–November 13, 2012–March 10, 2012
Studio 54
136 Performances
28 Previews

MUSICAL NUMBERS

Act 1

There You Are
A Man Could Go Quite Mad
Two Kinsmen
Moonfall
Moonfall Quartet
The Wages of Sin
Jasper's Vision/Smoke Ballet
Ceylon/A British Subject
Both Sides of the Coin
Perfect Strangers
No Good Can Come from Bad
Never the Luck
Off to the Races

Act 2

An English Music Hall
Settling Up the Score
The Name of Love/Moonfall (Reprise)
Don't Quit While You're Ahead
The Solution

CREATIVE TEAM

Book and Music and Lyrics by Rupert Holmes
Suggested by the unfinished novel by Charles Dickens

Directed by Scott Ellis
Choreographed by Warren Carlyle
Associate Director: Dave Solomon
Associate Choreographer: Angie Canuel

Music orchestrated by Rupert Holmes
Dance arrangements by Sam Davis
Musical Director: Paul Gemignani

Scenic Design by Anna Louizos
Costume Design by William Ivey Long
Lighting Design by Brian Nason
Sound Design by Tony Meola
Hair and Wig Design by Paul Huntley
Makeup Design by Angelina Avallone
Moving Light Programmer: Alex Fogel
Associate Scenic Design: Jeremy W. Foil
Associate Costume Design: Tom Beall
Associate Hair and Wig Design: Giovanna Calabretta
Assistant Scenic Design: Aimee Dombo
Assistant Lighting Design: Ken Elliott
Assistant Sound Design: Adair Mallory
Assistant Hair and Wig Design: Carrie Rohm
Assistant Makeup Design: Robert Amodeo

Dialect Coach: Kate Wilson
Fight direction by Rick Sordelet
Dance Captain: Justin Greer
Fight Captain: Kyle Coffman
Production Stage Manager: Lori M. Doyle
Stage Manager: Scott Taylor Rollison

CAST

Stephanie J. Block—Edwin Drood/Miss Alice Nutting
Will Chase—John Jasper/Mr. Clive Paget

Gregg Edelman—The Reverend Mr. Crisparkle/Mr. Cedric Moncrieff

Jim Norton—Chairman/Mr. William Cartwright

Chita Rivera—The Princess Puffer/Miss Angela Prysock

Nicholas Barasch—Deputy/Master Nick Cricker

Peter Benson—Bazzard/Mr. Phillip Bax

Alison Cimmet—Beatrice/Miss Violet Balfour

Kyle Coffman—Mr. Christopher Lyon

Nick Corley—Stage Manager and Barkeep/Mr. James Throttle

Robert Creighton—Durdles/Mr. Nick Cricker

Janine DiVita—Wendy/Miss Isabel Yearsley

Andy Karl—Neville Landless/Mr. Victor Grinstead

Shannon Lewis—Miss Florence Gill

Jessie Mueller—Helena Landless/Miss Janet Conover

Spencer Plachy—Mr. Harry Sayle

Kiira Schmidt—Miss Gwendolen Pynn

Eric Sciotto—Mr. Alan Eliot

Jim Walton—Mr. Montague Pruitt

Betsy Wolfe—Rosa Bud/Miss Deirdre Peregrine

Understudies

Alison Cimmet (Helena Landless/Miss Janet Conover, The Princess Puffer/Miss Angela Prysock), Kyle Coffman (Deputy/Master Nick Cricker), Nick Corley (Bazzard/Mr. Phillip Bax, Durdles/Mr. Nick Cricker, The Reverend Mr. Crisparkle/Mr. Cedric Moncrieff), Janine DiVita (Edwin Drood/Miss Alice Nutting, Rosa Bud/Miss Deirdre Peregrine), Spencer Plachy (John Jasper/Mr. Clive Paget, Neville Landless/Mr. Victor Grinstead), Eric Sciotto (John Jasper/Mr. Clive Paget, Neville Landless/Mr. Victor Grinstead), and Jim Walton (The Reverend Mr. Crisparkle/Mr. Cedric Moncrieff, Chairman/Mr. William Cartwright)

NOTABLE REPLACEMENTS

Erin Davie—Rosa Bud/Miss Deirdre Peregrine

Banana Joe—Miss Alice Nutting's dog

Andrew Samonsky—Neville Landless/Mr. Victor Grinstead

AWARDS
67th Tony Awards
Nominations

Best Revival of a Musical
Best Actress in a Musical—Stephanie J. Block
Best Actor in a Musical—Will Chase
Best Direction of a Musical
Best Scenic Design of a Musical

58th Drama Desk Awards
Win

Outstanding Sound Design in a Musical

Nominations

Outstanding Revival of a Musical
Outstanding Actor in a Musical—Jim Norton
Outstanding Actress in a Musical—Stephanie J. Block
Outstanding Featured Actor in a Musical—Andy Karl
Outstanding Featured Actress in a Musical—Jessie Mueller
Outstanding Set Design

SHE LOVES ME

Two feuding perfume clerks are entangled in a web of love letters and mistaken identity.

February 19, 2016–March 17, 2016–June 10, 2016
Studio 54
132 Performances
31 Previews

MUSICAL NUMBERS

Act 1

Overture
Good Morning, Good Day
Sounds While Selling
Days Gone By
No More Candy
Three Letters
Tonight at Eight
I Don't Know His Name
Perspective
Goodbye, Georg
Will He Like Me?
Ilona
I Resolve
A Romantic Atmosphere
Dear Friend

Act 2

Entr'acte
Try Me
Where's My Shoe?
Vanilla Ice Cream
She Loves Me
A Trip to the Library
Grand Knowing You
Twelve Days to Christmas
Finale

CREATIVE TEAM

Book by Joe Masteroff
Music by Jerry Bock

Lyrics by Sheldon Harnick
Based on a play by Miklós László
Directed by Scott Ellis
Choreographed by Warren Carlyle
Associate Director: Stephen Nachamie
Assistant Choreographer: Jason Sparks

Musical Director: Paul Gemignani
Music orchestrated by Larry Hochman
Dance arrangements and Incidental Music by David Krane

Scenic Design by David Rockwell
Costume Design by Jeff Mahshie
Lighting Design by Donald Holder
Sound Design by Jon Weston
Hair and Wig Design by David Brian Brown
Makeup Design by Christian McCulloch
Associate Scenic Design: Dick Jaris and T. J. Greenway
Associate Lighting Design: Mike Riggs
Associate Sound Design: Jason Strangfeld
Assistant Costume Design: Jennifer Jacob
Assistant Lighting Design: Coby Chasman-Beck
Assistant Sound Design: Josh Millican
Moving Light Programmers: Caroline Chao and Alex Fogel
Production Stage Manager: Scott Taylor Rollison
Stage Manager: Zac Chandler
Dance Captain: Jenifer Foote

CAST

Laura Benanti—Amalia Balash
Gavin Creel—Steven Kodaly
Byron Jennings—Mr. Maraczek
Jane Krakowski—Ilona Ritter
Zachary Levi—Georg Nowack
Michael McGrath—Ladislav Sipos

Nicholas Barasch—Arpad Laszlo
Peter Bartlett—Headwaiter

Ensemble
Cameron Adams, Justin Bowen, Alison Cimmet, Benjamin Eakeley, Michael Fatica, Gina Ferrall, Jenifer Foote, Andrew Kober, Laura Shoop, and Jim Walton

Understudies
Justin Bowen (Arpad Laszlo, Busboy), Alison Cimmet (Ilona Ritter), Benjamin Eakeley (Steven Kodaly), Andrew Kober (Georg Nowack, Ladislav Sipos), Laura Shoop (Amalia Balash), and Jim Walton (Mr. Maraczek, Headwaiter)

NOTABLE REPLACEMENT
Tom McGowan—Ladislav Sipos

AWARDS
54th Tony Awards
Win

Best Scenic Design of a Musical

Nominations

Best Revival of a Musical
Best Actor in a Musical—Zachary Levi
Best Actress in a Musical—Laura Benanti
Best Featured Actress in a Musical—Jane Krakowski
Best Direction of a Musical
Best Orchestrations
Best Costume Design of a Musical

45th Drama Desk Awards
Wins

Outstanding Revival of a Musical or Revue
Outstanding Featured Actress in a Musical—Jane Krakowski

Outstanding Orchestrations
Outstanding Set Design of a Musical

Nominations

Outstanding Actor in a Musical—Zachary Levi
Outstanding Actress in a Musical—Laura Benanti
Outstanding Featured Actor in a Musical—Nicholas Barasch
Outstanding Costume Design for a Musical
Outstanding Wig and Hair

2016 *Theatre World Awards*

Nicholas Barasch (Dorothy Loudon Award For Excellence)

Kiss Me Kate 2019

A divorced couple reunite to perform in a musical adaptation of The Taming of the Shrew

February 14th 2019–March 14th 2019–June 30th 2019
Studio 54 Theatre
125 Performances
30 Previews

Musical Numbers

Act 1

Another Op'nin' Another Show
Why Can't You Behave
Wunderbar
So in Love
We Open in Venice
Tom, Dick or Harry
I've Come to Wive It Wealthily in Padua
I Hate Men
Were Thine That Special Face
Cantiamo D'Amore
Kiss Me, Kate

Act 2

Too Darn Hot
Where Is the Life That Late I Led?
Always True to You (In My Fashion)
From This Moment On
Bianca
So in Love (Reprise)
Brush Up Your Shakespeare
Pavane
I Am Ashamed That Women Are So Simple
Kiss Me, Kate (Reprise)

Creative Team

Music and Lyrics by Cole Porter
Book by Sam Spewack and Bella Spewack
From "The Taming of the Shrew" by William Shakespeare
Additional Material by Amanda Green
Directed by Scott Ellis

Choreographed by Warren Carlyle
Associate Choreographer: Jason A. Sparks
Associate Director: Nikki DiLoreto

Music orchestrated by Larry Hochman
Dance arrangements by David Chase
Additional Orchestrations by Michael Starobin and Ned Paul
    Ginsburg
Musical Director: Paul Gemignani

Scenic Design by David Rockwell
Costume Design by Jeff Mahshie
Lighting Design by Donald Holder
Sound Design by Brian Ronan
Hair and Wig Design by David Brian Brown
Make-Up Design by Christian McCulloch
Associate Scenic Design: Dick Jaris and T.J. Greenway
Associate Lighting Design: Coby Chasman-Beck
Associate Sound Design: Patrick LaChance
Assistant Scenic Design: Gaetane Bertol
Assistant Costume Design: Jennifer Jacob
Assistant Lighting Design: Christopher Annas-Lee
Moving Light Programmer: Jay Penfield and Jeff Englander

Technical Supervisor: Steve Beers
Production Stage Manager: Jeffrey Rodriguez
Stage Manager: Larry Smiglewski
Assistant Stage Manager: Pamela Remler

CAST

Kelli O'Hara—Lilli Vanessi/Katharine
Will Chase—Fred Graham/Petruchio
Corbin Bleu—Bill Calhoun/Lucentio
Stephanie Styles—Lois Lane/Bianca
Terence Archie—Harrison Howell

Mel Johnson, Jr.—Harry Trevor/Baptista
James T. Lane—Paul
Adrienne Walker—Hattie
Lance Coadie Williams—Second Man
John Pankow—First Man

Ensemble

Darius Barnes, Preston Truman Boyd, Will Burton, Derrick Cobey, Jesmille Darbouze, Rick Faugno, Haley Fish, Tanya Haglund, Erica Mansfield, Marissa McGowan, Justin Prescott, Christine Cornish Smith, Sherisse Springer, Sam Strasfeld, Sarah Meahl, and Travis Waldschmidt

Understudies

Preston Truman Boyd (Fred Graham/Petruchio, First Man, Second Man), Will Burton (Bill Calhoun/Lucentio), Derrick Cobey (Harrison Howell, Harry Trevor/Baptista), Jesmille Darbouze (Hattie), Marissa McGowan (Lilli Vanessi/Katharine), Justin Prescott (Paul) and Christine Cornish Smith (Lois Lane/Bianca)

NOTABLE REPLACEMENTS

Tom McGowan—Second Man
Richard Kind—Second Man

AWARDS

73rd Tony Awards

Nominations

Best Revival of a Musical
Best Actress in a Musical—Kelli O'Hara
Best Choreography
Best Orchestrations

64th Drama Desk Awards

Wins

LaDuca Award for Outstanding Choreography

Nominations
    Outstanding Revival of a Musical
    Outstanding Featured Actor in a Musical—Corbin Bleu

2019 Theatre World Awards
    Stephanie Styles

Index